ROADMAP™ A2+

STUDENTS' BOOK

with digital resources and mobile app

Lindsay Warwick and Damian Williams

Contents

FAST-TRACK ROUTE

EXTENDED ROUTE

Contents

FAST-TRACK ROUTE

EXTENDED ROUTE

1A Getting to know you

> **Goal:** get to know someone
> **Grammar:** word order in questions
> **Vocabulary:** question words

Reading and vocabulary

1 **Work in pairs and discuss the questions.**

1. Do you share information online? What sort of things do you share?
2. How and why do you share this information?

2 a **You're going to read a social media post by Magda. Look at her photos. What topics do you think she writes about (e.g. holidays)?**

b **Read Magda's post and check your ideas. Then answer the questions.**

1. Which topics in the post are not in the photos?
2. Where does Magda work?
3. Is Abby a good friend?
4. What do Magda's friends and family not know about her? Why?

3 a **Match the question words with the answers.**

1 How	a tomorrow
2 How long	b a phone
3 How many	c I like Italian food
4 What	d two hours
5 What kind of	e five
6 When	f that one
7 Where	g by train
8 Which	h It's his
9 Who	I in Los Angeles
10 Whose	J because I'm tired
11 Why	K John

Magda Fisher

Yesterday at 21.33

Ten things about me

1. **Where do you like to relax?** At the beach. I love the sound of the sea.
2. **How do you travel to work or college/school?** I walk.
3. **How long does your journey to work take?** About 20 seconds – from my bedroom to my home office.
4. **What's your favourite drink?** Coffee. I have five or six cups a day. Shh, don't tell anyone!
5. **Whose name is first in your phone contacts?** Abby – she's my sister's best friend! **Do you know the person well?** Actually, I've only met her once!
6. **When are you happiest?** When I'm visiting somewhere new. **Why?** Because new places are exciting.
7. **What kind of music do you like**? 1970s rock music. Thanks, a lot, Dad!
8. **Which animals do you like?** Cats, especially my cat Bubble!
9. **How many pairs of shoes do you own?** I've got over 30, but I always wear the same pair of trainers. My family and friends think they're my only shoes – but that's only because I never wear the others!
10. **Who is your oldest friend?** Nina. We have so much fun together. **Are you a good friend to him or her?** I think so ... most of the time!

b Match Diego's answers a–j with questions 1–10 in Magda's post.

a About five. Who needs more than that?
b Someone I work with called Alex. I know him quite well.
c By bike when it's sunny. By car when it's raining.
d When I'm playing my guitar. I love music.
e About 30 minutes.
f At home, in my living room, with some music on.
g Two people, actually – Sofia and David. We're great friends.
h Anything with a guitar – rock, mostly.
i Fresh juice, especially on a hot day.
j I love horses!

c **Work in pairs. Take turns to ask and answer six questions in Magda's post.**

Go to your app for more practice.

Grammar

4 a **Read the grammar box and choose the correct alternatives.**

Word order in questions

Order questions in the present simple like this:
(Question word +) *do* + subject + infinitive
How do you travel *to work or college/school?*
How long [1]*do/does the journey take?*
[2]*Does/Do you know the person well?*
Order questions with *be* like this:
(Question word +) *be* + subject
What is your favourite drink?
Who [3]*are/is your oldest friend?*
[4]*Are/Do you a good friend to him or her?*

b **Check your answers in Magda's post in Exercise 2.**

5 a 1.1 **Listen to the questions. Does the speaker's voice go up or down at the end of each question?**

1 What kind of pizza do you like?
2 Who's your favourite singer?
3 Where do you live?
4 Why are you tired?
5 How long is this lesson?

b **Listen again and repeat.**

6 a **Put the words in the correct order to make questions. Use capitals where necessary.**

1 spend online / you / do / how many hours / each day / ?
2 who / you / online / talk to / do / ?
3 look at / whose photos / you / do / online / ?
4 like / what kind of / do / websites / you / ?
5 you / this area / from / are / ?
6 your normal working day / how long / is / ?

b **Make questions using the prompts. Choose an appropriate question word or expression.**

1 your birthday? *When's your birthday?*
2 your favourite TV show at the moment?
3 films / like?
4 languages / you / speak?
5 you / go / at weekends?
6 this lesson / finish?

c **Work in pairs. Take turns to ask and answer three questions in Exercise 6a and three questions in Exercise 6b.**

Go to page 116 or your app for more information and practice.

Speaking

PREPARE

7 a 1.2 **You're going to get to know your classmates better. First, listen to Becky and Josh and answer the questions.**

1 How many films does Josh talk about?
2 Why is Becky surprised?

b **Listen again. What questions does Becky ask?**

8 **Think of some topics that you're interested in and write some questions to ask your classmates.**

Do you like sport?
Are you a student?

SPEAK

9 a **Work in groups. Take turns to ask your questions to each other. Ask some follow-up questions and use the Useful phrases to help you respond.**

A: *Do you like sport?*
B: *Yes, I really like football and tennis.*
C: *Really? Me too! Do you play football?*

Useful phrases
That's interesting/nice.
Really?
Me too!
Great!

b **Tell the class one or two interesting things about the people in your group.**

Develop your listening page 86

1B Successful people

- **Goal:** describe habits and routines
- **Grammar:** Adverbs of frequency
- **Vocabulary:** success

Roger Federer

Alicia Keys

Stephen Hawking

Natalia Os

Listening and vocabulary

1 **Look at the photos and discuss the questions.**

1. What do you know about these people?
2. Why do you think they are/were successful?
3. What habits do you think successful people have?

I think they get up early and work late.

2 a 1.7 **Listen to a podcast about successful people. Does it include any of your ideas?**

b **Listen again. Number the tips in the order you hear them. Do you agree with them?**

- take care of yourself
- plan your time well
- try new things
- have clear goals *1*
- take time off
- start again
- ask a lot of questions
- listen carefully

3 a **Complete the questions with an expression in Exercise 2b.**

1. Do you *plan your time well*, or do lots of things at the same time?
2. Do you like to __________, or repeat the same experiences?
3. When things go wrong, do you __________?
4. Do you __________ to what other people tell you?
5. Do you __________ when you want to know something?
6. Do you __________? Do you know what you want in life?
7. Do you think it's more important to work all the time, or __________ and enjoy yourself?
8. Do you __________? Do you eat well and do exercise?

b **Work in pairs. Take turns to ask and answer the questions. Do you have similar habits?**

Go to your app for more practice.

Grammar

4 a **Listen to the podcast again and choose the correct alternatives.**

Successful people ...

1. *always/never* know what they want in life.
2. are *sometimes/rarely* bored.
3. are *often/always* good listeners.
4. *don't often/don't usually* do lots of things at the same time.
5. *sometimes/rarely* check their messages only once a day.
6. *usually/hardly ever* have busy and stressful lives.
7. *hardly ever/always* work at weekends.
8. *sometimes/never* stop trying.

b **Number the adverbs of frequency in the box from 1 (most frequent) to 6 (least frequent). Use Exercise 4a to help you.**

always *1*	hardly ever/rarely	never	often
sometimes	usually		

Meryl Streep

5 a **Read the grammar box and choose the correct alternatives.**

Adverbs of frequency

Use adverbs of frequency to talk about [1]*how often/ when* you do something.

Adverbs of frequency usually come [2]*before/after* the verb *be*.

Successful people ***are often*** *good listeners.*

They usually come [3]*before/after* other verbs.

... they ***always look for*** *new and exciting experiences.*

You can use *always, usually* and *often* with verbs in the negative. They come [4]*before/after* the negative verb.

Successful people ***don't often do*** *lots of things at the same time.*

There are other expressions of frequency that you can use, e.g. *every day, once a week, all the time.* These usually come [5]*at the end/in the middle* of a sentence.

They sometimes check their messages only ***once a day****.*

b 1.8 **Listen to the sentences. What do you notice about the two letters in bold?**

1 He doesn'**t o**ften try new things.
2 He sometimes asks **a l**ot **of** questions.
3 I'**m o**ften bored at weekends.
4 She goes to the cinema on**ce a** week.
5 You hardl**y e**ver **a**sk questions.

c **Listen again and repeat.**

6 a **Complete the sentences with the adverbs in brackets.**

1 Ben does one activity at a time. (always)
Ben always does one activity at a time.
2 Ana tries a new activity. (once a month)
3 I'm successful in exams. (hardly ever)
4 We don't have a clear goal. (often)
5 I take time off in June. (sometimes)
6 Jon works hard. (all the time)
7 They're not busy in the morning. (usually)
8 I check my work emails at weekends. (rarely)

b **Work in pairs. Take turns to ask and answer questions with *How often* and a phrase in the box.**

be late	be really busy	eat pizza	get angry
go for a swim	go to the cinema		
send something by post	sing in the shower		

A: *How often are you late?*
B: *I'm hardly ever late. I always leave early for everything. How often do you go to the cinema?*

Go to page 116 or your app for more information and practice.

Speaking

PREPARE

7 a 1.9 **You're going to tell other students about a successful person. First, listen to Alex talking about a successful person he knows. Answer the questions.**

1 Who is the person?
2 How old is she?
3 Why does Alex think she is successful?

b **Listen again. How often does the person do these things?**

1 get up early
2 go for a long walk
3 use public transport
4 look after her great-grandchildren

c **Make notes about a successful person. It can be someone you know (e.g. a friend) or someone you don't know (e.g. someone famous). Think about:**

- who the person is
- what they do
- why you think they are successful

SPEAK

8 **Work in groups. Take turns to tell each other about your successful person. Ask people questions to get more information and use the Useful phrases to help you.**

A: *My friend Dani often wins short film competitions.*
B: *That's great! What else does she do?*

Useful phrases

He/She sounds amazing/brilliant/fantastic!
Tell me/us more.
That's great!
What else does he/she do?

Develop your writing page 87

1C A new lifestyle

- **Goal:** describe everyday activities
- **Grammar:** present simple and present continuous
- **Vocabulary:** everyday activities

Reading

1 a Marek and Kim are trying a new lifestyle. Look at the photos. What kind of things do you think they do?

b Read Marek's blog post and check your ideas.

Hi everyone! Kim and I are trying a new lifestyle. We usually live in the city, but this month we're living in a forest without electricity, internet, phones and things like that.

So, how am I writing this blog? Well, we come into town once a week to use the internet and buy some things we need. The town is about 10 km away and we always walk here – it's great exercise! I'm using the computer in the library at the moment, to check my email and to write to you. Kim's looking for some blankets in a shop because it's really cold at night!

We're living in a really simple house which has a nice vegetable garden. Life is good, but it's hard work. We get up at 5.30 a.m. every day. We have a simple breakfast then work for most of the day. We pick vegetables in the garden and we collect wood in the forest. We finish work at about 6 p.m. In the evenings, we play cards, read or just sit in the garden ... when the weather's nice. We go to bed early, too, usually around 9 p.m. We're not missing TV at all! Anyway, we're really enjoying it so far!

2 a Read Marek's post again and answer the questions.

1. How often do Marek and Kim go into town?
2. Where is Kim at the moment?
3. What time do they get up?
4. What do they do in the evenings?
5. What time do they go to bed?

b Work in pairs and discuss the questions.

1. Would you like to try this lifestyle?
2. Where would be a good place to do this in your country?
3. What do you think are the positive and negative things about this lifestyle?

Grammar

3 a Read the grammar box and choose the correct alternatives.

Present simple and present continuous

Use the present [1]*simple/continuous* to talk about facts, things which are generally true or something that happens regularly.

*The town **is** about 10 km away.*
*We usually **live** in the big city.*
*We **get up** at 5.30 a.m. every day.*

Use the present [2]*simple/continuous* to describe something happening now.

***I'm using** the computer in the library.*

You can also use the present continuous to describe a [3]*permanent/temporary* situation happening around now.

*Kim and I **are trying** a new lifestyle.*

It is common to use time expressions like *at the moment*, *right now* and *these days* with the present continuous.

***I'm using** the computer in the library **at the moment**.*

b Find and underline three more examples of the present simple and three of the present continuous in Marek's post in Exercise 1.

4 a 1.10 **We usually contract *be* in the present continuous. Listen and choose the alternative you hear.**

1. *We are/We're* having a great time.
2. *She is/She's* eating a sandwich.
3. *I am/I'm* working in the garden.
4. *They are/They're* working outside.

b 1.11 **Listen to the sentences with contractions and repeat.**

5 **Complete Marek's latest post with the correct forms of the verbs in brackets.**

Hi all! Sorry for not writing. Town is very far and we [1]______ (not have) time to walk here every week. Anyway, only one week left! I [2]______ (sit) in the library, again. Things are the same here. Every day, we [3]______ (work) very hard from morning until night and we [4]______ (feel) tired all the time. To be honest, we [5]______ (want) to go home because we [6]______ (be) quite bored of this lifestyle. I [7]______ (think) about our TV and comfortable sofa right now!

6 a **Complete the sentences so they are true for you.**

1. I'm ... at the moment.
2. I ... every day.
3. My family always ...
4. I'm ... these days.
5. I'm not ... right now.

b **Work in pairs. Share your ideas and ask questions to find out more information.**

A: *I'm learning Chinese at the moment.*
B: *Really? Is it difficult?*

Go to page 116 or your app for more information and practice.

Vocabulary

7 a **Complete phrases 1–8 with the words in the box. Use Marek's posts in Exercises 1 and 5 to help you.**

check get have play spend start/finish ~~take~~ watch

1. *take* a break/a picture
2. ______ cards/video games
3. ______ TV/a film
4. ______ a shower/lunch
5. ______ work/school
6. ______ up/dressed
7. ______ your email/social media
8. ______ time with friends/family

b **Add the words in the box to phrases 1–8.**

a good time a language course a show ~~a taxi~~ home money the answers the piano

1 *take a break/a picture/**a taxi***

c **Work in pairs. Student A: say a verb from the box in Exercise 7a. Student B: say a noun in Exercise 7a or 7b that goes with it.**

Go to page 136 or your app for more vocabulary and practice.

Speaking

PREPARE

8 a 1.12 **You're going to describe a change in lifestyle. First, listen to a conversation between Paul and Stephanie. Which change of lifestyle below is Stephanie trying?**

- trying a new diet
- living in a different place/country
- living with little money
- living without technology
- working at night

b **Listen again and answer the questions.**

1. What is Stephanie doing when Paul phones her?
2. What different things does she do these days? Does she miss anything?
3. How does she feel about it?

9 **Imagine you're making a change to your lifestyle. Choose one of the topics in Exercise 8a or use one of your own ideas. Answer the questions below and make notes.**

- What change are you making? How is it different to your usual lifestyle?
- How do you feel about it? Do you miss anything?

SPEAK

10 **Work in pairs. Take turns to describe your change in lifestyle. Use your notes in Exercise 9 and the Useful phrases to help you.**

Useful phrases

How's it going?
Guess what I'm doing (at the moment)?
Wow, that sounds (amazing/brilliant/great).
I'm trying (a new sport).
I miss (chocolate).

Develop your reading page 88

1D English in action

Goal: ask for and check information

1 **Look at the pictures and answer the questions.**

1 What's happening in each picture?
2 What kind of help does each person need?
3 Have you ever been in any of these situations?

2 a 1.13 **Listen to three conversations. Match them to three of pictures A–D.**

b **Listen again and answer the questions.**

1 Where does the man in Conversation 1 want to go?
2 Which bus does the girl in Conversation 2 need to take?
3 Which exercise does the girl in Conversation 3 need do?

3 a 1.14 **Listen and tick (✓) the phrases you hear.**

Useful phrases

Asking for information
What do I need to do?
Can you help me?

Giving information
It's this one here.
You need to (buy a ticket).

Checking someone understands
Did you get that?
Is that clear?

Checking details
Which (one) is it?
Can you repeat that, please?

b **Listen again and repeat.**

4 **Complete the conversations. Use the Useful phrases to help you.**

1 **A:** Excuse me, I'm looking for somewhere that sells paper. Can you _help_ me?
B: Sure. You ______ to go to *Clips* on the High Street.

2 **A:** Is ______ clear?
B: No, sorry, can you ______ that, please?
A: Sure. Take the 9.52 train.

3 **A:** Sorry, I missed that. What ______ I need to do?
B: Read the paragraph, then answer the questions.
A: Which paragraph is it?
B: ______ this one here.

Speaking

PREPARE

5 **Work in pairs. Practise the conversation below.**

A: Hi. Can you help me? I'm not sure how to get to the transport museum.
B: You need to take the 59 bus to Springfield Park, then change to the 342. Is that clear?
A: I think so. I need to take the number 59, then the 342.
B: Yes, that's right.
A: Thanks again.

SPEAK

6 **Student A go to page 151 and Student B go to page 153.**

Go online for the Roadmap video.

Check and reflect

1 **Complete each question with one word.**

1 What time you get up in the morning?
2 What your favourite food?
3 Whose pen this?
4 Long is the lesson?
5 Which film do want to watch?
6 How brothers and sisters have you got?

2 a **Look at the topics below. Write a question for each one to ask another student. Use a different question word each time.**

- music/films/TV
- family/friends
- free time
- birthday
- work/studies
- food/drink

b **Work in pairs and ask each other the questions you wrote. Ask some follow-up questions.**

3 a **Choose the correct alternatives.**

1 *What/Who*'s your favourite actor?
2 *How long/How many* does it take you to get ready in the morning?
3 *Whose/Who's* birthday do you always remember?
4 *How long/How many* hours of TV do you watch every day?
5 *How/What* do you like to relax in the evening?

b **Work in pairs. Ask and answer the questions.**

4 a **Complete the sentences with one of the adverbs in the box so that they are true for you. You can use them more than once.**

always hardly ever never often rarely sometimes usually

1 I get up early at the weekend.
2 I listen carefully to other people.
3 I arrive late to class.
4 I plan my time well.
5 My teacher gives me homework.
6 I'm happy when I wake up in the morning.
7 I work/study at the weekend.
8 My friends are busy at the weekend.

b **Work in groups. Compare your sentences. Are any of them similar?**

5 a **Match verbs 1–8 with endings a–h.**

1 have	a care of yourself
2 take	b your time well
3 take	c new things
4 listen	d clear goals
5 start	e again
6 ask	f a lot of questions
7 try	g carefully
8 plan	h time off

b **Choose five of the phrases and write sentences about you for each one.**

6 **Choose the correct alternatives.**

A: Hi Janice, what [1]*do you do/are you doing* at the moment?
B: Nothing really, I [2]*just watch/'m just watching* TV.
A: Can I ask you a favour? I [3]*have/'m having* my dance class tonight but my babysitter just cancelled. Can you help?
B: Sure! I [4]*don't do/'m not doing* anything important right now.
A: That's great! Kieran [5]*does/is doing* his homework at the moment, but then he [6]*usually plays/'s usually playing* video games for an hour before bed. I should be back by then. Thanks a lot!
B: No problem!

7 a **Complete the questions with the correct form of the words in brackets.**

1 What time ______ (you / usually go) to bed?
2 What ______ (you / study) in English class this week?
3 What ______ (you / do) right now?
4 How often ______ (you / listen) to podcasts?
5 What ______ (you / wear) today?

b **Work in pairs. Ask and answer the questions.**

8 a **Complete the everyday activities with a verb.**

1 I always ______ my email first thing in the morning.
2 I ______ work/school at 9 a.m.
3 I ______ time with my friends every weekend.
4 I never ______ up early at the weekend.
5 I ______ video games in my free time.
6 I don't always ______ breakfast.
7 I try to ______ a break every hour when I'm studying.
8 I ______ TV every evening.

b **Which of the sentences are true for you? Change the others so they are true.**

c **Work in pairs. Compare your sentences. Ask some follow-up questions to find out more information.**

Reflect

How confident do you feel about the statements below? Write 1–5 (1 = not very confident, 5 = very confident).

- I can get to know someone.
- I can describe habits and routines.
- I can describe typical everyday activities.
- I can ask for and check information.

Want more practice?
Go to your Workbook or app.

2A One of those days

> **Goal:** describe a memorable day
> **Grammar:** past simple
> **Vocabulary:** feelings

Vocabulary and listening

1 **Look at the photos. Do you think the people in the photos are having a good or a bad day? Why/Why not?**

2 a **Which adjectives in the box can you use to describe the people in the photos? More than one answer may be possible for each photo.**

afraid angry bored excited happy nervous relaxed stressed surprised worried

b **Choose the correct alternatives.**

1 Sadie is *angry/nervous* about her big presentation – there are 600 people in the room.
2 Hamza is quite *relaxed/worried* about his interview. He's not nervous.
3 I'm so *bored/stressed* here. There's nothing to do except watch TV.
4 Pablo is so *surprised/excited* about his holiday – he talks about it all the time.
5 She's very *stressed/afraid* at the moment. I think she's having a very difficult time at work.
6 Matteo is *nervous/afraid* because he has an exam tomorrow.

3 a **How would you feel in these situations? Think of as many adjectives as possible for each one.**

1 You find out that someone at work is saying bad things about you to your colleagues.
2 You're lying on your sofa at the end of a long day, watching a film.
3 You have a job interview tomorrow morning.
4 You're lost in a big city at night.
5 You're graduating from university.
6 You're having a fun day with your friends.
7 You receive a present in the post from someone you don't know.
8 You have to pay a bill but you don't have any money.

b **Work in pairs and compare your answers.**

4 a **Choose three of the adjectives in Exercise 2a. For each one, write a sentence describing a situation when you feel this way.**

When I feel like this I talk a lot, I walk around the room and I can't relax. (nervous)

b **Work in pairs and read your sentences to your partner. Guess which adjective your partner is describing.**

Go to page 137 or your app for more vocabulary and practice.

5 a 2.1 **Listen to Lynn talking about her job interview. Tick (✓) how she felt that day.**

angry bored happy nervous relaxed stressed surprised

b **Listen again and decide if the sentences are true (T) or false (F).**

1 Lynn woke up late because her alarm didn't go off.
2 She had a big breakfast.
3 She went to her job interview by bus.
4 She used her computer in the presentation.
5 The interview went well.

Grammar

6 **Read the grammar box and choose the correct alternatives.**

Past simple

Use the past simple to talk about [1]*finished/unfinished* actions or states in the past.

*I **took** the bus to the interview.*

*I **was** angry.*

Use *was/wasn't* and *were/weren't* to make the past simple of [2]*be/have*.

*The interviewers **weren't** happy.*

Regular past simple verbs end in [3]*-ed/-ing*.

*It **started** badly.*

Some verbs are irregular.

*I **woke** up late.*

*I **got** into my car.*

7 a 2.2 **Listen to the pronunciation of the past simple verbs in the box and complete the table.**

arrived decided deleted ended played looked showed stopped talked tried wanted watched

/d/	/ɪd/	/t/
showed	*decided*	*looked*

b **Listen again and repeat.**

8 a **Complete the text with the past simple form of the verbs in brackets.**

Several years ago, I [1]_______ (go) to a dinner party at a colleague's house. When I [2]_______ (arrive), he took my coat and umbrella, and [3]_______ (show) me to my seat at the table. Looking around, I realised that I was the only person from work. Even worse, his friends all [4]_______ (know) each other really well – I [5]_______(try) to join in the conversations, but it [6]_______ (be) hard. However, I [7]_______ (notice) a woman at the other end of the table. I [8]_______ (think) she was beautiful, and I really [9]_______ (want) to talk to her, but she was too far away. Anyway, I was bored after dinner so I [10]_______ (decide) to leave early. I put on my coat, picked up my umbrella, and [11]_______ (walk) to the bus stop. But when I opened the umbrella, I saw it wasn't mine. Just then, I [12]_______ (hear) a voice behind me say, 'I think you've got my umbrella.' I looked round, and it was the beautiful woman from the dinner party. That was ten years ago, and now we're happily married!

b **Work in pairs. Talk about a time when you felt:**

- nervous
- excited
- bored
- suprised

Go to page 118 or your app for more information and practice.

Speaking

PREPARE

9 **You're going to describe a memorable day. Choose a day you want to describe and think about:**

1. Was it a good or bad day?
2. What happened at the start of the day?
3. What were the main events?
4. How did you feel during the day?
5. What happened in the end?

SPEAK

10 **Work in groups. Describe your day to your group. Use the Useful phrases to help you. Are any of your days similar?**

Useful phrases

It started well/badly.

First of all, (I woke up late).

Then, (I missed my bus).

After that, (I got lost).

Finally, (I went home).

Develop your reading page 89

2B You're never too old

A

- **Goal:** ask about and describe past events
- **Grammar:** past simple negative and questions
- **Vocabulary:** past time expressions

B

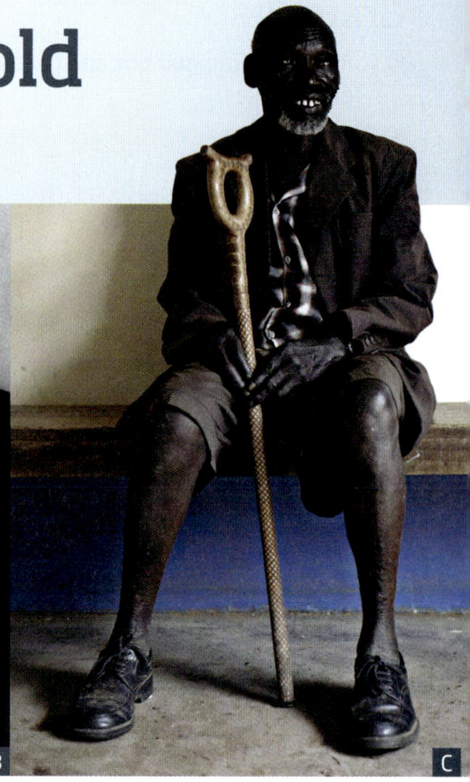
C

YOU DON'T HAVE TO BE YOUNG TO DO AMAZING THINGS

This week we're looking at three people who did something amazing later in their lives. Who were they? What did they do? Why did they do it?

1 Kimani Maruge
Kimani Maruge was born in Kenya. When he was a child, people in his country had to pay to go to school, so he didn't learn to read and write. Then, in 2003, primary schools became free so he decided to get an education. He started school for the first time at 84 years old. Learning wasn't easy for him but he worked hard. This experience completely changed his life. In fact, in 2005, he travelled to New York to talk to people at the United Nations about free education.

2 Harriette Thompson
Harriette Thompson was born in 1923 in the US. She worked as a piano player for most of her life. On 23 May 1999, one of Harriette's friends decided to walk the San Diego marathon for charity. Harriette joined her but she didn't walk – she ran. She was 76 years old. She ran the marathon every year between 1999 and 2015, except for one year when she was very ill. When she was 94 years old, she became the oldest woman to complete a marathon. It took her 7 hours, 24 minutes and 36 seconds and she collected more than $100,000 for charity.

3 Laila Denmark
Laila Denmark was born in 1898 in Atlanta, USA. She wanted to become a doctor so she could help children. Studying medicine wasn't usual for women at the time. In fact, she was the only woman in a class of 52 students. Most people stop working when they're about 65, but Dr Denmark didn't retire until she was 103 years old! She lived for 11 more years.

Reading and vocabulary

1 **Look at the photos. What amazing thing do you think you each person did?**

2 a **Read the article. Match descriptions 1–3 to photos A–C and answer the questions in the introduction.**

b **Read the article again and answer the questions.**

1. When did Kimani Maruge start school?
2. When did he travel to the US?
3. When did Harriette first run a marathon?
4. When did she become the oldest woman to run a marathon?
5. When did Laila Denmark retire?
6. How old was she when she died?

c **Work in pairs. Who do you think did the most amazing thing? Why?**

3 a **Put the time expressions in order from the most recent (1) to the oldest (6).**

in 2018 | last month *1* | on 23 May 2017
six weeks ago | until 2015 | when I was five

b **Complete the expressions with the words in the box.**

ago | in | last | on | until | when

1 ______ I was a child
2 ______ week
3 A few years ______
4 ______ my 10th birthday
5 ______ last year
6 ______ 2015

c **Write six sentences using each expression.**

When I was a child, I loved playing outside.

d **Work in pairs. Tell each other your sentences. Give more information.**

When I was a child, I loved playing outside. I always played football in the park with my brother.

Go to your app for more practice.

Grammar

4 Read the grammar box and choose the correct alternatives.

Past simple negative and questions

Use [1]*didn't/doesn't* + infinitive to make past simple negative sentences.

*She **didn't walk** – she ran.*

*Dr Denmark **didn't retire** until 2001.*

Use [2]*isn't and aren't/wasn't and weren't* with the verb *be*.

*Schools **weren't** free.*

*Learning **wasn't** easy for him.*

Use [3]*do/did* + infinitive to make past simple questions.

*What **did** they do?*

*Why **did** they do it?*

Use [4]*did/was and were* in past simple questions with *be*.

*Who **were** they?*

5 a 2.3 **Listen to the conversations. Notice the pronunciation of *did/didn't* and *was/wasn't*.**

1 **A:** Did you learn to sing at school?
  B: Yes, I did.
2 **A:** Did she finish the marathon?
  B: No, she didn't.
3 **A:** How old were you?
  B: I wasn't very old, actually.
4 **A:** Was he from Italy?
  B: No, he wasn't?

b **Work in pairs. Listen again and repeat.**

6 a **Use the prompts to make questions with *did, was* or *were*.**

1 How / you / learn to play the piano?
  How did you learn to play the piano?
2 it / difficult to get into your university?
3 When / you / get your driving licence?
4 you / happy with your exam results?
5 you / enjoy water skiing?
6 he / win the race?

b **Complete each answer with *didn't, wasn't* or *weren't*.**

a When I was 35. I ______ have lessons until I was in my 30s.
b It was really hard. Maths ______ an easy exam.
c I taught myself. I ______ have a teacher.
d No, we ______ .
e I loved it. It ______ scary at all.
f No, he ______ . He came second.

c **Work in pairs. Take it in turns to ask a question in Exercise 6a and answer with a response from 6b .**

Go to page 118 or your app for more information and practice.

Speaking

PREPARE

7 a 2.4 **You're going to talk about something special you did in the past. First, listen to Dan and Megan. What did Megan do?**

b **Write three questions Dan could ask Megan to find out more information.**

c 2.5 **Listen to the rest of their conversation. Did Dan ask any of your questions? What other things did you learn about Megan?**

8 **Think of something special that you did in the past, for example: an event, learning something new or doing something for the first time. Answer the questions below.**

- What did you do?
- When did you do it?
- Where did you do it?
- Who did you do it with?
- Why did you do it?

SPEAK

9 a **Work in pairs. Tell each other about what you did. Ask each other questions to find out as much information as possible.**

b **Work in different pairs. Tell each other what you learnt about your first partner.**

Develop your writing page 90

2D English in action

Goal: show interest and excitement

A

B

1 **Look at the photos. What are the people doing? How are they feeling?**

2 a 2.14 **Listen to four conversations and answer the questions.**

1 Why is Ali happy?
2 How did Marco help Fran?
3 What time is Ricky's party?
4 What did Simone win?

b **Choose the correct alternatives to complete the extracts from the conversations.**

1 80 percent? *That's/What's* brilliant!
2 *It's/They're* lovely. Thanks!
3 That *looks/sounds* great!
4 I love your curries. They're *really/so* good.
5 No way! That's *amazing!/great!*

c **Listen to the conversations again and check your answers.**

3 a 2.15 **Listen to the sentences. Does speaker 1 or speaker 2 show interest/excitement in each one?**

1 That sounds fantastic!
2 Amazing!
3 How exciting!
4 What a great idea!
5 That sounds really interesting!

b 2.16 **Listen to the speakers showing interest/excitement again and repeat.**

4 a **Complete the conversations with an appropriate response. Use the Useful phrases to help you. More than one answer might be possible.**

1 **A:** I'm going to run a marathon next month.
B: Really? That ______ exciting! And difficult!
2 **A:** We were in Mexico this time last week.
B: ______ ! ______ you have a good time?
3 **A:** I've just got my dream job!
B: Really? That's ______ !
4 **A:** I'm making your favourite pasta for dinner.
B: ______ !
5 **A:** We went to that new Italian restaurant last night.
B: Really? What ______ you think of it?
A: It was ______ !

Useful phrases

Creating interest
Guess what (happened to me)!?
Guess what I did/where I went?

Responding to information
Great!/Brilliant!/Fantastic!/Amazing!
It's/They're (delicious/lovely).
That's (amazing/great).
How (exciting/amazing/fantastic)!
What a (good idea).
That sounds (lovely/wonderful)!
No way!

Asking follow-up questions
What happened (exciting/next/after that)?
How did that/it go?
Who did you go with?

b **Work in pairs. Practise the conversations with the appropriate intonation.**

Speaking

PREPARE

5 a **Work in pairs. You're going to share some exciting news. It can be real or imagined. Student A go to page 151 and Student B go to page 152.**

SPEAK

b **Share your news with each other. Show interest and excitement when appropriate. Use the Useful phrases to help you.**

Go online for the Roadmap video.

Check and reflect

1 a Complete the sentences with the correct form of the verbs in the box.

be get up go have meet play take watch

1 I ______ a really good film last month.
2 My family and I ______ on holiday last summer.
3 I ______ a great meal last night.
4 My sister ______ a train to Moscow two weeks ago.
5 I ______ some video games last night.
6 My friend and I ______ at a coffee shop last week.
7 I ______ late yesterday, after 10am.
8 I ______ bored yesterday.

b Work in pairs. Which sentences are true for you? Give more information about them.

2 a Complete each sentence with an adjective of feeling. The first and last letter of each word are given.

1 I've got so much work to do. I'm really s____d.
2 Our holiday starts tomorrow. I'm so e____d!
3 I'm a____d of spiders. I hate them.
4 Jon never gets stressed. He's always r____d.
5 When Sam dropped Abi's phone, she got really a____y with him.
6 I've got my driving test tomorrow and I'm really n____s.
7 Billy just won a competition. He's really h____y.
8 Everyone was s____d when they heard the news.

b Work in pairs. Choose five of the adjectives and talk about when you last felt like that.

I was angry last week when I lost my keys.

3 a Make each sentence negative.

1 We went to the gym last night.
2 Sara was happy yesterday.
3 I went to bed late last night.
4 They were very busy last week.
5 We played cards yesterday.
6 Jimmy lived in San Diego when he was a child.

b Work in pairs. Tell each other three things you wanted to do yesterday but didn't do.

I wanted to go to the gym but I didn't have time.

4 a Put the words in the correct order to make questions.

1 last night / you / did / do / what / ?
2 you / who / chat to / yesterday / did / ?
3 were / last weekend / you / where / ?
4 did / go / what time / last night / to bed / you / ?
5 have for dinner / what / yesterday / you / did / ?
6 was / your / what colour / first car / ?
7 TV / last / you / did / night / watch / ?
8 this English course / decide / why / you / did / do / to / ?

b Work in pairs. Take turns to ask and answer the questions.

5 a Match the sentence halves.

1 I didn't learn to swim until I was
2 Cara was born on
3 We first met each other last
4 Liam started a new job a few weeks
5 I moved to Rome in
6 I didn't study English when

a year.
b 17 April 1999.
c ten years old.
d I was at school.
e ago.
f 2017.

b Work in pairs. Tell each other some things you did in the past using some past time expressions.

I went to France last week.

6 a Choose the correct alternatives.

This is a meal that I cook for friends. It's simple but delicious and they love it!

I make pasta with a tomato sauce. I cook [1]*some/a few* spaghetti and then I fry half [2]*an/some* onion in [3]*a little/a few* oil. Then I add [4]*a few/any* herbs and [5]*a few/a little* garlic but not too much. Finally, I mix the spaghetti and sauce together. I then put [6]*a/a lot of* parmesan cheese on top because I love it so much. There isn't [7]*any/a little* meat in this dish because I'm vegetarian but you can put [8]*an/some* in if you like.

b Work in pairs. Describe your favourite meal. What is it? What's in it?

7 a Put the letters in italics in the correct order to make adjectives.

1 This orange juice is really *etswe*.
2 This sandwich doesn't taste of anything. It's very *ialpn*.
3 I love this chocolate cake. It's *coleusidi*.
4 Let's eat something *thigl* like a salad.
5 Aargh! This lemon juice is really *orus*!
6 Is this milk *shref* or old?
7 I can't eat this cake. It's too *meaycr*.

b Work in pairs. Think of other food that you can describe with each adjective in Exercise 7a.

c Tell each other three foods you think are delicious and three foods you think are plain. Do you agree?

Reflect

How confident do you feel about the statements below? Write 1–5 (1 = not very confident, 5 = very confident).

- I can describe a memorable day.
- I can ask about and describe past events.
- I can describe a special dish.
- I can show interest and excitement.

Want more practice?
Go to your Workbook or app.

3A Urban escapes

- **Goal:** compare places to visit
- **Grammar:** comparatives
- **Vocabulary:** adjectives to describe places

Vocabulary and reading

1 **Look at the pairs of photos A–C and discuss the questions.**

1. Do you know any of the places in the photos?
2. Which place would you most like to visit? Why?

2 a **Do you think the adjectives in the box are positive (P) or negative (N)?**

beautiful *P* cheap clean crowded dirty exciting interesting lively modern noisy old peaceful popular

b **Work in pairs and compare your answers. Do you agree?**

3 a **Complete each sentence with an adjective in Exercise 2a.**

1. This area has become very ______ . Everybody likes to come here.
2. Look at that view, it's really ______ !
3. I love this city, but the air is so ______ .
4. Don't visit the museum on a Saturday, it gets very ______ .
5. There's a nice mix of both ______ and old buildings by the river.

b **Work in pairs and discuss the questions.**

1. Which of the adjectives could you use to describe the places in Exercise 1?
2. Which of the adjectives could you use to describe where you live?

4 a **Read the travel forum posts and decide which photos in Exercise 1 the people are discussing.**

JOIN

1

Simone
Hey! I'm in London for the weekend. Where are the best places to eat out?

Elisabeth
Camden Market! There are lots of choices, with food from all over the world, and it's quite cheap. It's a really lively area, with lots of exciting things to do. It's an interesting area, too – there's a mix of old and modern buildings.

Rebecca
Camden Market is great, but it can get very crowded. I'd recommend St Katharine's Docks, a bit further away. It's a lovely little area where you can relax and have a nice meal, and it's not as noisy as Camden Market. I think it's cheaper and quieter, too!

2

Barry
Hi everyone, my wife and I are going to Rio de Janeiro next month. Can you recommend which beaches to go to?

Pedro
Well, I just love Copacabana. It's longer than the other beaches in the city, so there's lots of space to play volleyball or just relax. It's livelier than other beaches, too – you can have lots of fun there!

Patrizio
I'd recommend Grumari or Prainha – these two beaches are a few kilometres out of Rio. They're cleaner than the city beaches, too, which are noisier and more crowded.

Bethany
I agree with Pedro. You should definitely visit Copacabana and other beaches in the city, but Prainha and Grumari are better. They're less noisy and more beautiful, in my opinion.

b **Read the forum posts again and decide if the sentences are true (T) or false (F).**

1 Camden Market is a peaceful place.
2 Camden Market is a popular place.
3 St. Katharine's Docks is near Camden Market.
4 Copacabana beach is busy.
5 Grumari and Prainha are outside the city.

c **Work in pairs. Are there any similar places in your country?**

Go to page 138 or your app for more vocabulary and practice.

Grammar

5 a **Read the grammar box and choose the correct alternatives.**

Comparatives

Use *be* + comparative adjective + *than* to compare two things.
*The market **is more popular than** the park.*
To make comparatives, add *-er* or *-ier* to [1]*short/long* adjectives.
*The castle is **older** than the bridge.*
*This exercise is **easier** than the last one.*
Use *more* or *less* before [2]*short/long* adjectives.
*South Beach is **more beautiful** than North Beach.*
*Campbell's restaurant is **less popular** than Gino's.*
Some adjectives are [3]*regular/irregular*, e.g. *good – better*.
*Woodland Park is **better** than the riverside.*
You can use *(not) as* + adjective + *as* to say two things are or aren't the same.
*This restaurant is **as good as** the one we went to yesterday.*
*This shop **isn't as cheap as** the supermarket, but I like it.*

b **Find and underline one example of each comparative form in the forum posts.**

6 a **3.1 Listen to the sentences and notice how the weak forms of *-er* and *than* are pronounced.**

1 The streets are dirtier than they were five years ago.
2 The north of the city is older than the south of the city.
3 This part of the beach is cleaner than the other part.
4 My town is busier than yours.

b **Listen again and repeat the sentences.**

7 **Complete the description with the correct form of the adjectives in brackets.**

One of my favourite places to escape to in Munich is the Viktualienmarkt, a fresh food market in the centre of the city. It's [1]______ (quiet) than the area around it and some products are [2]______ (cheap) as those in the supermarket – sometimes cheaper!
But when I really want to escape the city, I go to the English Garden. It's [3]______ (peaceful) than the Viktualienmarkt, and the air is [4]______ (not dirty) as the rest of the city. You can always find a quiet place to relax because it's so big. In fact, it's [5]______ (big) than Central Park in New York!

8 a **Compare the places using the adjectives in Exercise 2a.**

1 Rio de Janeiro / Madrid
I think Rio de Janeiro is more beautiful than Madrid.
2 my town or city / Paris
3 the desert / the mountains
4 the parks in my town or city / the countryside
5 the cities in my country / the cities in the US

b **Work in pairs and compare your ideas.**

Go to page 120 or your app for more information and practice.

Speaking

PREPARE

9 a **3.2 You're going to make a list of top ten places to visit. First, listen to Mark and Sandra talking about an article they have to write. Which two places do they choose to write about?**

b **Listen again and answer the questions.**

1 Why doesn't Sandra like Mark's first choices?
2 Why does Mark like the Louvre?
3 What does Sandra say about the British Museum?

10 a **Make your own list. Write two places for each of the categories below. They can be places in your own country or other countries.**

- famous buildings
- street markets
- places to eat
- beaches
- parks
- shopping areas

b **Write some adjectives next to each place.**

SPEAK

11 a **Work in pairs. Compare your lists using the adjectives you wrote and agree on two places for each category.**

A: *Bondi Beach is really beautiful, but I think South Bay is more beautiful and more peaceful*
B: *OK, let's choose South Bay*

b **Share your list with the rest of the class. Did anyone else make the same choices as you?**

Develop your reading page 92

3B A place to stay

> **Goal:** choose a place to stay
> **Grammar:** superlatives
> **Vocabulary:** hotels and places to stay

Vocabulary and reading

1 Work in groups and discuss the questions.

1 Do you like staying in hotels? Why/Why not?
2 What are the most important things for you when you choose a hotel?

2 a Work in pairs. Match words 1–10 with a–j.

1 airport	a room
2 breakfast	b service
3 organised	c star
4 free	d out
5 room	e included
6 double	f reception
7 sea	g transfer
8 four-	h tour
9 24-hour	i view
10 check	j parking

b Complete the sentences with one of the phrases.

1 We don't need to take a taxi. The hotel provides a free ____________ .
2 Is there a late ____________ ? I don't want to get up yet!
3 Here are your keys. There's ____________ in the price, but not lunch and dinner.
4 Excuse me. We asked for a ____________ , but we can only see the car park from our window.
5 Let's order some ____________ – I'm hungry!
6 Is there a ____________ ? We're going to arrive in the middle of the night.
7 We'd like to visit the city tomorrow. Can you recommend an ____________ ?
8 We have a ____________ for the same price as a single – would you like to book it?

3 a Think about the last time you stayed in a hotel and make notes. Use the phrases in Exercise 2a.

b Work in pairs. Tell each other about your hotels. Ask questions to find out more information.

A: I stayed in a modern five-star hotel for work.
B: Was it nice?
A: Not really, it was too big.

Go to page 138 or your app for more vocabulary and practice.

4 a Look at the photos in the magazine article. What do you think you can do in each place?

b Read the article and check your ideas.

We asked you to share your interesting hotel experiences with us from around the world. Here are our top choices.

BELA VISTA HOSTEL Peru

Shaun Tyson

We had a great time at the Bela Vista. It had some of the best views of anywhere we stayed in South America – we booked the room at the top of the hostel because you can see the furthest from it. Also, it's the biggest room. We spent an hour or two there every day, relaxing with a cold drink and enjoying the view. We loved their organised tours of the forest – they were amazing! But the best thing is, it's the least expensive place to stay in the area (with breakfast included every day!).

MATAHARI VILLAGE Indonesia

Juliette Wilson

Last year we travelled through South-East Asia and stayed in lots of modern hotels. So, when we came to Matahari Village, it was a really nice change. Actually, it was the nicest place we stayed in. We learnt about local cooking in the day, met people from the area, and at night we stayed in beautiful wooden houses. The beds inside didn't look very comfortable, but in fact it was the most comfortable place we stayed in all holiday!

THE PRINCESS MARGARITA RESORT Seychelles

Tristan Norris

This summer, my wife and I wanted to do something a bit special. We stayed in the 'Water Room' at The Princess Margarita Resort. The room is actually in the sea and you can see tropical fish through the glass floor. It's the most beautiful view ever. So if you're looking for a peaceful place to stay, then I definitely recommend it. Fish are the quietest neighbours in the world! At the end of our holiday, we didn't want to check out.

5 a Read the article again and match the descriptions to the places.

1 It's cheaper than other local places.
Bela Vista Hostel
2 You can learn something new there.
3 There isn't any noise.
4 You have a view under your feet.
5 You can see a long way from one of the rooms.
6 It's a traditional experience.

b Work in pairs and discuss the questions.

1 Which of these places would/wouldn't you like to stay in? Why? Why not?
2 Are there any places like this in your country?

Grammar

6 a Read the grammar box and choose the correct alternatives.

Superlatives

Use *the* + superlative adjective to compare.
*Hostels are **the cheapest** places to stay in the city.*
To make superlative adjectives, add *-est* or *-iest* to [1]*short/long* adjectives.
*It's the **biggest** hotel in the area.*
*He's the **funniest** person I know.*
Use *the most* or *the least* before [2]*short/long* adjectives.
*TenX is **the most modern** hotel in the city.*
*It was **the least comfortable** room in the hotel.*
Some adjectives are irregular, e.g. *bad - worse - worst.*
*It's **the worst** hotel in the city.*

b Find and underline nine superlatives in the article.

7 a 3.3 Listen to the sentences and notice how the superlatives are pronounced.

1 It's the easiest place to find.
2 It's the oldest building in the area.
3 This is the ugliest hotel in town.
4 They have the nicest food.

b Listen again and repeat.

8 Complete each sentence with the superlative form of the adjective in brackets.

1 This is ____ (small) room in the hotel, but it's very quiet.
2 The New Hotel is ____ (modern) hotel in the area. It was built last year.
3 Where's ____ (good) place to stay in this town? I've never been here before.
4 The hotels here are quite cheap, but the hostel next door is ____ (expensive) option – it's only £15 a night!
5 This is ____ (pretty) part of town.
6 There are the ____ (amazing) views from the roof. I took lots of photos!

9 a Complete the questions about the places in the article with the superlative form of the adjective in brackets.

Which place do you think ...
1 is ____________ (expensive)?
2 is ____________ (cheap)?
3 has ____________ (good) restaurant?
4 has ____________ (nice) rooms?
5 is ____________ (easy) to get to?
6 is ____________ (difficult) to get to?
7 has ____________ (interesting) organised tours?
8 is ____________ (far) from your country?

b Work in pairs and ask and answer the questions. Do you agree with each other?

Go to page 120 or your app for more information and practice.

Speaking

PREPARE

10 3.4 You're going to plan a trip. First, listen to Pat, Andrea and Shannon discussing three places to stay: Casa Tranquila, The Happy Campers Village and The Mantra Resort. Answer the questions.

1 Which hotel is the most expensive?
2 Which hotel is the cheapest?
3 Where do they decide to go?

11 a Imagine you're planning a class trip to New York and you need to decide where to stay. First, decide how important these things are for you (1 = not important and 5 = very important).

- close to the centre
- noise
- cost
- modern
- size of the room
- facilities (wifi, parking, etc.)

b Go to page 152. Read the information about three hotels and choose where you want to stay.

SPEAK

12 Work in groups. Explain your choice with the other students in your group and try to agree on a place to stay. Use the Useful phrases to help you.

A: *I think we should stay at the Homestyle because it's close to the centre and it's the cheapest.*
B: *I'm not sure. I'd like somewhere quiet and it's the noisiest!*

Useful phrases

I think we should stay at (the Miramar) because it (has the best views).
Why don't we (stay in this hotel)?
That one is too (expensive/noisy).
This one is (nearer) than (that one).

Develop your writing page 93

3D English in action

> **Goal:** give and respond to news

1 Work in pairs. What kind of news do people usually share with each other? Use the topics below to help you.

- family
- friends
- holidays
- home
- interests
- technology
- travel
- work

People often talk about work or their children.

2 a 3.13 Listen to three conversations. Which topic is each conversation about?

b Look at the Useful phrases. Then listen to the conversations again. In which conversation 1–3 do you hear each phrase?

Useful phrases

Giving news

Guess what!

Have you heard about ... ?

Asking for news

How are things? *1*

How have you been?

Responding to good news

That's (brilliant/great/fantastic)!

That's (fantastic/great/good) news.

Lucky you!

Sounds (amazing/brilliant/great)!

Responding to bad news

Sorry to hear that.

What a shame/That's a shame.

That's (awful/sad/not good).

3 a 3.14 Listen to two different speakers responding to some news. Do you think Speaker 1 or 2 uses the appropriate intonation in each phrase? Why?

1 Oh, that's a shame.
2 Really? That's a surprise!
3 Oh, I'm sorry to hear that
4 Really? That's not good!
5 Lucky you!

b 3.15 Listen and repeat. Copy the intonation.

4 a Read the sentences. Think about how to respond to each one. Use the Useful phrases to help you.

1 Guess what! I've won a trip to Paris!
2 Have you heard from Mike? He lost his phone last night!
3 I'm really sorry. I can't come to your birthday party.
4 We lost the match yesterday.
5 How are things with you?
6 My cat's missing. I can't find him anywhere.
7 Hey, I've got a new job!
8 Did you know that Tom's never read a book?

b Work in pairs. Take turns to read a sentence from Exercise 4a and respond.

B: Guess what! I've won a trip to Paris!
A: Lucky you!

Speaking

PREPARE

5 Imagine you're going to meet a friend to share some news. Choose three topics from Exercise 1 and make notes about some good or bad news – it can be real or imagined.

SPEAK

6 a Work in pairs and share your news with each other. Use the Useful phrases to help you.

A: Hey, how have you been?
B: Hi! I'm well, thanks. Guess what? I've got a new job!
A: That's brilliant! What is it?
B: I'm now head of sales.
A: Great! I have some good news, too – I've bought a new flat!
B: That's fantastic news!

b Work with a different partner and have another conversation.

Go online for the Roadmap video.

Check and reflect

1 a Complete each sentence with an adjective in the box.

dirty interesting lively modern noisy peaceful

1 The air in the city isn't very clean. It's quite ______ .
2 I know you find art galleries boring but I think they're ______ .
3 I like ______ restaurants with lots of people and noise.
4 I prefer ______ cities to old ones.
5 Most places are busy and noisy but the park is ______ .
6 This street's so ______ . I can't hear what you're saying!

b Work in pairs. Which adjectives can you use to describe the area where you are now?

2 a Complete the blog post with comparatives.

These days I live in London but I actually grew up on an island in the south of the UK called the Isle of Wight. The island's about 40 km long and 20 km wide with a population of 130,000 people so it's much [1]______ (small) than London. London's [2]______ (busy) and [3]______ (noisy) of course but it's also [4]______ (interesting) because there are so many things to do. There's a cinema on the island and lots of good places to eat out, but London has [5]______ (exciting) nightlife.

I feel lucky because I can enjoy London but also escape to the island for some weekends at the beach. The air there is [6]______ (fresh) than in London and I really feel that I can relax. I don't usually go there in summer though because the beaches feel [7]______ (crowded) as London! It's [8]______ (good) to go in spring or autumn when it's [9]______ (busy).

b Work in pairs and compare two places that you know.

3 a Complete each sentence about where you live with a superlative and your own idea.

1 The ______ (good) place to meet new people is ______ .
2 The ______ (nice) time of year is ______ .
3 The ______ (quiet) place in the area is ______ .
4 The ______ (delicious) food around here is ______ .

b Work in pairs. Share your answers to 3a. Do you agree?

4 a Complete the hotel description with the words below.

airport transfer breakfast included five-star free parking organised tours room service sea view 24-hour reception

The Ambassador Hotel is a [1]________ hotel with excellent service. There is a [2]________ so guests can check in at any time. Our rooms are comfortable and most of them have a [3]________ . There's [4]________ in the price and [5]________ is available if you want to eat in your room. There's [6]________ for people who want to drive here, and we offer a free [7]________ when you need to get your flight home. While you're with us, make sure you go on one of our fantastic [8]________ around the city to see some of the sights.

b Work in pairs. Describe your dream hotel. Where is it? What is in it? What can you do there?

5 a Choose the correct alternatives.

1 She's so lazy. She *has/have* never worked a day in her life!
2 Have you *ever/never* been to Greece?
3 We've never *saw/seen* so many people on this beach.
4 Luke *been/went* to the Maldives last year.
5 *I never/I've never* had a birthday party when I was a child.
6 *Did/Have* you ever tried sushi?
7 He *have/has* never played basketball.
8 They *spoke/have spoken* to a famous person at the weekend.

b Work in pairs. Take turns to ask *Have you ever ... ?* questions with the activities below and ask some follow-up questions.

- see an elephant
- cook dinner for more than ten people
- play chess
- win a competition
- ride a motorbike

A: *Have you ever seen an elephant?*
B: *Yes, I have.*
A: *When was that?*
B: *Last year in India.*

6 a Complete each sentence with an appropriate verb in the correct form. More than one answer might be possible.

1 I've never ______ on TV but I was once on the radio.
2 My mum's never ______ how to swim.
3 I ______ asleep on the bus yesterday.
4 My brother's never ______ a bike. He prefers walking!
5 Last year I ______ my uncle's sports car. It was fast.
6 I ______ Chinese food for the first time last night.

b Write a list of six activities you think everyone should do in their lifetime.

c Work in pairs and compare your lists. Which activities have you done? Which haven't you done?

Reflect

How confident do you feel about the statements below? Write 1–5 (1 = not very confident, 5 = very confident).

- I can compare places to visit.
- I can choose a place to stay.
- I can describe past expediences.
- I can give and respond to news.

Want more practice?
Go to your Workbook or app.

4A Special days

- **Goal:** talk about plans for a special day
- **Grammar:** *be going to, want* and *would like*
- **Vocabulary:** celebrations

A

B

C

Reading and vocabulary

1 **Work in pairs and look at the photos. What can you see? Which countries do you think these celebrations happen in?**

2 a **Read the text and check your ideas in Exercise 1. Match each celebration to a photo.**

b **Read the article again and answer the questions.**

1. When do people celebrate each day?
2. What do people do on these days?
3. On which day do people not go to work?

Celebrations around the WORLD

Friend's Day

Friend's Day in Argentina is on 20th July each year. It's a really important day and people start preparing a long time before. It's not a public holiday so people still work, but in the evenings they meet up with friends. It's popular to go out for a meal and restaurants are always full. People often contact old friends and give gifts to each other.

Moon Festival

This is one of the most famous festivals in China. The date changes every year but people celebrate it every autumn. It happens at this time of year because it's when farmers collect the food from their fields. It's called the Moon Festival because people thank the moon for the seasons and the food. It's a public holiday so people enjoy themselves all day. Some people celebrate at home, others go out to look at the moon, and lots of people eat traditional mooncakes.

Burn's Night

Robert Burns was a famous Scottish poet in the 18th century. Every 25th January, on his birthday, friends and family get together to celebrate Burns' Night. People work during the day, so in the evening they have dinner parties and invite friends and family to their homes for a Burn's Supper. They eat traditional food such as haggis and read some of Robert Burns' poems. They have fun on a cold winter's night.

3 a **Complete each question with a word or phrase in the box. Use the text in Exercise 2 to help you.**

celebrate	contact old friends	festivals	~~get together~~	give gifts	go out for a meal	have dinner parties	have fun	public holiday	traditional

1. How often do you *get together* with your friends and family?
2. Do you ever ________? How do you find them?
3. Do you like to ________ at your home? Are you a good cook?
4. What's your favourite ________? Does everyone have a day off work?
5. When did you last ________? Where did you go? What did you eat?
6. Do you prefer to ________ or receive them?
7. Are there any good ________ in your area? What do people do at them?
8. How do you like to ________ your birthday?
9. Do you prefer ________ festivals or modern ones?
10. How do you like to ________ and celebrate? What kinds of things do you do?

b **Work in pairs and take turns to ask and answer the questions.**

Go to your app for more practice.

Grammar

4 a 🔊 4.1 **Listen to Ben and Jane talking about Burn's Night. What are their plans?**

b Listen again and choose the correct alternatives.

1. I'm *going/want* to invite my neighbours to my house.
2. My mum *would like/'s going* to cook for the whole family.
3. I'd *like/want* to make a traditional meal.
4. I'm *not going/don't want* to cook haggis though.
5. I *would like/want* to ask my neighbours to bring a dessert.
6. What poems *are you going to/do you want* to read?

5 Read the grammar box and choose the correct alternatives.

> ### *be going to, want* and *would like*
> Use *be* + *going to* + [1]*infinitive/-ing form* to talk about future plans.
> ***I'm going to invite*** *my neighbours for dinner.*
> Use *want* and *would like* + [2]*infinitive/-ing form* to talk about things we want to do.
> ***I'd like to make*** *a traditional meal.*
> ***I want to ask*** *my neighbours to bring a dessert.*
> Use these time expressions to talk about the future:
> *in an hour, this Friday, next week, in two weeks/in two weeks' time.*

6 a 🔊 4.2 **Listen to the sentences. Notice the pronunciation of *to* in each one. Is it strong or weak?**

1. Dan wants to have a dinner party next week.
2. Kelly's going to contact her old school friends.
3. I'd like to go out for a meal later.

b Listen again and repeat.

7 a Complete the conversation with the correct forms of the verbs in the box.

be going to/do ~~be going to/celebrate~~
be going to/have be going to/get together
want/find would like to/go

A: Have you had any ideas for Friend's Day? How [1] *are* you [2] *going to celebrate* ?

B: I [3]__________ with some old school friends. We [4]__________ a dinner.

A: That's nice. Where are you going?

B: We [5]__________ to a great restaurant near my flat, if there are any tables available.

A: What [6]__________ you [7]__________ if it's full?

B: I'm not sure. We [8]__________ somewhere nice and quiet so we can chat.

A: Well, Chesco's Pizza is really nice, and in a quiet part of town. You could go there.

B: Great idea! Thanks!

b Work in pairs. Practise the conversation.

8 a Put the future time expressions in order from nearest (1) to furthest (8) in time.

- in two months' time
- next April
- at two o'clock tomorrow
- the day after tomorrow
- the year after next
- in 2060
- in an hour *1*
- this Saturday

b Complete the sentences with your own ideas and a time expression.

1. I'm going …
   I'm going to start a new job next month.
2. I'm not going …
3. I want …
4. I don't want …
5. I'd like …
6. I wouldn't like …

c Work in pairs and compare your sentences. Ask each other questions to find out more.

A: *I'm going to start a new job next month.*
B: *That's great. What are you going to do?*

Go to page 122 or your app for more information and practice.

Speaking

PREPARE

9 You're going to talk about a celebration (e.g. a birthday, a graduation or a public holiday) happening soon. It can be real or imagined. First, make notes and answer the questions.

- When is it?
- What are you going to do?
- Where are you going to celebrate it?
- Who are you going to celebrate with?

SPEAK

10 a Work in groups. Take turns to tell each other about your celebration. Ask each other questions to find out more. Use the Useful phrases to help you.

> **Useful phrases**
> A big celebration for me is (my daughter's birthday).
> I'm going to have fun (with friends/my family).
> We're going to (have a picnic).
> I'd also like to (play some games).
> What do you (want to do)?

b Who has the most interesting plans in your group? What are they going to do?

Develop your writing page 95

4B Planning events

Goal: organise an event
Grammar: *will/ won't* for decisions and offers
Vocabulary: organising events

Reading

1 **Work in pairs. Have you ever done any of the things below? Tell your partner about them.**
- cooked a meal for lots of people
- organised a surprise birthday party
- organised your own birthday party
- organised a work event

2 a **Work in pairs. How organised are you? Give yourself a score from 1–30 (30=very organised).**

b **Do the quiz. Then go to page 153, add up your score and read your results. Do you agree? Why/Why not?**

3 **Work in pairs and discuss the questions.**
1. Can you think of any other important things that you have to do when organising an event?
2. What's the best event you've ever been to? Why was it so good?

Grammar

4 **Read the grammar box and choose the correct alternatives.**

will/ won't for decisions and offers

To make a decision or an offer, use *will* + infinitive [1]*with to/without to.*

***I'll book** another restaurant.*
***I'll change** it if you need me to.*

Will is contracted to *'ll* and *will not* is contracted to *won't.*

***I'll** start now.*
***I won't** organise anything for a month or two.*

5 a 4.3 **Listen and choose the sentence you hear.**
1. a I'll drive to work.
   b I drive to work.
2. a We'll help them clean.
   b We help them clean.
3. a I'll call Ella every day.
   b I call Ella every day.
4. a We'll play on Sunday.
   b We play on Sunday.

b **Listen again and repeat.**

Are you organised?

1 **Your boss wants you to organise a party for your colleagues in three months' time. What do you think?**

a I'll start now. It's important to organise everything early.
b I'll think about some ideas now, but I won't organise anything for a month or two.
c Three months is a long time. I can forget about it for now.

2 **You want to organise a party to celebrate your Dad's birthday, but you don't have any money. What do you think?**

a I'll get my dad to pay for it. I'll suggest he cooks a meal for everyone or takes us to a restaurant.
b I'll hire a big room and book a DJ, then sell tickets to pay for it.
c I'll ask other family members to help with the cost.

3 **You're organising a party in a restaurant for thirty people. Two days before, you find out the restaurant doesn't have any vegetarian options and you know that ten of the people you invited are vegetarians. What do you think?**

a I'll ask the vegetarians not to come.
b I'll book another restaurant.
c I'll speak to the manager and ask them to prepare a vegetarian option. Thirty people is good business for them.

4 **You're organising a sports event and you've got too much to do. You're worried you can't do everything. What do you think?**

a I'll ask people to help.
b I'll cancel the event.
c I'll make it a smaller event, with fewer sports.

5 **You sent out invitations to your friend's surprise birthday party two weeks ago, but no one's replied. What do you think?**

a 'Why didn't you reply? I'll have to cancel the party now.'
b 'Did you get the invitation? I'd really like you to come.'
c 'Is that date difficult for you? I'll change it if you need me to.'

6 **You're organising a big party and two hours before the DJ calls you to say he can't come. What do you think?**

a 'Don't worry, I've got some music on my phone.'
b 'Why didn't you tell me earlier? I'll see if my friend can play instead.'
c 'I won't ever call you again!'

6 **Complete the conversations with *'ll* and a verb in the box.**

carry clean come do make

1 **A:** These bags are really heavy.
B: I __________ them for you.
2 **A:** Hello Jamie? I've missed the last bus.
B: Don't worry, I __________ and get you.
3 **A:** Mum, I'm hungry.
B: OK, I __________ you a snack.
4 **A:** Right, we need someone to book the restaurant.
B: OK, I __________ it – I've got their number.
5 **A:** What have you done to my car – it's really dirty!
B: Sorry, we __________ it now.

Go to page 122 or your app for more information and practice.

Vocabulary

7 a **Work in pairs. Imagine you're organising a surprise party for someone. Make a list of the things you need to do.**

b **Complete the 'to do' list with the verbs in the box.**

bake book ~~choose~~ plan ~~make~~ remind send set

Kate's party – to do list
1 ______ a date – 30th March?
2 *choose* a place – restaurant? club? town hall?
3 ______ a DJ
4 ______ invitations
5 ______ a cake (chocolate!)
6 *make* some food – lasagne? pizza? sandwiches?
7 ______ activities/things to do – games?
8 ______ people one week before!

c **Were any of your ideas in Exercise 7a on the list?**

8 **Choose the correct alternatives.**

A: Right, so we need to [1]*set/plan* a date. Kate's birthday is on 1st April, but that's a Monday. What about having a party on the Saturday before?
B: Sounds good. I'll [2]*bake/book* a DJ if you want.
A: Great. We also need to [3]*remind/choose* a place. What about the town hall?
C: Good idea. I work near there so I'll book it.
A: OK, I'll [4]*make/send* invitations to everyone. What about food?
C: Oh, I'll [5]*plan/bake* a cake! Kate loves chocolate!
B: Yes, and I'll [6]*make/set* lasagne – it's her favourite.
A: Brilliant. I'll [7]*send out/plan* some games to play after dinner, too … OK, anything else?
C: I'll [8]*remind/choose* everyone a few days before so they don't forget!

Go to your app for more practice.

Speaking

PREPARE

9 a **Work in groups. You're going to plan an event together. First, decide what kind of event you want to organise. Use the ideas below or think of your own idea.**
- a birthday party
- a class party to celebrate the end of the course
- a work summer party
- a sports event
- a music festival

b **Make a 'to do' list of things you need to organise.**

SPEAK

10 **Organise your event. Decide who will do what and when they will do it. Use the Useful phrases to help you.**

Useful phrases
We need to (send out invitations).
I'll (book a band) if you want.
Can you (call the restaurant)?
What about (food and drink)?

11 **Tell the class about your event.**
We're going to have a party for Ana's birthday. Marcelo's going to bake a cake.

Develop your listening page 96

4C Rules of the race

› **Goal:** present an idea for an event
› **Grammar:** *can* and *have to*
› **Vocabulary:** *-ed* and *-ing* adjectives

Listening

1 a Have you ever taken part in a race or do you know someone else who has? What kind of race was it?

b Read about an extreme race. Which of the activities can you see in the photos? Why do you think people want to do this race?

2 4.7 Listen to Felicity asking her colleague Lucas about the race. Answer the questions.

1 Which things in the box does Felicity ask about?

breaks	cost	health	location	start time
teams	visitors	what to wear		

2 Does Felicity decide to run in the race?

3 a Listen again and tick (✓) the statements that are true.

You need to …

1 be very fit.
2 see a doctor before the race.
3 do all parts of the race.
4 wear special clothes.

It's possible to …

5 bring food.
6 have a rest during the race.
7 run in a team.
8 get your money back after paying.

b 4.8 Listen to the extracts and complete the sentences.

1 Do I ______ to be very fit?
2 You don't have ______ see a doctor before you do it but it's a good idea.
3 Runners ______ to do everything on the course.
4 You ______ have to wear any special clothes.
5 ______ people bring their own food?
6 ______ I have a rest during the race?
7 But if you don't want to run on your own, you ______ run in a team.
8 After you pay, you ______ get your money back.

c Work in pairs and discuss the questions.

1 Would you like to take part in a race like this?
2 Do you know about any other unusual races?

Grammar

4 Complete the grammar box with *can*, *can't*, *have to* and *don't have to*. Use Exercise 3b to help you.

can and *have to*

Obligation

Use [1]______ to say that something is necessary.
*Runners **have to** do everything on the course.*
Use [2]______ to say that something is not necessary.
*You **don't have to** see a doctor before the race.*

Possibility

Use [3]______ to talk about things that are possible.
*You **can** run in a team.*
Use [4]______ to talk about things that are not possible.
*After you pay, you **can't** get your money back.*

5 a 4.9 **Listen to the sentences. When are *can* and *can't* stressed/not stressed?**

1 **A:** Can I take my own food?
B: Yes, you can.

2 **A:** Can we get our money back?
B: No, we can't.

3 **A:** Can we run together in a team?
B: Yes, we can.

b Listen again and repeat.

6 a Complete the descriptions with *can, can't, have to* or *don't have to* in the correct form and the verb in brackets.

1 Every May, in the UK, someone throws a cheese from the top of Cooper's Hill and runners [1]_______ (try) and catch it. There [2]_______ (be) more than 15 runners in a race because people often fall down and have accidents.

2 The Colorado Pack Burro race is a marathon with a difference. Each runner [3]_______ (take) a donkey up a 29-mile path. However, there's one important rule – they [4]_______ (push) the donkey, pull the donkey or even carry the donkey, but they can't ride it.

3 In the wife-carrying race in Finland, runners [5]_______ (carry) their wives along a 253.5 metre track. The wife [6]_______ (run) at all, only the man can. She [7]_______ (be) the runner's own wife – it's OK if she's a friend's wife, for example.

b Which race do you think is the most unusual?

7 a Complete the sentences so they are true for you.

1 Most days, I have to ...
2 I don't have to ...
3 Usually, I can ...
4 I can't ...

b Work in pairs. Tell each other your sentences and ask some questions.

A: Most days, I have to get up at 5.30.
B: Why do you have to do that?

Go to page 122 or your app for more information and practice.

Vocabulary

8 a Which of the adjectives in bold in sentences 1–4 describe a feeling and which describe a thing?

1 I'm **interested** in running the Massive Mud Run.
2 It's an **interesting** course.
3 The race is really **tiring**.
4 The race lasts 12 hours so you'll be **tired**.

b Choose the correct alternatives.

1 Which sports do you think are *bored/boring*?
2 Do you feel *relaxed/relaxing* after you do exercise?
3 When was the last time you were *excited/exciting* about a sport?
4 What *interested/interesting* things do you enjoy doing?
5 What do you sometimes feel *worrying/worried* about?
6 What's the most *tiring/tired* thing you've ever done?
7 What's the most *excited/exciting* sporting moment in your country's history?
8 What's the most *surprised/surprising* thing someone has done for you?

c Work in pairs. Take turns to ask and answer the questions in Exercise 8b.

Go to page 139 or your app for more vocabulary and practice.

Speaking

PREPARE

9 a 4.10 **You're going to present an idea for a race. First, listen to Marco and his classmates presenting their idea. Who is the race for?**

b Listen again and answer the questions.

1 Where is the race?
2 Do the runners run alone or in teams?
3 Do the runners have to wear anything special?
4 What are the rules of the race?
5 What prizes do the winners get?

10 Work in groups. Plan a race for your town or city.

SPEAK

11 a Present your race to the class. Use the Useful phrases to help you.

b Vote for the best idea. You can't vote for your own!

Useful phrases

The (event) is (in June).
The winners get (a prize).
It starts at (9 a.m.) in Dublin.
(Runners) have to/don't have to/can/can't (bring water).

Develop your reading page 97

4D English in action

> **Goal:** make plans to meet

A

B

C

Listening

1 **Look at photos A–C and answer the questions.**

1. How often do you do these things with your friends?
2. What other things do you like to do?
3. How do you organise to meet?
4. How often do you do the things in the photos?

2 a **4.11 Listen to conversations 1–3 and match each one to the places in photos A–C.**

b **Listen again and answer the questions.**

1. Why doesn't Lucy want to meet at the park entrance?
2. Where do Lucy and Susan decide to meet?
3. Why can't Jimmy meet on Friday?
4. Why can't Chris meet on Sunday?
5. Why doesn't Tanya want to go to the concert by taxi?
6. Why does Paul think this isn't a problem?

3 **Look at the Useful phrases and then listen again. In which conversation (1, 2 or 3) do you hear the phrases in the box?**

Useful phrases

Inviting people

Would you like to come? *1*
Do you want to meet up (this Friday)?
Do you want to join us?

Responding to invitations

I'd love to!
Yes, that sounds (fun/great).
I don't think I can, sorry.
I'm sorry I can't, I'm busy.

Organising when and where to meet

Where/What time shall we meet?
Shall we meet (at ten/at the park)?
Let's meet (in front of the bank/at five o'clock).

Responding to suggestions

That's a good idea.
I'm not sure about that.

4 a **4.12 Listen to the phrases and underline the stressed words.**

1. Would you like to come?
2. Do you want to join us?
3. I'd love to.
4. Where shall we meet?
5. Shall we meet at ten?
6. That's a good idea.

b **Listen again and repeat.**

5 a **Use the prompts to write questions.**

1. like / go / cinema / tomorrow?
2. want / play football / us / weekend?
3. Shall / go / a restaurant?
4. time / shall / meet?
5. Shall / meet / seven o'clock?

b **Work in pairs. Practise saying the questions and responding in different ways.**

Speaking

PREPARE

6 **You're going to organise something to do with your classmates. First, make notes about what you'd like to do (e.g. have lunch, go for a run). Answer the questions below to help you.**

- What are you going to do?
- What time would you like to meet?
- Where would you like to meet?

SPEAK

7 a **Go around the class and invite people to meet up. Respond to other people's invitations. Use the Useful phrases to help you.**

A: Would you like to come to our picnic?
B: I'd love to. Where is it?
A: It's in Parco Centrale. It starts at one o'clock.

b **Did you make any interesting plans? Which Useful phrases did you find the most useful?**

Go online for the Roadmap video.

Check and reflect

1 a Find five mistakes and correct them.

1 I'm going move to another country after I graduate.
2 I'd like to go away somewhere nice this weekend.
3 I going to finish this lesson in 30 minutes.
4 My parents want retire when they're 70.
5 I'm going to have dinner at eight o'clock tonight.
6 I like to visit Denmark one day.
7 The teacher's going to give us lots of homework.
8 Two of my friends is going to get married next year.

b Change the sentences so that they're true for you.

1 I'm going to move to Istanbul next year.

2 Match the halves of each phrase.

1 public	a gifts
2 go out	b holiday
3 give	c old friends
4 have	d for a meal
5 have a dinner	e together
6 contact	f fun
7 get	g party

3 Work in pairs and discuss the questions.

1 What was the last special day you celebrated?
2 Which of the things in Exercise 2 did you do?

4 a Choose the correct alternatives.

1 I'll *carry/to carry* it for you.
2 *I won't/I'll* pick you up if you want.
3 We'll *looking/look* after the kids tonight.
4 I'll *lend/to lend* you some money.
5 *I/I'll* help her.

b Work in pairs. What do you think the other person says before each offer in Exercise 4a?

5 Put the sentences and questions in the correct order.

1 party / I'd / Sam's / go / to / to / like
2 you / do / go / to / running / want / ?
3 August / to / this / Mark's / Ibiza / going
4 Saturday / are / watch / on / you / to / going / match / the / ?
5 dinner / come / she'll / after / home
6 tonight / I'm / late / going / stay / to / out / not
7 doesn't / to / change / Kate / want / job / her
8 world / like / would / the / you / travel / around / to / ?

6 Complete the sentences with the missing word.

1 I need to p______ some games for my son's fifth birthday.
2 Let's b______ a cake for Ella's birthday.
3 My mum always m______ a special dish at New Year.
4 I'm going to s______ the invitations next week.
5 Did you r______ everyone about the party?
6 Have they s______ a date for their wedding?

7 Work in pairs. Think of the last time you planned an event. Tell each other what you did.

8 a Complete the sports rules with *can, can't, have to* or *don't have to*.

1 Football: You ______ touch the ball with your feet, legs and head but you ______ touch it with your hands.
2 Running: You ______ use any special equipment, but there are lots of things you ______ use if you want to.
3 Swimming: You ______ use your body to move through the water.
4 Tennis: You ______ hit a ball with a racket.
5 Basketball: You ______ touch the ball with your hands but you ______ carry the ball while you move.
6 Golf: You ______ hit the ball into a hole. You ______ kick it with your foot or move it with your hand.
7 Volleyball: You ______ to hit the ball over the net with your hands. You ______ use your feet or head. You ______ play it on the beach.

b Work in pairs. Think of another sport. What are the rules?

9 a Choose the correct alternatives.

1 I feel *worried/worrying* a lot about work.
2 I think horror films are very *frightened/frightening*.
3 I'd like to be more *relaxed/relaxing* about speaking English.
4 I was *surprised/surprising* when I read the news yesterday.
5 I think surfing is *excited/exciting*.
6 I'm not very *interested/interesting* in sport.
7 I never feel *bored/boring* when I'm at work.
8 For me, shopping is a really *tired/tiring* activity.

b Change the sentences so they're true for you.

Reflect

How confident do you feel about the statements below? Write 1–5 (1 = not very confident, 5 = very confident).

- I can describe plans.
- I can organise an event.
- I can present an idea for an event.
- I can make plans to meet.

Want more practice?
Go to your Workbook or app.

5A The right person

› **Goal:** describe a job

› **Grammar:** relative clauses with *who, which* and *that*

› **Vocabulary:** job skills and preferences

A

B

C

D

E

F

Vocabulary and listening

1 a Work in pairs. How many jobs can you think of? Write a list.

b Match the jobs in the box with photos A–F.

architect	businessperson	film extra
shop assistant	tour guide	writer

2 a Read the questionnaire and check you understand the phrases in bold. Then complete the questionnaire for you.

b Work in pairs. Compare your answers to the questionnaire. Do you have the same skills? Do you have similar work habits?

c Work in pairs and discuss the jobs in Exercise 1b.

1 Which jobs can you match with the sentences in the questionnaire?

2 Which jobs would you be good at? Why?

3 Which jobs would you like to do? Why?

Go to page 140 or your app for more vocabulary and practice.

Work and skills questionnaire

Mark the line with a cross to show how much you agree.

1 I am **creative.**
Disagree .... *Agree*

2 I have **good communication skills.**
Disagree .... *Agree*

3 I am a **good manager.**
Disagree .... *Agree*

4 I like **working in a team.**
Disagree .... *Agree*

5 I like **working from home.**
Disagree .... *Agree*

6 I like **working on my own.**
Disagree .... *Agree*

7 I'd like to **work part-time.**
Disagree .... *Agree*

8 I don't need **a job that is well-paid.**
Disagree .... *Agree*

9 I enjoy **working with customers.**
Disagree .... *Agree*

10 I don't mind **working long hours.**
Disagree .... *Agree*

3 a 5.1 **Listen to Cheryl talking to her friend James. Which of the jobs in Exercise 1b do they mention? Which job does Cheryl like?**

b **Listen again and answer the questions.**

1 Why is Cheryl looking for a new job?
2 What's important for her in a job?
3 Why doesn't she like the first two jobs that James suggests?
4 Why does she like the last job he suggests?

4 5.2 **Listen to the extracts and choose the correct alternatives.**

1 I'd like a job *that's/who's* completely different.
2 I want a job *which/that* is interesting.
3 They want someone *who/which* enjoys writing.
4 Well, they're looking for someone *that/who* can work part-time.

Grammar

5 **Read the grammar box and choose the correct alternatives.**

Relative clauses with *who, which* and *that*

Use defining relative clauses to give more information about people and things.

Use *who* for [1]*people/things*.

We need ***someone who*** *has good communication skills.*

Use *which* or *that* for [2]*people/things*.

I want a ***teaching job which*** *is well-paid.*

She wants a ***part-time job that*** *is interesting.*

It is sometimes possible to use *that* instead of *who*.

He's the man that we interviewed last week.

Also use defining relative clauses to combine two sentences.

He's a doctor. He works all over the world.

= He's ***a doctor who works*** *all over the world.*

6 a 5.3 **Listen to the relative clauses and notice the pronunciation of *who, which* and *that*.**

1 This job is for people who can work long hours.
2 I'd like a job which is interesting.
3 He wants a job that's well-paid.

b **Listen again and repeat.**

7 **Complete the sentences with a relative pronoun.**

1 This is the dress ______ I bought yesterday.
2 He's the man ______ fixed my computer.
3 This is the book ______ I read on holiday.
4 It's a job ______ you have to do at night.
5 She's the girl ______ lives next to me.
6 I like films ______ are about real people.
7 Paul is the person ______ told me about this restaurant.
8 This is the time of year ______ I like the best.

8 **Choose the correct alternatives to complete the text. What job does it describe?**

For this job we need someone [1]*which/who* is creative, so that they can plan activities [2]*who/that* are interesting for small children. The best person for this job is someone [3]*who/which* has good communication skills, because it's a job [4]*who/that* involves working with many different types of people, such as children, parents and managers. It's a job [5]*who/which* isn't usually well-paid, but it's very interesting. Nowadays, you also need to be someone [6]*which/who* is good with computers to do this job well.

9 **Work in pairs. Take turns to describe a type of job you would like to do. Use the phrases in the questionnaire to help you. Suggest some jobs for your partner.**

A: *I'd like a job which I can do from home.*
B: *How about an online teacher?*

Go to page 124 or your app for more information and practice.

Speaking

PREPARE

10 **You're going to describe a job for other students to guess. First, think of a job that you want to describe. Then complete the sentences below.**

- It's a job which ...
- It isn't a job that you ...
- You need to be someone who ...
- You can't be someone who likes/doesn't like ...

It's a job that you can do at home. You need to be someone who's creative ... (an artist).

SPEAK

11 a **Work in groups. Describe your job to the group. Can they guess which job you're describing?**

b **Would you like to do the jobs that other people described? Why/Why not? Use the Useful phrases to help you.**

Useful phrases

I'd like to be (a chef) because (I love food).
I wouldn't like to be a (journalist) because I don't like (writing).
I think I'd like this job because (it's creative)
I don't think I'd like this job because (it's not well-paid).

Develop your reading page 98

5B Appearances

A

D

- **Speaking:** describe people
- **Grammar:** *look like, look* +adjective, *be like*
- **Vocabulary:** appearance

Reading

1 Work in pairs and discuss the questions.

1. Do you use social media? What for?
2. Do you post photos on social media?
3. Have you ever tried to find anyone/anything using social media? Do you think social media is a good way to do this?

2 Read the post and answer the questions.

1. What did Gabriela find?
2. Where did she find it?
3. What does Gabriela want people to do?
4. Who does Katie think the person in the photo is?
5. How does Katie describe Eduardo's personality?

Gabriela Garcia
Hi everyone. I found a camera on Corona Avenue at about 3.00 p.m. today. This is the most recent photo on it. Does anyone know these people? Please share this post so we can find out whose camera it is. Thanks!

Katie Novak
The man in the middle looks like Eduardo's brother, but I'm not sure. You can ask Eduardo – he works in the library.

Gabriela Garcia
I don't know Eduardo. What does he look like?

Katie Novak
He's got dark hair and a beard like the man in the photo, but he doesn't look old. He looks around 35.

Gabriela Garcia
What's he like? Will he think I'm strange if I show him a photo and ask if it's his brother?!

Katie Novak
No, don't worry, he won't think you're strange. He's really nice.

Grammar

3 Read the grammar box and choose the correct alternatives.

look like, look + adjective, *be like*

Use *look like* + [1]*adjective/noun* to describe people and things that are similar.
*The man in the middle **looks like Eduardo's brother**.*
Use *look* + [2]*adjective/noun* to describe appearances and feelings.
*You all **look** (really) **happy** in the photo.*
Use *look* + [3]*noun/number* to say how old we think someone or something is.
*He **looks** (around) **35**.*
Use *What do/does* (*he/she/they*) *look like?* to ask about the [4]*appearance/character* of a person or thing.
A: What does he look like?
B: He's got dark hair and a beard.
Use *What is/are* (*he/she/they*) *like?* to ask about a person's [5]*appearance/character*.
A: What's he like?
B: He's lovely.

4 a 5.4 Listen to the sentences. What do you notice about the letters in bold?

1. Oh dear. You loo**k a**ngry!
2. He look**s r**eally sad.
3. She look**s l**ike a runner.
4. They loo**k e**xcited.

b Listen again and repeat.

B

C

E

F

5 a **Match the sentence halves.**

1 I don't know Tom. What does
2 Is Sam OK? He doesn't
3 I don't think Evan is 30. He
4 The new manager started today. What's
5 Has Cecile had some good news? She
6 What's your dad's job? He

a he like?
b looks really happy.
c look well.
d looks like a businessperson.
e looks about 25.
f he look like?

b **Complete the questions and answers with the correct form of *be, like, look* and *look like*.**

1 **A:** What does he look like?
B: He ______ quite young and he has really short hair.
2 **A:** Does she ______ anyone in her family?
B: Yes, like her dad.
3 **A:** How old does he ______ ?
B: He looks about 40.
4 **A:** What's she like?
B: She ______ really nice.
5 **A:** Does she ____ like her twin sister?
B: Yes, they look exactly the same.
6 **A:** Is she like her brother?
B: Yes, they ____ both very funny.
7 **A:** What's your new boss ____?
B: He's very nice!
8 **A:** How old is Anthony?
B: I don't know, but he ____ really young.

Go to page 124 or your app for more information and practice.

Vocabulary

6 a **Match the words in the box with the categories below.**

bald beard blonde casual curly dark long moustache slim smart straight tall tattoo

- clothes
- body
- face
- hair

b **Think of some more words for each category.**

c **Work in pairs and compare your ideas.**

7 a 5.5 **Listen to Marcus telling Alessia about his family. Tick (✓) the words in Exercise 6a that he uses to describe them.**

b **Listen again. Make notes about what each member of Marcus's family looks like.**

c **Work in pairs and compare your notes. Then go to page 154 and check your ideas.**

8 a **Work in pairs. Look at photos A–F and take turns to describe one of the people. Try to guess which person your partner is describing.**

This person has short, dark hair and a moustache.

b **Make some guesses about each person's job, age and character with your partner. Use *looks* and *looks like*.**

A: *The man in photo C looks like a rock star.*
B: *Yes, he looks quite creative.*

c **Go to page 154 and read about each person. Did you guess correctly? Is there any surprising information?**

Go to your app for more practice.

Speaking

PREPARE

9 **You're going to describe three people who are important to you. First, make notes about the things below.**

- who each person is
- why each person is important to you
- each person's appearance
- each person's character
- each person's job, interests, etc.
- who each person is similar or different to

SPEAK

10 **Work in pairs. Take turns to describe the people you want to talk about. Ask your partner questions. How similar or different are the people you described?**

A: *I want to talk about my friend, Ella. We aren't very similar, but she's really important to me because she's my oldest friend.*
B: *That's great! Where did you meet her?*

Develop your listening page 99

5c Shopping tips

- **Goal:** give advice about shopping
- **Grammar:** *should, shouldn't* and imperatives
- **Vocabulary:** shopping

Vocabulary

1 Look at photos A–E and discuss the questions.

1. What do you usually buy in these places?
2. Where do you like to go shopping? Why?
3. Do you prefer shopping alone or with someone else?
4. Have you ever had a problem with something you've bought?

2 Work in pairs. Read the shopping tips and check you understand the meaning of the phrases in bold. Do you agree with the tips? Why/Why not?

TOP shopping tips

- **Pay by credit card** – you can collect points!
- Always **ask for a discount**.
- Always **keep the receipt**.
- If you don't have much time when buying clothes, don't **try them on** in the shop. You can always **return something** later (if you kept the receipt!)
- When buying electronic products, **read reviews** first.
- **Compare prices** before you buy – you might find something cheaper **in a sale**.

3 a Complete the questions with the phrases from Exercise 2.

1. Do you prefer to ________ or in cash? Why?
2. When is the best time to buy something ________ in your country? Are things a lot cheaper?
3. When was the last time you had to ________ to a shop? What was the problem?
4. Do you often ________ or do you usually just pay full price?
5. Do you ________ after you buy something? Or do you throw it away?
6. Do you like to ________? Do you think other people's opinions are important?
7. Do you use any websites to ________? Do you think this is a good way to save money?
8. When you buy clothes, do you always ________ first?

b Work in pairs and ask and answer the questions.

Go to your app for more practice.

Listening

4 a You're going to listen to Jenny and Luke describing problems with a coffee machine and a shirt. What kinds of problems do you think they'll describe?

b 5.9 Listen and check your ideas. Who bought each product? What was each person's problem?

c Listen again and answer the questions.

1 Was the coffee machine that Jenny bought cheap?
2 How much cheaper was the coffee machine on another day?
3 What happened to Luke's shirt on the morning of his interview?
4 Why didn't Luke try the shirt on before he bought it?
5 What was wrong with the shirt?

5 Who gives each piece of advice? Write Jenny (J) or Luke (L).

1 You should always try clothes on in the shop.
2 You shouldn't just buy the first thing you see.
3 Keep the receipt.

6 Work in pairs and discuss the questions.

1 Whose problem do you think was the worst? Why?
2 Have you ever had any problems like these?
3 Do you agree with their advice? Why/Why not?

Grammar

7 Read the grammar box and choose the correct alternatives.

should/shouldn't and imperatives

Use *should* + infinitive to say something is a [1]*good/bad* idea.

*You **should ask** for a discount.*

Use *shouldn't* + infinitive to say something is a [2]*good/bad* idea.

*You **shouldn't buy** something if you're not sure about it.*

Use an imperative for [3]*strong/weak* advice. Make imperatives with the infinitive [4]*with to/without to*.

***Look for** sales!*

It's also possible to use *always* or *never* before an infinitive.

***Never pay** by credit card.*

8 a 5.10 Listen to the advice. Is *should* or *shouldn't* stressed?

1 You should ask for a discount.
2 You shouldn't pay the full price.
3 You should return it.
4 You shouldn't buy a used phone.
5 You should read the description carefully.
6 You shouldn't buy that online.

b Listen again and repeat.

9 a Put the words in the correct order to make sentences.

1 old / an / Never / car / buy
2 clothes / buy / online / Don't
3 something / always / you / before / should / You / it / try / buy
4 the / supermarket / discount / Always / a / ask / for / in
5 things / You / cash / pay / expensive / shouldn't / for / in
6 market / buy / You / food / fresh / a / should / from

b Work in pairs. Do you agree with the advice? Why/Why not?

10 a Choose one of the topics below and write three tips for it.

- buying a mobile phone
- buying clothes
- buying a new car
- finding something in a sale
- shopping in your city
- shopping online

b Work in groups. Read out your tips to other students. Can the others guess which topic they're for? Do you agree? Why/Why not?

Go to page 124 or your app for more information and practice.

Speaking

PREPARE

11 You're going to talk about a shopping experience you've had. It can be real or imagined. First, answer the questions below.

- What did you buy/want to buy?
- Was it a good or bad experience?
- Why was it good/bad?
- What happened?
- What advice would you give to someone in the same situation?

SPEAK

12 Work in groups. Tell each other about your experiences and give your advice. Then agree on the two best pieces of advice.

Develop your writing page 100

5D English in action

Goal: make and respond to suggestions

Listening

1 **Look at the photos and discuss the questions.**

1 Which item would you most like to receive as a gift?
2 Are you good at finding gifts for people? Why/Why not?

2 a 5.11 **Listen to Simon and Tina. Who are they buying gifts for? Why?**

b **Match the sentence halves. Use the Useful phrases to help you.**

1 How	a him some gardening books.
2 What about	b some jewellery?
3 You could get	c the department store on West Street.
4 Why don't	d about some flowers?
5 Why don't we	e you get him a nice sun hat?
6 Let's try	f go shopping together at the weekend?

Useful phrases

Making suggestions
How/What about (some flowers)?
Why don't you/we (get her a watch)?
You could (buy him a ball).
Let's (get something on Saturday).

Responding to suggestions
Great!
(That's a really) good/fantastic idea.
Maybe/Perhaps.
I think I'd prefer to (get some flowers).

c **Listen again and check your answers.**

3 a 5.12 **Listen to the suggestions. Which word is the most stressed in each one?**

1 Why don't we make him a cake?
2 You could get her a book.
3 Why don't you buy them a game?
4 What about a new pair of trainers?
5 I think I'd prefer to get her some chocolates.

b **Listen again and repeat.**

4 a **Complete each suggestion with an appropriate idea.**

1 **A:** I'd like to buy my English teacher a gift.
B: How about *some chocolates* ?
2 **A:** What shall we do after class?
B: Let's ________ .
3 **A:** I need to get to class but my car won't start.
B: Why don't you ________ ?
4 **A:** What shall we have for dinner?
B: What about ________ ?
5 **A:** It's my friend's birthday but I don't have much money.
B: You could ________ .

b **Work in pairs. Take turns to read the sentences from Exercise 4a and respond with suggestions.**

5 **Work in groups. Take turns to tell each other about a person you'd like to buy a gift for. Give suggestions.**

A: I'd like to buy a present for my friend Greg. He loves football.
B: Which team does he like? You could buy him their shirt!

Speaking

PREPARE

6 **Work in pairs. Student A go to page 151 and Student B go to page 156. Follow the instructions.**

SPEAK

7 **Have a conversation and give each other gift suggestions. Try to use as many of the Useful phrases as possible.**

A: I need to buy a gift for Gail. She's 50, she's a doctor and she likes running. Do you have any ideas?
B: What about some nice running socks?

Go online for the Roadmap video.

Check and reflect

1 a Choose the correct alternatives.

1 A tour guide is a person *who/which* shows people around a city.
2 Police officers do a job *who/that* is sometimes dangerous.
3 I have a job *which/who* I like.
4 That's the man I *which/who* I work with.
5 Teaching is a job *who/which* is important.

b Write some definitions for jobs using *who* and *which*.

c Work in groups. Read out your definitions. The other students guess what you're describing.

A: *It's a person who looks after your teeth.*
B: *Is it a dentist?*
A: *Yes!*

2 a Match the sentence halves.

1 It's a	a well-paid job.
2 You need to be a good	b a team.
3 You need to be	c manager.
4 Most people who do this job like working in	d creative.
5 People who do this job usually work	e from home.

b Think of a job for each sentence.

3 a Choose the correct alternatives.

1 What does your closest friend *like/look like*?
2 What's your neighbour *like/look like*?
3 Who in your family *are/do* you look like?
4 What *was/were* you like when you were a child?
5 What did you *like/look like* when you were young?

b Match questions 1–5 to answers a–e.

a I was shy and didn't talk much.
b He's a nice man. I like him.
c She's tall with dark hair. She wears glasses.
d I had longer hair ... and I was thinner!
e My son. We have similar faces.

c Work in pairs. Take turns to ask and answer the questions in Exercise 3a.

4 Complete the description with the words in the box.

curly fair moustache slim tall

People say my brother Nik and I look similar, but I don't agree. Nik's [1]______ but I'm short. He's got dark hair but mine's [2]______ – also, his is straight but mine's [3]______. He's got a [4]______ but I haven't. One thing we do have in common is that we run a lot, so we're both quite [5]______.

5 a Sheila needs to buy a nice dress for a wedding but she hasn't got enough money. Complete the advice with the words in the box.

don't make should (x3) shouldn't tell

1 You ______ explain the situation to your friend. I'm sure she won't mind what you wear.
2 ______ your friend that you can't go. ______ waste your money!
3 You ______ buy new clothes. You ______ look for some nice used clothes.
4 You ______ go online and find a website that sells cheap clothes, or ______ a dress yourself!

b Work in pairs. Can you think of any other advice for Sheila?

6 a Choose the correct alternatives.

1 I never really compare *money/prices* before I buy something.
2 Most people I know pay *by/on* credit card.
3 I keep the *recipe/receipt* for most things that I buy.
4 I never *put/try* on clothes before I buy them.
5 I often ask for *sales/discounts*.
6 I often buy something and then *return/try* it to the shop the next day.
7 I prefer to buy clothes in a *bargain/sale*.

b Work in pairs. Which sentences do you agree with?

7 a Match words in the box to the definitions.

bald casual a discount work part-time good communication skills

1 a price which is lower than usual
2 the ability to speak to other people so they understand you well
3 without hair
4 work for only a few days a week
5 informal clothes/style

b Work in pairs. Choose three words or phrases from this unit. Take turns to give a definition and guess the word/phrase.

Reflect

How confident do you feel about the statements below? Write 1–5 (1 = not very confident, 5 = very confident).

- I can describe a job.
- I can describe people.
- I can give advice about shopping.
- I can make and respond to suggestions.

Want more practice?
Go to your Workbook or app.

6A Happiness

- **Goal:** make predictions about the future
- **Grammar:** *will* for predictions
- **Vocabulary:** happiness

Vocabulary and listening

1 Match photos A–G to statements 1–7 about what makes a happy life.

1 *I **earn lots of money** so I can do what I want. And I like having expensive cars and lots of nice things.*

2 *It's great to have enough money, but I think being healthy is more important. I always try to **eat well** and **keep fit**.*

3 ***A happy family life** is the only thing I need. There's nothing I love more than spending time with my wife and kids.*

4 ***A good career** is important. I really enjoy my job, which makes me feel good.*

5 *You've got to **have a lot of interests** and a **busy social life**. I couldn't live without my friends.*

6 ***A sense of humour** is very important. You have to laugh, even when life is difficult.*

7 ***A simple life** and plenty of **free time**. The simple things are the most important and we need time to enjoy them.*

2 Match the phrases in bold in Exercise 1 with sentences 1–10.

1 I'm meeting Jack for lunch on Thursday, then it's Sally's birthday on Friday and I'm going to a party on Saturday.
2 I ran 15 km and played a bit of tennis last weekend.
3 My company pays me just over €100,000 a year.
4 I'm going to spend some time in the garden next weekend, that's all.
5 Flora knows about lots of different things. She plays chess, likes music and enjoys football.
6 Jamie fell over in the street, but when he got up he just laughed about it. It was very funny.
7 Velia's job is going really well. She's very happy about it.
8 I only work three days a week – I think it's important not to work too much.
9 I cook my own meals and try to eat lots of fruit and vegetables.
10 We had a big dinner at home last night - children, grandparents, aunts and uncles. It was lovely!

3 Work in pairs. Discuss the statements in Exercise 1. What else is important for your happiness?

Go to your app for more practice.

F

G

4 a 6.1 **Listen to five people answering the question 'Will we be happier in the future?' Does each speaker 1–5 think we'll be happier?**

b **Listen again. Number the predictions in the order you hear them.**

1 It won't be hard to make friends.
2 It'll be easier to earn lots of money.
3 I don't think we'll have as much free time.
4 I think we'll be more careful about what we eat.

c **Work in pairs. Which predictions do you agree/disagree with? Why?**

Grammar

5 **Read the grammar box. Match statements a–d with predictions 1–4 in Exercise 4b.**

will for predictions

[a] Use *will* + infinitive to make predictions about the future.
***It'll be** more difficult to find a good job.*
[b] Use *won't* + infinitive for negative sentences.
*In the future, we **won't have** so many problems.*
[c] We often use *I think* + *will* in spoken English.
***I think we'll** be healthier.*
[d] The negative form is *I don't think* + *will*.
***I don't think we'll** work as much.*

6 a 6.2 **Listen to the sentences and choose the alternatives you hear.**

1 I don't think *people will/people'll* be less happy.
2 People *will not/won't* go out much.
3 I think *we will/we'll* have more time for our friends.
4 *It will/It'll* be easier to meet new people.
5 I don't think *we will/we'll* sleep as much.

b **Listen again and repeat.**

c **Use the prompts to write predictions.**

1 Most people / not have / lots / money
Most people won't have lots of money.
2 Technology / make / us / happier
3 I / think / we / travel / more
4 I / don't think / we / have / much / free time
5 People / have / more / fun
6 People / not eat / unhealthy food
7 I / don't think / people / have / simple lives
8 I / think / we / work / harder

d **Work in pairs. Do you agree with the predictions Why/Why not?**

Go to page 126 or your app for more information and practice.

Speaking

PREPARE

7 **You're going to discuss the question 'Will we be happier in the future?'. First, make predictions for the topics below. Use the phrases in Exercise 1 and the Useful phrases to help you.**

- health and exercise
- family and friends
- travel
- work
- social life/interests
- money

Useful phrases

We'll (have more free time).
I think (we) will (be healthier).
I (don't) think (people) will (do much exercise).
We won't (work as much as we do now).

SPEAK

8 a **Work in groups. Tell your group your predictions. Say if you agree or disagree with other students' predictions.**

b **As a group, decide which three predictions are the most important.**

c **As a group, discuss the question 'Will we be happier in the future?'**

Develop your listening page 101

6B A busy week

B

> Goal: make arrangements
> Grammar: present continuous for future arrangements
> Vocabulary: *make, do, have*

A

Reading and vocabulary

1 a Look at the people in the photos and discuss the questions.

1 How do you think the people feel? Why?
2 What do you think their daily lives are like?
3 Is your daily life similar?

b Read the forum post and answer the questions.

1 What's the writer's problem?
2 Which things in the photos does the writer mention?
3 Whose advice do you think is the best? Why?

Managing a busy week

I feel stressed just looking at my calendar! I have lots of meetings every day next week – including lunchtime! On Monday evening I'm making a birthday meal for a friend and on Tuesday evening I'm looking after my two nieces. Then I'm having dinner with my parents on Wednesday evening, and on Thursday evening my boss is having a leaving party (I tried to make an excuse but he got upset).
That's a typical week for me and I know I'm not alone. I never have time to do exercise, make a dentist's appointment or have a haircut. When I do have time, I'm too tired. How do you all manage a busy week? I need some ideas!
Rita

I feel your pain! I try to do at least one relaxing thing a day. For me that's doing some exercise, doing some cooking, making cakes, etc. I even find that doing some housework is relaxing, but not everyone agrees!
Grace

I always have lunch away from the office. Walking is good exercise and I can do some shopping on the way, too. I also have a day off each month to do something fun.
Marco

I do some work on the train in the morning – that way I can leave early and go to the gym. At the weekends, I get some fresh air and do some exercise, and in the summer I have a barbecue or a picnic with friends. Then I'm ready for Monday – more or less!
Nancy

2 a Find the nouns in the box in the forum post. Does each one go with *do*, *make* or *have*?

an appointment	a barbecue/picnic	a cake
(some) cooking	a day off	(some) exercise
an excuse	a haircut	(some) housework	lunch
a meal	a meeting	(some) shopping	(some) work

b Complete the questions with *do*, *make* or *have*.

1 Who do you usually ______ lunch with?
2 Do you ______ an excuse when you're late? Or do you say nothing?
3 Do you usually ______ appointments by phone or online?
4 Do you ever ______ your food shopping online?
5 How often do you ______ a haircut?
6 Do you ever ______ some work at the weekend?
7 How often do you ______ a day off?
8 When do you usually ______ housework?

c Work in pairs. Take turns to ask and answer the questions. Ask follow-up questions.

A: Who do you usually have lunch with?
B: Friends from my class.
A: Where do you eat?
B: We usually go to a café near the college.

3 Work in pairs. Which action in Exercise 2a would you do in each situation?

1 Your friend has invited you for dinner but you don't want to go. *make an excuse*
2 You need some help from your colleagues with a project.
3 You don't feel well today. You need some rest and you don't think you can go to work.
4 Your kitchen is full of dirty dishes and you don't have any clean clothes.
5 You want to get fit.
6 You have toothache and need to see a dentist.
7 You want shorter hair.
8 It's a lovely day and you want to eat outside.

Go to your app for more practice.

C

D

Grammar

4 a Read the grammar box and choose the correct alternatives.

Present continuous for future arrangements

Use the present continuous (*be* + *-ing*) to talk about future [1]*predictions/arrangements*. These are often plans we have with another person. We usually [2]*know/don't know* the time and place.

***I'm making** a birthday meal for a friend on Monday evening.*

It's common to use future time expressions with the present continuous, such as *tonight*, *on* (*Thursday evening*), *next* (*week*), *a week on* (*Friday*), *on the* (*24th*) with the present continuous.

b Underline four examples of the present continuous in the forum post in Exercise 1.

5 a 6.7 Listen to the sentences and choose the alternatives you hear. Is the *-ing* verb stressed or unstressed?

1 They*'re/are* having a meeting at 4.
2 She*'s/is* seeing her dentist on the 16th.
3 I *'m/am* making dinner for Ed tomorrow.
4 He*'s/is* starting a university course in March.

b Listen again and repeat.

6 a Complete the sentences with the correct form of the words in brackets.

1 What ________ (you/do) at lunchtime today? Shall we eat together?
2 Erin's a bit nervous. ________ (she/start) a new job on Monday.
3 We haven't got any food but ________ (my dad/go) to the shop soon.
4 John's busy tomorrow. ________ (he/do) some work on his house.
5 Louisa and I have decided to get fit so ________ (we/go) for a swim tomorrow.
6 ________ (I/make) dinner for some friends on Thursday but ________ (I/not/cook) anything special.

b Work in pairs. Tell your partner about some arrangements you have:

- tomorrow
- next week
- next month

I'm meeting a friend for dinner tomorrow evening.

Go to page 126 or your app for more information and practice.

Speaking

PREPARE

7 a 6.8 You're going to make some arrangements with other students. First, listen to Jade and Sam. What time tomorrow do they decide to meet?

b Listen again. Number the suggestions in the order you hear them.

1 Sure, I can do twelve o'clock.
2 I'm meeting Professor White at eleven. Can we meet before that?
3 Maybe Wednesday then?
4 Shall we go for a coffee tomorrow? *1*
5 Okay, let's meet tomorrow at twelve.

8 Go to page 155 and follow the instructions.

SPEAK

9 a Go around the class and try to make arrangements with other students. Add them to your calendar.

A: *Do you want to go for a coffee on Monday?*
B: *Sounds good. What time?*
A: *What about ten o'clock?*
B: *Sorry, I can't at ten o'clock, I'm playing tennis then.*

b Go around the class and try to make as many arrangements as possible.

c Who has planned the busiest week?

Develop your reading page 102

6c A quiet weekend

- **Speaking:** discuss weekend plans
- **Grammar:** *may* and *might*
- **Vocabulary:** weekend activities

Vocabulary and reading

1 **Look at photos A–E and discuss the questions.**

1. What do you usually do at the weekend?
2. Do you do any of the things in the photos?
3. What's a perfect weekend for you?

2 **Read the article about weekend activities. Do the people do the same things as you?**

3 a **Which of the nouns in the box go with *do, go* and *play*?**

activities clubbing/dancing cycling
gardening golf/tennis/volleyball
homework nothing out
running/swimming shopping
the guitar/in a band video games yoga

b **Read the article again and check your answers.**

HOW DO YOU SPEND YOUR *Weekend*?

According to a recent survey, the top five weekend activities are sleeping, watching TV, watching sport, going shopping and doing housework. But is that what people really do at the weekend? We asked a few people around the city to find out.

'I usually go shopping with some friends on Saturday. Then we go out in the evening – we usually go clubbing. I visit my family most Sundays and we have a big lunch together.' **Emily**

'I like playing golf but most of the time I do nothing. I sleep, I watch TV and then I sleep again!' **Hiroki**

'I play the guitar and I spend most of my time at the weekend writing songs, recording them and then sharing them online. I play in a band, too, so we get together in my flat to practise.' **Natalia**

'I love the outdoors and I go cycling whenever possible. If I'm too tired I just spend time in my garden. I grow a lot of plants and vegetables and I do some gardening most weekends. Sometimes I do yoga out there, or I just sit and relax.' **Lewis**

'I go to a friend's house and we play video games and do our homework together … every weekend.' **Audrey**

'I do lots of activities at the weekend. I go running or swimming in the morning. Then I spend the rest of the time at home, playing football with my kids, watching TV, chatting to my wife. The usual things.' **David**

4 Work in pairs and discuss the questions. Ask follow-up questions.
1 Which activities in Exercise 3a do you often do?
2 Which activities do you never or hardly ever do?
3 Do you agree with the top five weekend activities in the article? Can you think of any others?

Go to page 141 or your app for more vocabulary and practice.

Listening

5 a 6.9 Listen to Isabel and Ruth talking about their plans for the weekend.
1 Which activities in Exercise 3a do they mention?
2 How many people is Isabel cooking for on Sunday?
3 Who's having a quieter weekend, Isabel or Ruth?

b Listen again and complete each sentence with a verb.
1 Olly and I may ______ a game of tennis after lunch.
2 We may not ______ much on Sunday.
3 We might ______ a Turkish dish we like but we haven't decided yet.
4 That evening, we may ______ out.
5 I might ______ in the garden and read if it's a nice day.
6 On Sunday mornings we usually play cards, but we might ______ this weekend.

Grammar

6 Read the grammar box and choose the correct alternatives.

may and *might*

Use *may* and *might* to talk about future actions and events that we are [1]*sure/not sure* about.
*Olly and I **may play** a game of tennis after lunch.*
*We **might make** a Turkish dish we like, but we haven't decided yet.*
After *may* and *might*, use the infinitive [2]*with/without to*.

7 a 6.10 Listen to the sentences. What happens to the /t/ sound in bold before a consonant sound? What happens before a vowel sound?
1 I migh**t** meet Will for coffee tomorrow.
2 Bruna may no**t** come out with us later.
3 I may no**t** see you this evening.
4 We migh**t** eat out tonight.
5 Lorenzo migh**t** arrive at ten.

b Listen again and repeat.

8 Complete the message with *may/might* (*not*) and the correct form of the verb in brackets.

I have the day off tomorrow so I [1]______ (go) and see a film. My sister wants to come too but she has to finish some work so it [2]______ (be) possible. We're not sure what to see though. We [3]______ (see) the new superhero film but I'm getting a bit bored of those. There's a horror film on but my sister gets frightened easily so she [4]______ (enjoy) it. We [5]______ (choose) the comedy just because we don't like the others! We'd like to go somewhere to eat after the film. We [6]______ (go) to the Italian place next door for pizza.

9 a Think of five things you *may/might do* in the next 24 hours. Write some notes.

b Work in pairs and share your ideas. Are they similar?
I might go running tomorrow morning but I won't if the weather's bad.

Go to page 126 or your app for more information and practice.

Speaking

PREPARE

10 You're going to have a conversation about what you're doing next weekend. First, make notes about:
- your plans and arrangements
- things you're not sure about

SPEAK

11 a Work in groups. Talk about your plans for the weekend. Ask each other questions. Use the Useful phrases to help you.

Useful phrases

What are you doing at the weekend?
That sounds (nice/lovely/great).
Lucky you!
Where will you do that?
Who are you (going) with?

A: *What are you doing at the weekend?*
B: *I'm seeing a friend on Saturday. We're having a coffee together.*
A: *Oh, that's nice. Where are you going?*
B: *I don't know yet. We might go to the shopping centre.*

b Who is having the quietest weekend? Who is having the busiest weekend?

Develop your writing page 103

6D English in action

> Goal: leave a phone message

Listening

1 **Work in pairs and discuss the questions.**

1 How often do you check your phone? Do you always answer your phone/reply to text messages immediately?

2 When was the last time you left a voice message? Why?

3 Do you prefer texting or leaving voice messages? Why?

2 a 6.11 **Listen to five voice messages. Match each speaker 1–5 to the reason for their message a–e.**

a to check someone remembers an important date

b to change the time of a meal

c to talk about work

d to offer an earlier appointment

e to invite someone to do something

b **Listen again and complete the extracts.**

1 It's Chris ______ . I'm really ______ but I have to cancel our lunch tomorrow.

2 ______ me to let me know when you're free.

3 This is a ______ for Mr Williams.

4 Call us ______ on 0208 4654 7212.

5 I'm ______ to remind you about Aunt Claire's birthday.

6 ______ is Gareth.

7 Can you call me back when you ______ this?

8 I'm calling ______ the meeting on Friday.

c **Check your answers in the Useful phrases box.**

Useful phrases

Saying who it is

It's (Chris) here.

This is (Gareth).

Giving a reason for calling

This is a message for Mr Williams.

I'm really sorry but (I have to cancel our lunch tomorrow).

I'm calling to (remind you about Aunt Claire's birthday).

I'm calling about (the meeting on Friday).

Asking for a reply

Text me to let me know (when you're free).

Can you call me back (when you get this)?

Call (us) back on (0208 4654 7212).

3 6.12 **Listen to the extracts and repeat.**

1 It's Chris here.

2 This is a message for Mr. Williams.

3 Can you call me back when you get this?

4 I'm calling about the meeting on Friday.

4 **Work in pairs. Write the appropriate messages for instructions 1–8.**

1 Say who you are and why you are calling.
Hi, it's Navid here. I'm calling about the concert tonight.

2 Find out if your friend wants to come to a party you're having on Saturday evening.

3 Remind your son to do his homework before he goes out.

4 Cancel an appointment.

5 Ask someone to call you back. Give them your number.

6 Ask someone to text you to say if they can come to your party.

7 Ask someone to call you back as soon as they can.

Speaking

PREPARE

5 **Work in pairs. Go to page 155 and follow the instructions.**

SPEAK

6 a **Take turns to leave messages for each other. When you listen to your partner, make some notes for each message.**

- Who's calling?
- Why are they calling?
- What do you need to do?

b **Show your partner your notes. Did you write the correct message?**

Go online for the Roadmap video.

Check and reflect

1 a Complete the predictions with *will/won't* and the verbs in the box in the correct form.

be do get better have have to live

1 I think the weather ________ next week.
2 I don't think people ________ as many children in the future.
3 I think robots ________ a lot of our jobs.
4 We ________ on another planet.
5 Cities ________ too expensive to live in.
6 We ________ work as much.

b Work in pairs. Do you agree with the predictions?

2 Complete the predictions with your own ideas.

1 We'll ...
2 We won't ...
3 I think we'll ...
4 I don't think we'll ...

3 a Choose the correct alternatives.

1 I go to the gym to *keep/make* fit.
2 My parents always wanted to *have/be* a happy family life.
3 I don't mind if I don't *get/earn* lots of money, but I would like a good *career/work*.
4 I love having a really *busy/noisy* social life, but I'd also like some more free *time/life*.
5 My friend has got a good sense of *funny/humour*.
6 Ada has a *busy/simple* life – she has lots of free time

b Work in pairs. Which of the sentences are true for you? Change the others so they are also true.

4 a Look at Katrina's diary for next week. Write sentences about all of her arrangements.

Monday	*10 a.m. organise team meeting*
Tuesday	*2 p.m. go to dentist's*
Wednesday	
Thursday	*12.30 p.m. have lunch with Diana*
Friday	*6 p.m. fly to Trieste*
Saturday	*10 a.m. visit museum*
Sunday	*2 p.m. catch train to Bologna*

She's organising a team meeting on Monday at 10 a.m.

b Work in pairs. Talk about your arrangements for next week.

5 Put the words in order to make present continuous sentences and questions.

1 isn't / Dallas / to / month / Dani / travelling / next
2 today / leaving / work / you / What time / are / ?
3 pizza / tonight / making / I'm
4 Frankfurt / two weeks' time / moving / she's / to / in
5 they / are / party / coming / the / on Friday / to / ?
6 next week / London / aren't / we / in / working

6 a Correct one mistake in each sentence.

1 I need to do an appointment to see my doctor.
2 I did an important meeting this morning.
3 You need to make more exercise if you want to lose weight.
4 For my wife's last birthday, I had a meal at home for her.
5 Every summer, I do a barbecue with my friends.

b Which of the sentences are true for you?

7 Reorder the prompts to make statements.

1 at home / I / may / this evening / stay
2 visit / My brother / might / weekend / me / this
3 may / My parents / on holiday / this year / go / for three weeks
4 go / might / I / tonight / running

8 a Complete the sentences so they're true for you.

1 This weekend I might ...
2 Tonight I may ...
3 Next month I might not ...

b Work in pairs. Share your sentences and find out if you have anything in common.

9 a Complete the questions with the correct form of *do*, *play* or *go*.

1 Do you ________ any activities? Which ones?
2 When was the last time you ________ swimming? Where did you go?
3 Did you ________ a musical instrument when you were a child?
4 Do you prefer to ________ cycling or running?
5 Who do you like to ________ shopping with?
6 Do you ever like to just ________ nothing? When?
7 Are you ________ clubbing tonight?
8 Do you like ________ gardening?

b Work in pairs and ask and answer the questions.

Reflect

How confident do you feel about the statements below? Write 1–5 (1 = not very confident, 5 = very confident).

- I can make predictions about the future.
- I can make arrangements.
- I can discuss weekend plans.
- I can leave a phone message.

Want more practice?
Go to your Workbook or app.

7A The building project

- Speaking: give opinions
- Grammar: *too* and *enough*
- Vocabulary: features of city life

Vocabulary and reading

1 **Work in pairs. What are the bad things about living in a city?**

2 **Read the advert. Would you like to live in Horton Fields? Why/Why not?**

3 a **Complete the questions about where you live with the words in the box. Use the advert to help you.**

~~area~~ cycle paths flats local location neighbours nightlife pollution public transport traffic

1. Do you like your *area*? Why/Why not?
2. Are your ____________ friendly?
3. Do you live in a good ____________? What can you do there?
4. Do most people in your area live in ____________ or houses?
5. Is there a good ____________ system? E.g. buses, trains, etc.
6. Is it safe for people on bikes? Are there ____________?
7. Is there a lot of ____________ on the roads?
8. Is there a lot of ____________? Is the air clean or dirty?
9. Do you prefer to go to ____________ shops, cafés and restaurants? Or do you go to a different part of town?
10. Is the ____________ good? Can you stay out late in your area?

b **Work in pairs. Ask and answer the questions.**

Go to your app for more practice.

4 **Read the social media posts about the Horton Fields development. Does each writer think the new homes are a good or bad idea?**

Max
We have enough space here for more homes so why not welcome more people to our lovely area? We should share what we have.

Lisa
I think Horton Fields is a terrible idea. There isn't enough space for people to play sport in the city. Also, the west side of the park isn't big enough for 300 new homes!

Diana
Horton was a lovely area. These days there are too many people on the streets and too much traffic on the roads. 200 new families will make it worse.

Nic
Young people leave the area because they don't have enough money to buy a home and it's too expensive to rent. We need to build homes that are cheap enough for young people so they stay here. In my view, that's a good thing.

5 **Read the posts again.**

Which writer ...

1 is worried about people moving to other areas?
2 talks about the location of the new homes?
3 talks about the cost of living in the area?
4 believes the area was nicer in the past?
5 would like more people in the area?

Grammar

6 **Read the grammar box and choose the correct alternatives.**

too and *enough*

Use *too* + adjective, *too many* + countable noun and *too much* + uncountable noun to say that something is [1]*less/more* than necessary.

*It's **too expensive** to rent.*
*These days there are **too many people** on the streets and there's **too much traffic** on the roads.*

Use *enough* + noun and adjective + *enough* to say that something is the [2]*right/wrong* amount.

*We have **enough space** for more homes.*
*We need to build homes that are **cheap enough**.*

Use *not* + adjective + *enough* and *not enough* + (adjective) + noun to say it's [3]*less/more* than necessary.

*The west side of the park **isn't big enough**.*
*Young people **don't have enough money**.*

7 a 7.1 **Listen to the sentences. Notice the pronunciation of *too* and *enough*. Do they have long or short vowel sounds?**

1 The flats are too small.
2 There are too many buildings in this area.
3 There's enough space for everyone.
4 There aren't enough cheap homes.

b **Listen again and repeat.**

8 a **Choose the correct alternatives.**

1 My flat's small but there's *enough/too* space for me.
2 There are *not enough/too many* cats around here. I don't like them.
3 There's *too many/too much* traffic on the roads.
4 The school's *too/enough* small for all the children.
5 There isn't *many/enough* space for another shopping centre in this town.
6 The park isn't *big enough/too much* for everybody.

b **Complete the sentences about your area.**

1 It's too ...
It's too expensive.
2 There are too many ...
3 There's too much ...
4 There aren't enough ...

c **Work in pairs. Talk about some things you would like to change in your area and say why. Use the vocabulary in Exercise 3a to help you.**

I think we need a better public transport system. There are too many cars on the road and not enough buses.

Go to page 128 or your app for more information and practice.

Speaking

PREPARE

9 a 7.2 **You're going to discuss a new development in your area. First, listen to Mia and Colin discussing Horton Park. Do they think the homes are a good idea?**

b **Listen again. Does Mia (M) or Colin (C) give each reason?**

1 We need to build homes that young people can buy.
2 What about the location of these homes? It's terrible!
3 There aren't many parks in town.
4 It seems like the only place possible to me.

10 a **Imagine the local government has decided to build 300 new flats in your town. Read the information below and make notes about the good and bad things about the development.**

- It will take three years to build the flats.
- They will build in the park.
- The flats will be modern and the buildings will be very tall.
- They will improve public transport.
- They will build a new school near the flats.
- Lots of new people will move to the area.

b **Work in pairs and compare your notes.**

SPEAK

11 a **Work in groups. Have a discussion about the new development. Explain why you think it is a good or bad idea. Use the Useful phrases to help you.**

Useful phrases

I think it's a (good) idea because (we need more homes in the area).
We (don't) need these homes because (we already have lots available).
I understand/That's true, but (the development will improve the area).
I (don't) agree with that.

b **Is your opinion still the same? Do you think the development is a good or bad idea? Vote as a class.**

Develop your listening page 104

7C A favourite room

> **Goal:** describe a place
> **Grammar:** articles
> **Vocabulary:** prepositions

Reading and vocabulary

1 **Work in groups. Look at the photos and discuss the questions.**

1. What type of person do you think lives in each place?
2. What do you think they do in these rooms?
3. Which of the rooms do you like/dislike? Why?

A

B

2 a **Read the text about Angela's favourite room. Which photo is she describing?**

b **Read the text again. Are the following sentences true (T) or false (F)?**

1. The main reason Angela likes the room is because it's warm.
2. The chair in the room was expensive.
3. Angela has plants in her room because she likes the way they look.
4. Angela doesn't travel to go to work.
5. Angela only uses this room for work.

A SPACE OF MY OWN

Angela Chapman

This is my favourite room. I love it because it gets a lot of light from those big windows behind the sofa. I took the picture from opposite the windows because I think it's the best view of the room.

As you can see, black and white are my favourite colours. There's a black and white rug in the middle of the room, black and white cushions on the sofa and a black and white bin under my desk! I bought the chair in front of my desk in Milan – I paid a lot for it! In the corner of the room there's a bookcase and a tall lamp. This gives a lovely light in the evening and in winter.

I think it's really important to have plants inside – they're good for you. There's a plant on my desk (I keep it next to my computer because it makes me happy while I work). If you look carefully, there's a plant on the bookshelves, too.

My favourite thing in this room is the black wall. I work from home and whenever I have a new idea, I just write it on there. I also stick notes and pictures on it, too. These are the only pictures in the room. There used to be a picture between the two windows, but I got bored of it so I took it down.

I spend most of my time in this room – I usually work here but it's also a great place to relax and have fun with friends.

c **Match the words in the box with pictures A–I. Use the description in Exercise 2a to help you.**

opposite *d*	behind	between	in front of
in the corner of	in the middle of	next to	
on	under		

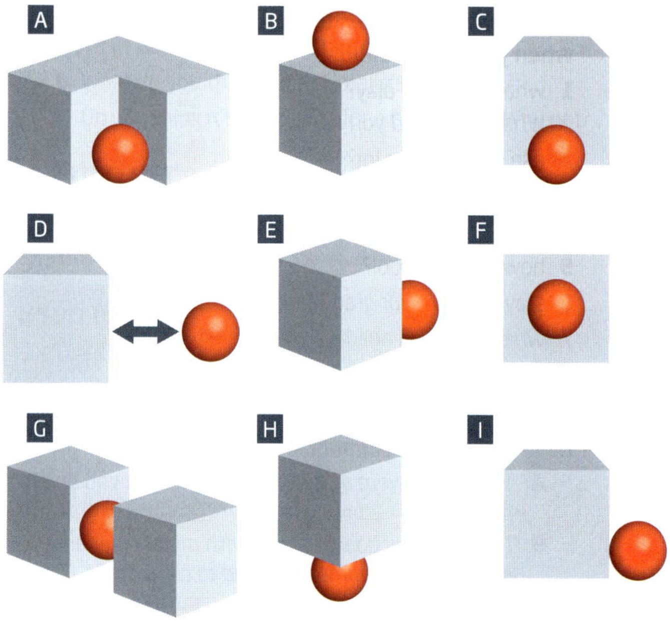

Go to page 142 or your app for more vocabulary and practice.

C

D

Grammar

3 **Read the grammar box and choose the correct alternatives.**

Articles

Use [1]*a or an*/*the* when talking about singular countable nouns for the first time.

*My friend has **an office** at home.*

*There's **a sofa** and **an armchair** in it.*

Use [2]*a or an*/*the* when both the speaker and the listener know which noun we are talking about.

*I want to buy **the sofa** that we saw yesterday.*

***The cat** wants to go outside.*

We also use it in some phrases with prepositions.

*It's in **the middle of the room**.*

We use [3]*a or an*/*no article* when talking about plural or uncountable nouns in general.

I love books!

Furniture is usually expensive.

4 a 7.8 **Listen to the sentences and notice how *a, an* and *the* are pronounced.**

1. There's a nice table in the room.
2. He has an office in the house.
3. I went to a shop to buy an armchair.
4. The garden is a lovely place to relax.

b **Listen again and repeat.**

5 **Complete the description with *a, an, the* or no article (-).**

I have [1]_____ room in my house which is just for games and sport. I love [2]_____ sport, especially basketball and football. There's [3]_____ basketball hoop on the wall at one end of [4]_____ room. On the other side of the room there's [5]_____ pool table. [6]_____ pool table is quite small but it's fine to play with [7]_____ friend. In [8]_____ middle of the room there's a big TV screen and two sofas, where I can watch [9]_____ films with my friends. Last week my friends came over to watch [10]_____ film and eat [11]_____ popcorn. [12]_____ film wasn't very good, but we had a great time. I love this room!

6 **Work in pairs. Describe one of the places in the photos to your partner. Listen and say which one your partner is describing.**

There's a big TV and a sofa. There's a pool table behind the sofa.

Go to page 128 or your app for more information and practice.

Speaking

PREPARE

7 7.9 **You're going to describe your favourite room. First, listen to Neil describing his. Number the things he mentions in the order you hear them.**

- where he relaxes.
- how much furniture there is
- the view from the window
- why he likes this room

8 **Think about your favourite room. Make notes about:**

- how much furniture there is
- where different things are in the room
- what you use it for
- why you like it

SPEAK

9 a **Work in pairs. Take turns to describe your favourite room. Use the Useful phrases to help you.**

Useful phrases

My favourite room is the (games room).
There's a (big plant in the corner of the room).
The room is (very bright/big/relaxing/colourful).
I like it because it's (a great place to relax/have fun with friends/work).

b **Are your rooms similar or different? How?**

Develop your writing page 106

7D English in action

Goal: make and respond to excuses

A

B

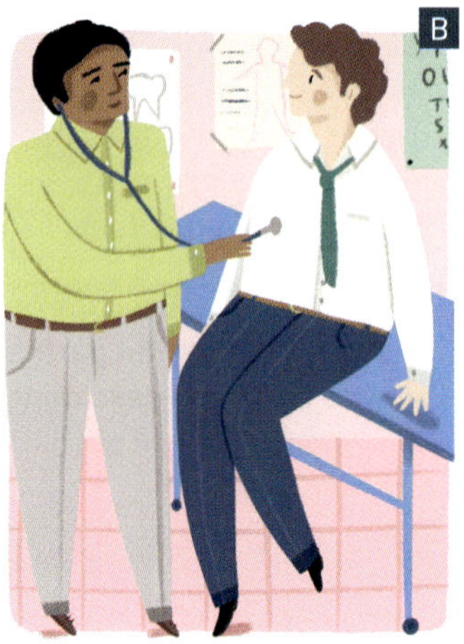

C

D

Listening

1 a Work in pairs and look at the pictures. What do you think is happening in each one?

b 7.10 Listen and check your ideas.

2 a 7.11 Listen to four more conversations. Why does each speaker say sorry?

b Listen again and complete the conversations with the words you hear.

1 **A:** I'm ______ sorry I'm late, Professor. I waited for the bus for half an hour but it still didn't come.
B: That's ______ , but your bus is seems to be late every week, Mr Young.

2 **A:** Really sorry, Tom, but I ______ come out tonight.
B: Oh, OK, no ______ .

3 **A:** Oh, no, sorry, I have a dentist's appointment ______ I can't today.
B: Don't ______ about it. Maybe another day?

4 **A:** Well, I'm ______ I lost it.
B: Oh well, ______ mind. It's just a shirt!

3 7.12 Listen to four excuses and responses. Are the speakers who respond happy or unhappy? How do you know?

4 a Match the excuses 1–4 with the responses a–d.

1 I'm so sorry, I drank your water by mistake. I thought it was mine.
2 I'm sorry, I can't come out with you tonight because I'm meeting Samantha.
3 I'm so sorry I'm late. The bus was twenty minutes late.
4 I'm afraid there's food all over your floor. I dropped my plate by mistake.

a Don't worry about it. I'll help you clean it up.
b That's OK. We ordered you a tuna sandwich.
c Never mind. Perhaps we can meet next week?
d No problem. I've got some more.

b Work in pairs. Take turns to make an excuse and respond. Use the Useful phrases to help you. Change the information in brackets when possible.

Useful phrases

Making excuses

I'm sorry (I can't come out tonight).
I'm really sorry (I'm late).
I'm afraid I (dropped your phone).
I ('m busy) so I can't (come for coffee), sorry.

Responding to excuses

Never mind.
Don't worry (about it).
That's OK/all right
No problem/worries.
It doesn't matter.

Speaking

PREPARE

5 Work in pairs. You're going to make and respond to excuses. Student A go to page 156 and Student B go to page 153. Follow the instructions.

SPEAK

6 Take turns to make your excuses and respond.

A: *I'm sorry, I lost your coursebook. My little brother took it and now I can't find it.*
B: *That's OK – I'll ask the teacher for a new one!*

Go online for the Roadmap video.

Check and reflect

1 a Make sentences from the prompts using the words and phrases in brackets.

1. There / coffee shops / in this area (too many)
2. This street / crowded / at the weekend (too)
3. My street / wide / for big cars (not enough)
4. Theatre tickets here / cost / for most people (too much)
5. There / nightlife around here (not enough)
6. There / car parking spaces / for everyone (enough)

b Complete the sentences about your home or where you work.

1. There's enough ...
2. There aren't enough ...
3. There's too much ...
4. There are too many ...
5. It's too ...

c Work in pairs and compare your sentences.

2 a Complete the description. The first letter of each word is given.

I love the [1]a______ where I live. The [2]l______ is good because it's close to the city. The [3]l______ people are really friendly and there are lots of great shops and cafés to go to with your friends. The [4]p______ t______ system is really good too with buses and trains into the city. The [5]t______ on the road isn't too bad because a lot of people cycle. It's safe because there are [6]c______ p______ everywhere. Finally, the [7]n______ is great because there are lots of cinemas, restaurants and a few theatres.

b Work in pairs. How similar or different is the description in Exercise 2a to your area? Why?

3 a Complete each sentence with *used to, didn't use to* or *use to* and a verb in the box.

be   eat   play   take   talk   watch

1. When I was young, I __________ the guitar in a band.
2. My older brother __________ to me much. He was really quiet.
3. Did you __________ a lot of TV?
4. I __________ tomatoes but I do now.
5. Did your parents __________ you to the cinema?
6. Sally __________ good at sport but she is now.

b Complete the sentences about your childhood.

1. I always used to ...
2. I sometimes used to ...
3. I didn't use to ...
4. My parents used to ...
5. My friends used to ...

c Work in pairs. Share your sentences and ask questions.

4 a Complete each sentence with a word in the box.

beach   forest   hill   river   stream   wood

1. Are you sure that's a ______? It looks more like a mountain!
2. There's a small ______ behind our house where the children climb the trees.
3. The ______ at the end of our garden becomes a river when it rains a lot.
4. Shall we go on a boat along the ______ at the weekend? Or shall we drive to the lake?
5. Let's walk along the ______ and then have a swim in the sea.
6. People get lost in that ______ because it's so big and the trees are close together.

b Work in pairs. Talk about a place you've visited and say:

1. where it was
2. what it was like
3. what natural features were there

5 a Choose the correct alternatives.

1. The sofa is in the middle *to*/*of* the room.
2. There's a coffee table *in front of*/*between* the sofa.
3. There's a green chair in *the*/*a* corner of the room.
4. There are some flowers *in*/*on* the coffee table.
5. There's a rug *in front of*/*in the middle of* the sofas and chair.
6. The picture is *between*/*on* two bookshelves.

b Work in pairs and describe the room you're in now.

6 Complete the description with *a, an, the* or no article (-).

My favourite space is my study. There's [1]______ desk in one corner of the room with [2]______ computer and printer on it. Next to [3]______ desk are some shelves full of [4]______ books. There's also [5]______ radio and [6]______ TV. On the other side of the room is [7]______ armchair. I only turn on [8]______ TV when I finish work.

Reflect

How confident do you feel about the statements below? Write 1–5 (1 = not very confident, 5 = very confident).

- I can give opinions.
- I can talk about where I grew up.
- I can describe a place.
- I can make and respond to excuses.

Want more practice?
Go to your Workbook or app.

8A Special photos

C

- **Goal:** describe a special photo
- **Grammar:** past continuous
- **Vocabulary:** verbs of movement

A

B

Listening

1 **Work in pairs and answer the questions.**

1 How often do you take photos?

2 What do you like taking photos of?

2 a **You're going to listen to some people talking about photos A–D. Why do you think the photos are special to them?**

b 8.1 **Listen to conversations 1–4 and check your ideas. Which photo is each speaker talking about? What is special about each photo?**

c **Listen again. Match sentences a–h with speakers 1–4.**

a My friend Al took this photo while I was sleeping in a train station in Hungary.

b I took this photo a couple of years ago when I was working in Argentina.

c We were trying to get to Bucharest but we missed the last train.

d She was crying so I told some funny stories to make her feel better.

e When I opened the door, he was sitting at a table on the beach!

f Well, I was taking a walk one morning when I went into a busy cafe.

g I took this photo while we were camping near some woods. e.g. *1*

h We listened to the sound of the sea while we were eating.

Grammar

3 **Read the grammar box and choose the correct alternatives.**

Past continuous

Use was/were + *-ing* to form the past continuous. It describes an action that was [1]*finished/in progress* in the past.

*I **was working** abroad in 2016.*

*We **were visiting** friends last night.*

This action is often interrupted by another a single action or event. This single action or event is in the [2]*past continuous/past simple*.

*I was working **when** Leo **got** home.*

*We met **while** we **were living** in France.*

*They arrived at the cinema **when** the film **was starting**.*

We often use when and while to connect the two actions. Use [3]*when/while* before the past simple. It is possible to use both *when* and *while* before the past continuous.

4 a 8.2 **Listen to the sentences. Are *was/were* stressed or unstressed?**

1 I was making dinner at seven.

2 We were travelling when we took that photo.

3 He lost his wallet while he was doing the shopping.

4 They were arguing when we saw them.

b **Listen again and repeat.**

5 a **Make sentences from the prompts using the past simple and past continuous and the words in brackets.**

1 I / have an accident / I / drive to work yesterday (while)
I had an accident while I was driving to work yesterday.
2 We / see a snake / we / run this morning (while)
3 I / get up this morning / it / snow (when)
4 It / start to rain / we / have our picnic. (while)
5 I / get home / my children / clean the house (when)
6 Dan / hurt his back / he / play with the children (while)
7 Leon / break his leg / he / ski (when)
8 I / tidy my room / I / find 50 euros (while)

b **Write three sentences about you using the past continuous, the past simple and *when* or *while*.**

I lost my credit card while I was shopping yesterday.

c **Work in pairs. Tell each other about your sentences. Give more information.**

I lost my credit card while I was shopping yesterday. When I got home, I called the bank to cancel it.

Go to page 130 or your app for more information and practice.

Vocabulary

6 **Work in pairs. Match the sentence halves and check you understand the meaning of the phrases in bold.**

1 I got dressed and **went out**
2 The door bell rang so
3 I **turned around** to see
4 I left the house early in the morning and
5 I **went into** the kitchen
6 Danny **fell over**
7 I'm a salesman,
8 I got home, **lay down**

a so I **travel around** the country a lot.
b on the sofa and went to sleep.
c and hurt his hand.
d what the strange noise was.
e she **got up** to see who it was.
f for a cup of coffee.
g **came back** at midnight!
h to make a cup of tea.

7 a **Choose the correct alternatives.**

1 I *got up/ lay down* really quickly because I was late.
2 I *came back/ fell over* while I was playing basketball.
3 I thought I heard someone say my name. But when I *turned around/ came back* no one was there.
4 I *lay down/ went out* one afternoon and woke up the next day!
5 I've travelled *around/ over* most of Europe, but I've never been to Poland.
6 I *turned around/ went into* a shop yesterday but I forgot what I was looking for.
7 I *went into/ went out* to buy milk and *came back/ got up* with several shopping bags!

b **Work in pairs. Has anything similar to the situations in Exercise 7a ever happened to you? Tell your partner what happened.**

A: *I once fell over while I was walking in the street.*
B: *Oh, no! How did you feel?*
A: *I just laughed – it was quite funny.*

Go to your app for more practice.

Speaking

PREPARE

8 a **You're going to talk about a special photo. First, answer the questions and make notes.**

- Who were you with?
- Where were you?
- When was it?
- What were you doing?
- Why is it special?
- How you did you feel?

b **Plan how to describe your photo. Answer the questions below and use the Useful phrases to help you.**

- What will you talk about first/last?
- When will you use the past simple and continuous?
- How will you use *when* and *while*?

Useful phrases

It's a special photo because (it shows my first day at university).
I took the photo (five years ago).
I was (working abroad) at the time.
I was with (all of my family).
It was (funny/embarrassing)!

SPEAK

9 **Work in groups. Take turns to tell each other about your photos. Ask each other questions to find out more.**

A: *I took this photo while I was walking around Rome.*
B: *What were you doing there?*

Develop your reading page 107

8B Getting around

C

> **Goal:** describe a journey
> **Grammar:** *because, so* and *to*
> **Vocabulary:** transport

A

B

Reading and vocabulary

1 Look at the photos and discuss the questions.

1. Where do you think the places are?
2. What kinds of transport can you see? What other kinds of transport can you think of?
3. Which journey in the photos would you most like to take?

2 a Read the travel article and match each journey 1–5 to a photo A–E.

b Read the article again. Write the name of each person next to the questions. Sometimes there is more than one answer.

1. Who travelled for their job?
2. Who travelled to do a sport?
3. Who saw a famous building?
4. Who went with their family?
5. Who travelled on water?
6. Who made the journey several times?

c Complete the phrases with the words in the box. Use the article to help you.

get in	get off	get on	get out of	miss	~~park~~	rent	take

1. *park* a bike/car
2. ______ and ______ a cable car/a car/a taxi
3. ______ and ______ a bike/a bus/a ferry/a tram
4. ______ a car/a bike/a boat
5. ______ a flight/a bus/a train
6. ______ a ferry/a taxi

d Work in pairs and discuss the questions.

1. What forms of transport do you usually use? When and where do you use them?
2. What's your favourite form of transport? Why?
3. What are your least favourite forms of transport? Why?

Go to page 143 or your app for more vocabulary and practice.

FANTASTIC *journeys*

Last month we asked you to tell us about your most memorable journeys around the world. Here are our five favourites:

1 Last year I went to Istanbul for a business trip. I had an afternoon free so I took a ferry across the sea, from one side of the city to the other. It was a lovely journey and I got to see some amazing sights, like the Topkapi Palace. I was having so much fun that I almost missed my flight home!
Nikki, PRAGUE

2 I worked in China for a few years. At the weekends, I used to get on my bike and cycle into the countryside. There was an especially beautiful lake which I used to cycle around. Sometimes I stopped, parked the bike and had a swim. It was a simple journey, but that's also why it was lovely.
Holly, SAN DIEGO

3 I went to La Paz in Bolivia for work. It's the highest capital city in the world and the cable car there is 4,000 metres above sea level. I didn't have much time, so I got in a cable car at the central station and travelled to the end of the line and back. I got out of it only 30 minutes later, but I'll never forget that view of the city.
Wiktor, WARSAW

4 I remember taking a tram in San Francisco. I was 11 and I was on holiday with my mum and dad. One day, we got on a tram near our hotel and got off down by the sea. The view of the sea and the city from the hill was fantastic – we could even see the Golden Gate Bridge!
Mo, SHANGHAI

5 A few years ago, I went skiing with some friends in Switzerland. The public transport there is amazing so we didn't need to take a taxi or rent a car. On the day we arrived, we took a train to our resort and it was such a beautiful journey. We passed by some of the highest mountains in the Alps and some really pretty villages. I enjoyed it almost as much as the skiing!
Dave, BRISTOL

D

E

Grammar

3 a 8.3 **Listen to Mac talking about a journey. What was the most memorable thing about the journey?**

b Listen again and choose the correct alternatives.

1 They went to the river to *take a walk/ go fishing.*
2 They slept in the car because *the hotel was full/ they didn't want to walk anywhere.*
3 The car wasn't very comfortable so Mac *didn't sleep/ went for a walk.*

4 Read the grammar box and choose the correct alternative.

because, so and *to*

Use [1]*because/ so/ to* + infinitive to say why we did something.
We also walked down to a river ***to go fishing****.*
Use [2]*because/ so/ to* to say what made something happen.
They got us there really quickly ***because they knew the area well****.*
Use [3]*because/ so/ to* to talk about the result of something.
It was getting dark, ***so we slept in the car*** *until morning.*

5 a 8.4 **Listen to the sentences. Notice the pronunciation of *because, so* and *to*.**

1 They hired a car to go to the beach.
2 She took out her money to pay for the ticket.
3 I took a bus because it was cheaper.
4 They went by train because it was quicker.
5 We were late so we called a taxi.
6 I get sea sick so we didn't take the ferry.

b Listen again and repeat.

6 a Complete each sentence with *because, so* or *to*.

1 We wanted to go to the beach _____ we walked to the nearest bus stop.
2 The train was late _____ there was a problem on the line.
3 Our car broke down _____ we walked to the garage.
4 We walked for two hours _____ find a place to camp.
5 I went on a cycling tour of Vietnam _____ I wanted to see the country.
6 Jan drove around for over two hours _____ give me a tour of her city.
7 Everyone looked out of the train window _____ see the amazing mountains.
8 There's a big storm _____ they've cancelled all ferries.

b Write three true sentences about you with *because, so* and *to*.

1 Yesterday I went to the shop to buy some chocolate.
2 Last week I didn't go to work because I was ill.
3 I missed the bus to the airport last month so I took a taxi.

c Work in pairs. Student A: say the first half of one of your sentences. Student B: guess the end of the sentence. Then swap roles and repeat.

A: *Yesterday I went to the shop ...*
B: *...to get some milk?*

Go to page 130 or your app for more information and practice.

Speaking

PREPARE

7 You're going to talk about a memorable journey that you've taken. It can be real or imagined. First, answer the questions and make notes.

- Where, when and why did you go on this journey?
- Who did you go with?
- How did you travel?
- What happened during the journey?
- Did you see anything interesting?
- How did this journey make you feel and why?

SPEAK

8 a Work in pairs. Tell each other about your journeys and ask questions. Make notes about your partner's journey.

b Work with another student. Tell them about your partner's journey. Did any of you go on similar journeys?

Develop your listening page 108

8C Dream holidays

- Goal: plan a special trip
- Grammar: verb patterns
- Vocabulary: travel

Vocabulary

1 Read the quotes and discuss the questions.

1 Which do you agree with? Why/Why not?
2 What else is important to you when you go on holiday?

1 I hate going on organised tours or cruises. It's much more fun just to do what you want when you go on holiday.

2 Some people do too much when they go on holiday – they try new things, go sightseeing or shopping, and visit museums. Not me, I'm happy just lying on a beach all day.

3 I plan my trips and journeys really well. I book the flights and hotel at least four months before. I always travel light, and usually alone. If I can't pack something in one small bag or suitcase, I don't take it with me.

2 a Complete the phrases with the words in the box. Use the quotes in Exercise 1a to help you.

book go ~~go on~~ pack plan travel try

1 *go on* a holiday/a cruise/an organised tour
2 ______ your bags/suitcase
3 ______ shopping/sightseeing
4 ______ new things
5 ______ alone/light
6 ______ a journey/trip
7 ______ a flight/a hotel

b Match sentences 1–7 with a phrase from Exercise 2a.

a I'm only taking two pairs of shorts, three t-shirts and my sunglasses! *travel light*
b There's someone to show you where to go and give you information.
c What's the phone number for the place we want to stay at? We need to see if they have a free room.
d I'm going to visit all the most important places and museums.
e We need to decide where we're going to go. The holiday is only one month away!
f I don't know anything about where we're going. I'm looking forward to trying the food, learning some of the language, finding out about the culture.
g It takes me so long to decide what I want to take on holiday! Then there's never enough space for everything!

c Work in pairs. Ask each other questions using the phrases in Exercise 2a.

A: Do you sometimes travel alone?
B: Yes, but only for a short time. I quite like it.

Go to your app for more practice.

Listening

3 a 8.7 **Listen to Renata and Keith planning a round the world trip. Tick (✓) the places they plan to visit.**

- London
- Paris
- Lisbon
- Casablanca
- Rio de Janeiro
- Bogotá
- Buenos Aires
- Miami

b **Listen again and decide if the statements are true (T) or false (F).**

1 They're going to Paris on the 9th.
2 Keith likes walking, but Renata doesn't.
3 They're going to drive from Paris to Lisbon.
4 Keith wouldn't like to go on a cruise.
5 The cruise will stop at each place for a few days.
6 They'd like to do different things in Rio de Janeiro.

4 8.8 **Listen to the extracts and choose the correct alternatives.**

1 We both hate *flying/fly*.
2 I love *travelling/travel* by land and sea.
3 I'd like *doing/to do* some sightseeing.
4 I don't mind *using/to use* the Metro.
5 I know you don't want *doing/to do* a cruise.
6 I wouldn't like *being/to be* on a normal ship for that long.
7 I enjoy *relaxing/to relax* on the beach.
8 You like *hiking/hike* in the mountains.

Grammar

5 **Read the grammar box and match the sentences in Exercise 4 to the rules.**

Verb patterns

¹Use *love, like, enjoy, don't mind, hate*, etc. + *-ing*.
***I love travelling** by train, but **I don't mind getting** the bus.*
*She **hates flying**.*
²Use *want/would like* + infinitive with *to*.
***I'd like to visit** Calcutta one day.*
*What do **you want to do** in California?*

6 a 8.10 **Listen and underline the stressed words in each sentence.**

1 I don't mind walking.
2 We'd like to study.
3 She doesn't want to stay.
4 I love cycling.
5 They enjoy relaxing.
6 I hate flying.

b **Listen again and repeat.**

7 **Complete the conversation with the correct form of the verbs in the box.**

cook	do	go	learn	stay	travel	try

A: I'd like ¹_______ on a special holiday this year.
B: Really? What do you want ²_______?
A: I'm not sure. But I enjoy ³_______ new things and different food on holiday.
B: Do you like ⁴_______? There are holidays in Italy where you can learn to cook with a local chef.
A: That's a great idea! I'd like ⁵_______ how to cook Italian food! How about you? Are you going away?
B: Oh no. I hate ⁶_______! I want ⁷_______ at home and relax!

8 a **Complete the sentences about holidays so they're true for you.**

1 Next year, I'd like …
2 I really enjoy … when I go on holiday.
3 I don't want …
4 I hate …
5 I'd like to … one day.

b **Work in pairs and compare your sentences. Do you have anything in common?**

Go to page 130 or your app for more information and practice.

Speaking

PREPARE

9 **You're going to plan a special trip with a classmate. Make notes about the questions below.**

- Where would you like to go?
- What would you like to do? Will you do anything special?
- How do you want to travel?
- What will you need?
- How long do you want to go for?

SPEAK

10 a **Work in pairs. Tell your partner about what you'd like to do. Agree on a trip you'd like to take together.**

A: *I'd like to go somewhere hot.*
B: *Me too. How about Greece?*
A: *Sounds good … but I hate flying.*

b **Work with another pair. Tell each other about your trips and ask questions. How are they similar/different?**

Develop your writing page 109

8D English in action

Goal: give directions

Listening

1 **Work in pairs. When was the last time you got lost? What happened?**

2 **Match phrases 1–5 with pictures A–E.**

1 Turn left.
2 Go straight on at the roundabout.
3 Take the second right.
4 It's on the left, opposite the bank.
5 At the traffic lights, turn right.

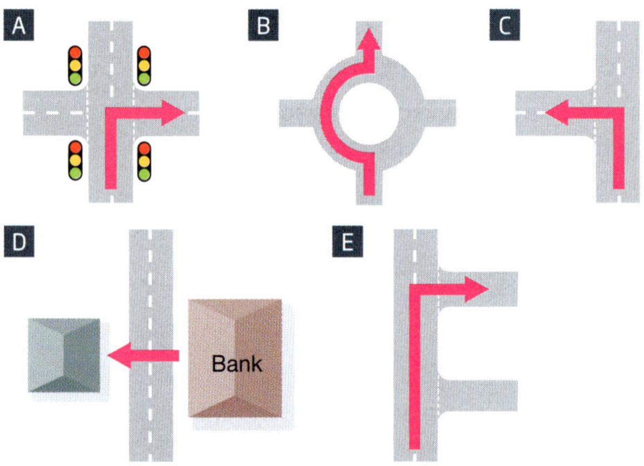

3 a 8.10 **Listen to Karen and Mike. What do they do when they get lost?**

b **Find START on the map and listen to Karen and Mike again. Where do they stop? Why?**

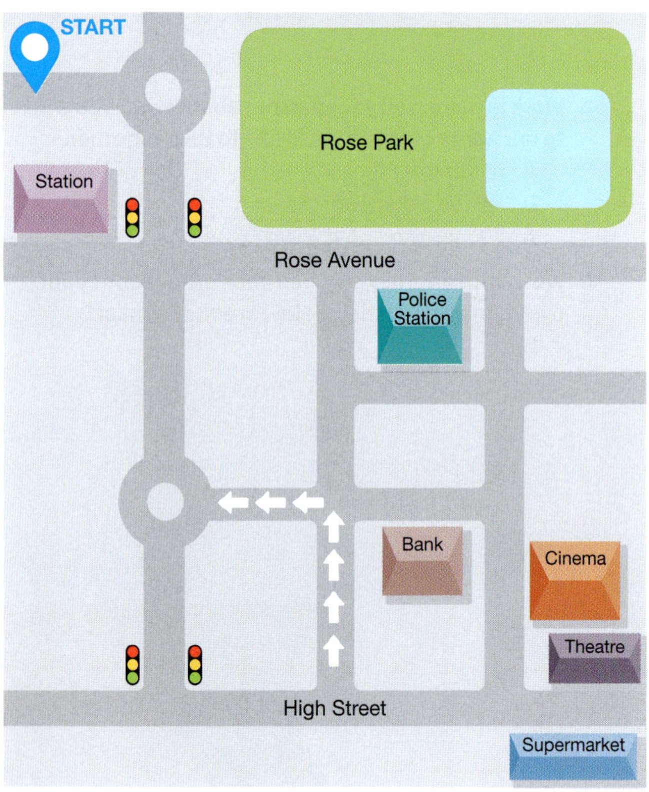

4 a 8.11 **Listen to Karen give directions. Follow their route on the map. Where do they go?**

b 8.12 **Choose the correct alternatives. Then listen and check.**

1 *Turn/Take* left into Rose Avenue.
2 You'll *see/have* a police station on the corner.
3 *Take/Turn* the second left.
4 *Turn/Go* straight on past the bank.
5 *At/On* the end of that street turn left.
6 It's *on/at* the left, *straight/opposite* the big supermarket.

c **Listen again and repeat.**

5 **Find START on the map in Exercise 3. Then follow the directions below. Where do you finish?**

Go straight on until the roundabout, then turn right at the roundabout. Go straight on and then turn left onto Rose Avenue. Go past the park and take the second right. Go straight on and it's on your left, just before the end of the road.

Speaking

PREPARE

6 **Work in pairs. Go to page 156 and follow the instructions.**

SPEAK

7 **Give each other directions and use the Useful phrases to help you.**

Useful phrases

Giving directions

Go straight on (at the roundabout).
Take the (second/third) left/right.
At the (traffic lights/roundabout/ police station) turn left/right.
Go straight on past (the library).
At the end of the road, turn left/right.

Saying where something is

It's on the left/right.
It's next to/opposite (the cinema).
You'll see a (big supermarket) on the right/in front of you.

Go online for the Roadmap video.

Check and reflect

1 Correct the mistakes in each sentence.

1 I fell over when I were taking this photo – that's why it's so bad!
2 After I got up, I was going downstairs and made some coffee.
3 Janice was meeting her husband when she was working in Toronto.
4 When we heard the noise, we all were stopping talking.
5 When I heard my name, I was turning around.
6 Billy was leaving while I arrived at the party.

2 Write sentences about what you were doing at these times.

1 10 p.m. last night
2 8 a.m. this morning
3 1 p.m. yesterday
4 on Saturday night
5 on Sunday morning

3 a Reorder the letters to complete the sentences.

1 I *lefl vreo* last month and hurt my leg. *fell over*
2 I always turn off the lights when I *og tuo* of a room.
3 I fell asleep as soon as I lya nwod last night.
4 When I wake up, I lie in bed for a while before I *etg pu*.
5 I always *emco kbca* before midnight when I go out.
6 I missed your call because I *wnte uto* to buy some bread.

b Work in pairs. Which of the sentences are true for you? Rewrite the ones that aren't true.

4 Match the sentence halves.

1 We really enjoyed our trip to the zoo because the
2 We liked all the animals but we went there to
3 Farah took her camera
4 Unfortunately, the lions stayed inside
5 After the zoo we were hungry so

a to take some photos of the lions.
b we went for a pizza.
c see the lions especially.
d animals were amazing.
e because it was raining.

5 Correct one wrong word in each of the sentences.

1 I hate flying, so I always get in the plane last.
2 I often make a taxi to work.
3 We need to park a car when we arrive so we can drive around Spain.
4 Get on the car, we need to leave now!
5 I'm always the last person to get on of the car – I'm never in a hurry.
6 We arrived at the airport late and lost our plane.

6 Choose the correct alternatives.

1 I love *doing/going* sightseeing on holiday.
2 It takes me a really long time to *make/pack* my bags before a holiday.
3 Roger is going *on/for* a cruise in May.
4 Fiona has *saved/booked us* a hotel in the city centre.

7 Choose the correct alternatives.

1 I'd like *to visit/visiting* Nepal one day.
2 I don't mind *to drive/driving*.
3 Do you want *to come/coming* with me?
4 We both enjoy *to see/seeing* new places.
5 Sarah hates *to travel/travelling* on her own.
6 Would you like *to stay/staying* in a hotel or go camping?
7 Do you like *to work/working* here?
8 We don't want *to leave/leaving* to late?

8 a Write four sentences. Choose from the ideas below.

- something you would like to do this weekend
- something you hate doing in the morning
- something you want to do this year
- something you enjoy doing on holiday
- something you don't mind doing
- a person you love travelling with

b Work in pairs and tell each other your sentences.

9 Choose the correct alternatives.

1 Have you planned the *journey/flight* yet?
2 Last month I went on a lovely *cruise/travel* around the Mediterranean.
3 I always *pack/plan* my bags the day before I leave.
4 Let's *book/try* our flights early, they'll be cheaper.
5 I'm going to *plan/try* so many new things when I go to Mongolia.
6 I never travel *light/small*. I like taking lots of things on holiday.
7 Did you *see/go* sightseeing in Paris?
8 Martin likes travelling *only/alone*.

10 a Choose two of the activities in the box and make notes about the last time you did them.

book a flight | book a hotel | a cruise | sightseeing

b Work in pairs and talk about your experiences.

Reflect

How confident do you feel about the statements below? Write 1–5 (1 = not very confident, 5 = very confident).

- I can describe a special photo.
- I can give a description of events and activities.
- I can plan a special trip.
- I can give directions.

Want more practice?
Go to your Workbook or app.

9A Good friends

> Goal: describe a friend
> Grammar: present perfect with *for* and *since*
> Vocabulary: describing a relationship

Listening and vocabulary

1 Work in pairs and discuss the questions.

1 How much time do you spend with your friends?
2 Do you prefer being in a big or small group of friends?
3 Why do you think friends are important?

2 9.1 Listen to three people talking about their friends and answer the questions.

1 Where did Fran meet Karen?
2 Why is Karen a good friend to her?
3 How do Nick and his friends know each other?
4 What do they do when they get together?
5 What's the name of Lewis's friend?
6 What interest do they both have?

3 a Complete the extracts with the words in the box.

argue text close friends disagree with got on keep in touch made friends meet up old friends see

1 I didn't like her at first but one day we sat together in class and we quickly became ____________ .
2 We ____________ maybe two or three times a week for coffee.
3 We ____________ each other a lot, too. We're always on our phones.
4 We're quite different people so we ____________ each other about quite a few things.
5 We still ____________ but we don't meet up very often.
6 But even if we don't ____________ each other for months, nothing changes.
7 I've ____________ with lots of people over the years, but I think ____________ are the best.
8 We met at work and we ____________ really well from the start.
9 He's really relaxed, like me. We never ____________ with each other.

b Listen again and check your answers.

4 a Complete the questions with a word or phrase in Exercise 3a.

1 How often do you *meet up* with your friends? What do you like doing together?
2 Do you think it's better to have a few ____________ or lots of friends that you don't know very well?
3 Do you think it's OK to ____________ your friends' opinions? How often do you argue with your friends?
4 Do you ____________ people much? Or do you prefer to speak on the phone?
5 How do you ____________ with friends who live far away from you?
6 How many ____________ from your childhood do you still meet up with? Are any of them close friends?

b Work in pairs. Take turns to ask and answer the questions.

Go to your app for more practice.

Grammar

5 a Read the grammar box and choose the correct alternatives.

Present perfect with *for* and *since*

Use the present perfect (*have/has* + past participle) to talk about things that started in the past and [1]*continue/don't continue* now.

*How long **have you known** her?*

*We**'ve known** each other since we were at school.*

*We**'ve lived** together for about nine months.*

Use *for* with the present perfect to talk about [2]*a period of time/when an action started.*

*I've only known Justin **for about two years.***

*We haven't done that **for a long time.***

Use *since* with the present perfect to talk about [3]*a period of time/when an action started.*

*I have a whole group of close friends that I've known **since I was at college.***

*We haven't argued once **since we met.***

b Complete the table with the words and phrases in the box.

~~2012~~ a few minutes a long time April years Monday over 20 years the 22nd ten o'clock three months

for	since
	2012

6 a 9.2 Listen to the sentences and notice the pronunciation of *for*.

1 She's lived here for years.

1 We've been here for hours.

2 He's worked at this school for 18 years.

3 I haven't seen her for a long time.

4 We've been friends for a few years now.

b Listen again and repeat.

Go to page 132 or your app for more information and practice.

7 a Make sentences using the prompts and *for* or *since*.

1 I / know / my closest friend / 60 years

I've known my closest friend for 60 years.

2 We / live / next door to each other / 1990

3 Ricky / work / at the post office / a long time

4 Tania / be married to Paco / she was 21

5 They / know / each other / they were six

6 My parents / live / here / last year

b Complete the sentences so they're true for you. Use a *for* or *since*.

1 I've lived …

I've lived in Oslo for about ten years.

2 I've studied/worked at …

3 I've known …

4 I haven't seen …

5 I've had …

c Work in pairs and compare your sentences. Ask each other questions to find out more.

Speaking

PREPARE

8 You're going to describe a close friend to another student. First, answer the questions below and make notes.

1 What's your friend's name? What's he/she like?

2 How long have you known your friend?

3 When did you meet?

4 How did you meet?

5 How often do you see your friend?

6 What do you do when you get together?

7 Why do you get on well?

8 Why is your friend important to you?

SPEAK

9 a Work in pairs. Take turns to describe your friend. Use your notes and the Useful phrases to help you.

Useful phrases

We've known each other (for ten years).

We met (at college).

We see each other (a few times a month).

We get on really well because (we're similar).

(He's/She's) important to me because (he/she makes me laugh).

b Are your friends similar or different?

Develop your listening page 110

9B What's on?

A

B

- **Goal:** talk about about films and TV
- **Grammar:** present perfect with *already, just* and *yet*
- **Vocabulary:** adjectives to describe films and TV programmes

Reading and vocabulary

1 Look at the photos and answer the questions.

1 What kind of programmes do they show?
2 Do you like these kinds of programmes?
3 What other kinds of programmes do you like watching?

2 Read the TV programme reviews.
Which reviewer 1–4 ...

a always watches the programme with other people?
b has different feelings when they watch the programme?
c didn't think they would enjoy the programme at first?
d advises people to watch the programme?

WHAT TO WATCH **TV**

Today's top 4!

1 Murder on 4th Street
This might be the most **exciting** thing on TV at the moment. A **serious** crime drama with a really **clever** story and brilliant acting – don't miss it!

2 Housemates
I love this programme. It's so **funny** it makes me laugh out loud. It's got a bit of everything – sometimes it's **silly**, sometimes it's **sad**. I can understand why it's so **popular**.

3 Brook Hill
I've watched this programme since it began a few years ago. It's a **long** story with lots of episodes, lots of characters, and lots of action. It is a bit **scary** though, so I never watch it alone!

4 Looking at the past
I really enjoyed this programme. I don't usually like historical programmes because I think they're **boring**, but my friend suggested this and I actually found it really **interesting**. What makes it even better is that it's a **true** story.

3 a Work in pairs. Decide if the adjectives in bold in the reviews are positive, negative or neutral.

b Choose the correct alternatives.

1 I don't usually watch comedies, but I saw a really *funny/serious* one recently.
2 I don't like documentaries. I think they're *boring/clever*.
3 I love really *long/boring* films – they're a good reason to spend three hours in front of the TV!
4 Documentaries are really *popular/silly* at the moment. There are so many on TV.
5 I hate watching *scary/interesting* films, I can't sleep afterwards!
6 The last TV programme I watched was very *sad/popular*, I cried at the end.

c Which of the sentences are true for you?

Go to page 144 or your app for more vocabulary and practice.

Listening

4 a 9.7 Listen to Mark and Claire talking about *Victoria* and *Game of Thrones* and answer the questions.

1 Which programme is about history?
2 What happens in *Victoria*?
3 How many series of *Game of Thrones* have they made?
4 Does Claire want to watch it?

b Listen again. Does Mark (M) or Claire (C) say each sentence?

1 I've just finished watching a really interesting drama.
2 I haven't seen it yet though.
3 They've already made an eighth series of it!

C

D

Grammar

5 **Read the grammar box and choose the correct alternatives.**

Present perfect with *already*, *just* and *yet*

Use *just* to describe something which happened a [1]*short/long* time ago.

***I've just seen** a great comedy.*

Use *already* to describe an action which [2]*has/hasn't* happened.

***They've already finished** making the new series.*

Use *yet* in negatives and questions to describe an action which [3]*has/hasn't* happened, but we think it might.

*Have you **watched it yet**?*

*I **haven't seen it yet**.*

6 a 9.8 **Listen and notice the pronunciation of *already*, *just* and *yet*.**

1 I've just seen that new film.
2 We've already finished dinner.
3 She hasn't left yet.
4 They've just turned the TV off.
5 I've already seen that.
6 Have you finished yet?

b Listen again and repeat.

7 **Choose the correct alternatives.**

1 I haven't seen that new comedy *already/yet*.
2 We've *just/yet* finished watching the first episode.
3 We've *yet/already* seen that film.
4 I've *just/already* watched an interesting documentary. It finished a few minutes ago.
5 Have they made the second series *just/yet*?
6 They've *already/yet* chosen the actors, but they haven't filmed it *just/yet*.

8 a **Complete the sentences about films or TV programmes so they're true for you.**

1 I haven't seen ... yet.
2 I've just started watching ...
3 I've already seen ...

b Work in pairs and compare your sentences.

Go to page 132 or your app for more information and practice.

Speaking

PREPARE

9 a 9.9 **You're going to plan what to watch on TV with another student. First, listen to Steve and Amy. Tick (✓) the programmes that they choose.**

- We All Love Sally
- One Night in June
- Westfield
- Galactic Empire
- No Time To Escape

b Listen again. Which adjectives do they use to describe the programmes/films?

c Think of some TV programmes/films that you would like to watch. Make some notes about why you want to watch them.

SPEAK

10 a **Work in pairs. Tell each other about the programmes/films you'd like to watch and explain why. Then choose two programmes to watch together. Use the Useful phrases to help you.**

b Tell the class which programmes/films you chose. Are any of them the same?

Useful phrases

Have you seen (*Game of Thrones*) yet?
Shall we watch (*Victoria*)?
Yes, that looks (interesting/funny/boring).
Oh, no, (I've already seen that).

Develop your reading page 111

9D English in action

Goal: ask for information

Listening

1 **Work in pairs. How do you usually get information about the things in the box?**

education films hotels places to eat
public transport tourist information

2 a 9.12 **Listen to conversations 1–4. What type of information is each person asking about?**

b **Listen again and choose the correct alternatives.**

1 *Could/Would* you tell me what the password is, please?
2 *Sir/Sure.* Are you a guest at the hotel?
3 Could you tell me when breakfast *is/starts*?
4 Do you know which platform the train to Leeds leaves *from/on*?
5 I'm not *know/sure*. I think it leaves in six minutes.
6 Yes, of *course/sure*. It's £120 for twelve weeks.
7 *Could/Do* you know if I need to buy a camera?
8 I'm *sure/afraid* I can't help you with that.
9 Do you know *if/when* it's open now?
10 *I'm sorry/Of course*, I don't know.

3 a 9.13 **Listen to the questions. Does the speaker's voice go up or down at the end of each one?**

1 Do you know where the bus station is?
2 Do you know if the library's open?
3 Could you tell me what time the film starts?
4 Could you tell me where the milk is?

b **Listen again and repeat.**

4 a **Put the words in the correct order to make questions.**

1 the time / tell / could / is / you / me / what / ?
2 finishes / the lesson / do / you / know / what time / ?
3 homework / if / do / have / you / know / we / any / today / ?
4 the next lesson / me / you / could / is / tell / when / ?
5 where / you / know / the train station / do / is / ?
6 is / you / could / me / the teacher's name / what / tell / ?
7 a bank / do / near / there's / if / you / know / here / ?
8 the way / tell / to / me / could / the nearest bus stop / you / ?

b **Work in pairs. Take turns to ask the questions. Use the Useful phrases to help you answer.**

5 a **Complete the first four sentences in the Useful phrases box in an appropriate way.**

1 Do you know what time it is?

Useful phrases

Asking for information
Do you know … ?
Could you tell me … ?
Do you know if … ?
Could you tell me if … ?

Giving information
Yes, of course. (It starts at 8).
Sure. (It's 1234).
I'm sorry/I'm afraid I don't (know).
I'm not sure. (I think it's at five o'clock)

b **Go around the class and ask your questions. Answer in an appropriate way.**

A: *Excuse me, Josef. Do you know what time it is?*
B: *Sure, it's a quarter to eleven.*

Speaking

PREPARE

6 **Work in pairs. Student A go to page 157 and Student B go to page 158. Follow the instructions.**

SPEAK

7 **Practise your conversations with your partner.**

Go online for the Roadmap video.

Check and reflect

1 Complete the description with a verb in the box in the present perfect or past simple.

be become know like live meet move

I [1]______ my neighbour for about three years. His name's Jun and he's from China. He [2]______ here to study at university and he [3]______ here since then. We [4]______ when Jun lost his key and he couldn't get into the house. Since then, we [5]______ close friends. Both of us [6]______ playing video games since we [7]______ children so he often comes round to my flat to play. Unfortunately, he's much better than me!

2 a Choose the correct alternatives.

1 I *argue/agree* with my brother all the time. We don't get on.
2 Graham and I became *close/near* friends at primary school.
3 I don't *see/watch* Molly very often, maybe once a year.
4 I didn't get *in/on* well with my best friend at first.
5 Andy and I are *old/long* friends. We met 25 years ago.
6 I always try to keep in *feel/touch* with people.

b Work in pairs. Make true sentences about you and your friends using some of the vocabulary in Exercise 2a.

3 Toby has invited some friends round for dinner at 8 p.m. It's now 7.05 p.m. Look at his 'to do' list. Write sentences with *already, yet* or *just* for each activity.

go to the supermarket ✓
clean the house ✓
have a shower ✓
put the meat in the oven at 7 p.m. ✓
cook the vegetables at 7.45 p.m.
make a playlist ✓
do the washing up

He's already been to the supermarket.

4 a Complete the sentences with the words in the box.

clever funny long popular sad serious silly true

1 The story wasn't very clever. In fact, it was very ______ .
2 Everybody went to see that film. It was so ______ .
3 It's not a funny film at all. It's quite ______ .
4 The things in the film really happened. It's a ______ story.
5 The story was ______ . It really made me think.
6 That comedy really made me laugh. It was so ______ .
7 We saw a really ______ film last night - almost four hours!
8 It was such a ______ story - I cried a lot.

b Work in pairs. Use the adjectives in Exercise 4a to describe some films you've seen. What are they?

5 a Complete the sentences with the words in the box.

at did for found got hard passed

1 I didn't understand geography so I ______ it really boring.
2 I didn't study very hard ______ exams so I never ______ them.
3 I ______ well at school but I didn't actually do much work.
4 I'm bad ______ anything with numbers so I found maths difficult.
5 I worked ______ at school so I ______ better at most subjects.

b Complete the prompts to make true sentences about your experience at school.

1 I was good at ...
2 I was terrible at ...
3 I found ... really boring.
4 I did well at ...
5 I found ... easy.
6 I worked hard at ...

c Work in pairs. Tell each other your sentences and give more information.

6 a Complete the sentences with *could/couldn't* and a verb in the box.

read speak ride swim

1 I ______ until I was 15 because I was afraid of water.
2 I ______ a skateboard when I was younger but I'm not good at it anymore.
3 My son ______ music when he was three and now plays in a band.
4 My daughter went on holiday with her Greek friend but they ______ each other's language.

b Work in pairs. What things could you do when you were younger that other people couldn't?

Reflect

How confident do you feel about the statements below? Write 1–5 (1 = not very confident, 5 = very confident).

- I can describe a friend.
- I can talk about TV and films.
- I can talk about my school days.
- I can ask for information.

Want more practice?
Go to your Workbook or app.

10A Save or spend?

- **Goal:** present money saving ideas
- **Grammar:** first conditional
- **Vocabulary:** money

Vocabulary

1 Work in pairs and discuss the questions.

1. Do you prefer spending or saving money? Why?
2. Are you careful about how much you spend?
3. What do/don't you like spending money on?

2 a Read the Money survey and answer questions 1–7. Check you understand the meaning of the words and phrases in bold.

b Complete the sentences with the words and phrases in the box.

borrow	cash	credit	cost	earn
lend	pay for	save	spend	waste

1. I don't *earn* much money in my job so it's hard for me to ______ money for the future.
2. I ______ all my money on video games because they ______ a lot!
3. I'm always happy to ______ money to friends if they need it.
4. I sometimes ______ money from my sister.
5. I usually ______ things with ______. When I use a ______ card I spend too much
6. I often ______ money on clothes I never wear.

c Work in pairs. Compare your answers to the questions in the survey. Do you have similar spending habits?

Go to page 145 or your app for more vocabulary and practice.

Money survey

We'd like to know a bit more about your habits. Do you think about what you spend? Do you try to save money? Please read questions 1–7 and answer yes (✓) or no (x).

1. Do you enjoy **spending money** on new things?
2. Do you ever **waste money** on things you don't need?
3. Do you prefer to **pay for** things by **credit card** or with **cash**?
4. Do you sometimes buy things which **cost a lot** of money without thinking about it?
5. Is it important for you to **save** some of the **money** that you **earn**?
6. Do you ever **borrow money** from friends?
7. Are you happy to **lend money** to friends?

Listening

3 a **Work in pairs. You're going to listen to a podcast about saving money. Look at the topics below and say what you think you'll hear about each one.**

- buying gifts
- food
- clothes
- waiting
- credit cards

I think they'll say that credit cards are not a good way to save money.

b 10.1 **Listen to the podcast and answer the questions.**

1 What five tips do the presenters give?
2 Do they mention any of your ideas?
3 Which do you think are the best tips?

c **Match the sentence halves. Then listen to the podcast again and check your answers.**

1 If you make a list,
2 If you sell your clothes,
3 If you make something,
4 If you still want it after a month,
5 You won't do that

a you'll spend more time on it but less money.
b you can earn some extra money.
c if you pay by card.
d you'll know it's a good decision.
e you'll only buy the food you need.

Grammar

4 **Read the grammar box and choose the correct alternatives.**

First conditional

Use the first conditional to talk about the result of an action in the [1]*past/future*.
Use *if* + [2]*will/present simple* + *will/won't* + [3]*infinitive/-ing* to form the first conditional.
***If you bake** something, **you'll spend** less money.*
It [4]*is/isn't* possible to use other modal verbs such as *can* and *should* instead of *will*.
***If you sell** your clothes, **you can** earn extra money.*
***If you want** to save money on transport, **you should** listen in.*
The *if* clause can come first or second.
***If you make a list**, you'll only buy the food you need.*
*You'll only buy the food you need **if you make a list**.*

5 a 10.2 **Listen to the sentences and notice the pronunciation of *'ll*.**

1 If you pay by cash, you'll spend less.
2 If you bake your own bread, you'll save money.
3 We'll save more if we go out less.
4 You'll save money if you turn lights off.

b **Listen again and repeat.**

6 **Complete the tips for eating out with *will* and the verbs in brackets.**

1 You *'ll find* (find) special offers if you *look* (look) online.
2 If you ______ dinner early (eat), you ______ (get) a discount.
3 If you go out for ______ (lunch) instead of dinner it ______ (be) cheaper.
4 You ______ (save) money if you ______ (drink) tap water.
5 Your bill ______ (be) lower if you ______ (share) a dessert with someone.
6 If you ______ (have) coffee at home you ______ (save) enough money to eat out.

7 a **Complete each sentence with your own ideas.**

1 If I have time tomorrow, I'll ...
2 If the weather's good/bad at the weekend, I'll/I won't ...
3 I won't ... next week if ...
4 I'll/I won't ... next month if ...

If I have time tomorrow, I'll go swimming.

b **Work in pairs. Tell each other about your plans.**

Go to page 134 or your app for more information and practice.

Speaking

PREPARE

8 a **Work in pairs. You're going to present some money-saving tips. Think of five ideas and make some notes. Use the topics in the box to help you.**

home clothes free time furniture going out phone shopping transport travel

b **Think about how you want to present your ideas. Use the Useful phrases to help you.**

Here are some some tips for when you want to save money. Firstly, going out is expensive. If you go out less, you'll save money quickly.

Useful phrases

Here are some tips for when you're (eating out).
You should (make lunch, not buy it).
If you (make lunch) you'll (spend less).
It's a good idea to (stop buying coffee).
If you (don't buy coffee), you'll (save over £10 a week).

SPEAK

9 a **Work in groups and take turns to present your tips. Listen and make notes.**

b **What was the best tip you heard?**

Develop your reading page 113

10B Everyday objects

- Goal: share information
- Grammar: present and past passive
- Vocabulary: time expressions

Reading

1 **Work in pairs and discuss the questions.**

1 What have you got in your bag or pockets at the moment?
2 What do you usually carry around with you?
3 Why are those things important?

2 a **Read the introduction to the factfile. What's it about?**

1 technology
2 how difficult life is
3 things we use all the time

b **Choose the correct alternatives in the factfile. Then work in pairs and compare your answers. Do you agree?**

c **Go to page 151 and check your answers. Which facts are the most surprising/worrying/interesting?**

Do you ever stop to think ... ?

Our lives are so easy today. There are objects to help us with everything we do. We have scissors to cut, pencils to write with and light bulbs to help us see in the dark. We can't really live without these objects, but do any of us ever stop to think about where they came from? Complete the facts below to find out how much you know about everyday objects.

1 Over *820 million/20 billion* pairs of shoes are bought worldwide each year.
2 Around the world, one million plastic bottles are sold each *hour/minute*.
3 Jeans were first made in 1873 by *Jacob Davis/Levi Strauss*.
4 Around *2,500/8,500* pencils are made from one tree.
5 The first scissors were used *350/3,500* years ago.
6 Bluetooth technology is named after a *king/shark*.
7 The first electric light was made by *Thomas Edison/Humphry Davy*.
8 Your mobile phone is powered by *more/less* technology than the Apollo 11 spacecraft that landed on the moon.

Grammar

3 **Read the grammar box and choose the correct alternatives.**

Present and past passive

Use [1]*be/have* and the [2]*infinitive/past participle* to form the passive.

Present passive: *Bluetooth technology* ***is named*** *after a king.*

Past passive: *The first scissors* ***were used*** *3,500 years ago.*

Use the passive when you [3]*know/don't know* who or what did an action (or if it's not important).

2,500 pencils ***are made*** *from one tree.*

If we want to say who or what did the action, we can use *by*.

Jeans ***were invented*** *in 1873* ***by*** *Jacob Davis.*

4 a 10.3 **Listen to the sentences. Notice the pronunciation of the verb *be*. Is it stressed or unstressed?**

1 Denim was first used in the 19th century.
2 Jeans are worn by lots of different people.
3 Jeans weren't invented until 1873.
4 A lot of money is spent on jeans each year.

b **Listen again and repeat.**

Go to page 134 or your app for more information and practice.

5 **Complete the facts about chocolate with the correct passive form of the verbs in brackets.**

- Chocolate [1]_____ first _____ (make) in the Americas.
- In those days, it [2]_________ (not eat), it was a drink.
- Cocoa beans [3]_________ (use) as money at that time.
- Chocolate [4]_________ (bring) to Europe by the Spanish in the 16th Century.
- Now, half of the world's chocolate [5]_________ (eat) by Europeans each year.
- Lots of sugar [6]_________ (add) to most chocolate today.
- These days, most cocoa beans [7]_________ (grow) in West Africa.
- Cocoa beans [8]_________ (not/ use) to make white chocolate.

Listening and vocabulary

6 10.4 **Listen to an interview about chocolate and choose the alternatives you hear.**

1 Chocolate was first made over 3,000 years *ago/ before*.
2 It wasn't the same as the chocolate we have *yesterday/ nowadays*.
3 *From/ For* a long time it was drunk cold.
4 It was in the sixteenth *century/ years*.
5 *These/ this* days lots of sugar is added to most of the chocolate we eat.
6 Chocolate wasn't sweet *about/ until* the 1500s.
7 *At/ During* the 1800s, milk was added to chocolate too.
8 Over two-thirds of cocoa beans are grown in West Africa *all/ each* year.

7 a **Complete the sentences with the words in the box. Use Exercise 6 to help you.**

ago century during each for nowadays these until

1 Electric lightbulbs weren't used ______ the late nineteenth century.
2 Gas was used to light homes ______ a hundred years.
3 Chocolate milk was sold as medicine in the eighteenth ______ .
4 ______ day, 27,000 trees are used to make toilet paper.
5 ______ no one uses the small pocket in jeans but they were originally designed for pocket watches.
6 ______ days, more chocolate is eaten in Switzerland than in any other country.
7 The first iPhone was made more than ten years ______ .
8 ______ the 1990s, most people listened to music on CDs.

b **Complete the sentences so they're true for you.**

1 During my school days, I ...
2 I used to ... but nowadays I ...
3 I didn't ... until ...
4 A few years ago, I ...
5 Each year, I ...
6 These days, I ...

During my school days, I did a lot of sport.

c **Work in pairs and compare your sentences.**

During my school days I did a lot of sport but nowadays I don't do any.

Go to your app for more practice.

Speaking

PREPARE

8 a **Work in pairs. You're going to read some information about four things: the ballpoint pen, tomato ketchup, chewing gum and paper. First, discuss anything you already know about them.**

I think there's a lot of sugar in ketchup.

b **Student A: turn to page 157. Student B: turn to page 158. Follow the instructions and check the meaning of any words you don't know.**

SPEAK

9 a **Student A: tell your partner about the ballpoint pen and chewing gum. Student B: Listen to your partner and make notes.**

b **Student B: tell your partner about tomato ketchup and paper. Student A: Listen to your partner and make notes.**

c **What were the most interesting things you found out?**

Develop your writing page 114

10C Unusual hobbies

- **Goal:** discuss hobbies and interests
- **Grammar:** review of tenses
- **Vocabulary:** hobbies and interests

Reading

1 a Look at the photos in the article and answer the questions.

1. Who do you think these people are?
2. What are they doing?

b Read the article and check your ideas. Would you like to try any of these hobbies?

2 Read the text again and choose the correct alternatives.

1. There are *more/fewer* Comic-Con conventions now than there used to be.
2. The writer thinks everyone who goes to the event *is crazy/has a good time*.
3. The Chrismans live in an old-fashioned house because *they want to/they don't have much money*.
4. Their fridge doesn't *work/use electricity*.
5. People from Little Woodham *think/live* like they are from the past.
6. Little Woodham is used for *education/shopping*.

Grammar

3 Read the grammar box. Then match statements A–H to the underlined sentences in the article.

Review of tenses

A Use the **present simple** to describe facts, things which are generally true or something that happens regularly. *7*

B Use the **present continuous** to describe something happening now or around now.

C Use the **past simple** to describe finished actions or states in the past.

D Use the **present perfect** to talk about unspecific actions in the past or an action which started in the past and is still true now.

E Use ***be going to*** + **infinitive** for future plans.

F Use ***will*** + **infinitive** to make predictions.

G Use the **past continuous** to describe actions in progress in the past.

H Use the **present continuous** for future arrangements.

I've just got back from Comic-Con. It's a popular comic book event which first started in San Diego in 1970, and now happens all over the world. People dress as their favourite comic characters. For example, when I walked in, [1]Superman and Spiderman were having a conversation. It was great!

But why do people do this? Some love it when people take their picture. Some like to meet people who have similar interests. Whatever the reason is, everyone has lots of fun! I really enjoyed it, and I'm sure [2]I'm going to go again.

In fact I had such a good time [3]I've decided to try something different myself, so at the moment [4]I'm looking for other unusual hobbies that people do. For example, [5]Sarah and Gabriel Chrisman are having a hiking and cycling holiday this summer. [6]They'll be very easy to notice because [7]they wear clothes from 100 years ago! They also eat old-fashioned food, and even have furniture from that time – they haven't used a modern fridge since 2010. Their fridge uses real ice to keep the food fresh! The Chrismans do these things because they're really interested in how people lived in the 1880s and 1890s.

But it's not just individual people that dress up, whole villages do too! Little Woodham in the UK is a seventeenth-century 'living village', full of people who live like they are from that time. International film studios have used it in their films and schools often take children there to learn about how people used to live. You can see people doing typical jobs from that time, such as making clothes and pots, and even listen to a mother telling stories to her children. A good time to visit is at the beginning of May when they have a May Day festival, [8]which was a big event in the seventeenth century.

4 a 10.5 **Listen to the sentences and notice the pronunciation of the contracted words (e.g. *We're*).**

1 We're having a party next week.
2 I'm learning about different lifestyles.
3 She's written many books.
4 They've lived like that since they were children.
5 I think you'll find it interesting.

b **Listen again and repeat.**

5 a **Use the prompts to write questions.**

1 What games / you / play / when / child?
What games did you play when you were a child?
2 What / you / doing / yesterday / 8 p.m.?
3 How long / live / your house?
4 What / you / do / this evening?
5 What / you / going / do / next weekend?
6 What / you think / the weather / like / tomorrow?
7 What / you / read / at the moment?
8 Where / you / live?

b **Work in pairs. Ask and answer the questions.**

Go to page 134 or your app for more information and practice.

Vocabulary

6 a **Read the tips about choosing a hobby. Which do you think is the best tip?**

Choosing a hobby

How do you choose the right hobby for you? Here are some ideas to help you:

1 Choose something you're interested in. It might sound simple, but you should be excited about trying something new. Remember that you're doing this for fun!
2 Before you start doing something seriously, make sure it's good for you.
3 Find out about the hobby. Go online or talk to people to learn about it.
4 Join a club. This will keep you interested and it's great to spend time doing something with other people who also enjoy being part of a team.
5 If it gets hard, don't give up! It might be difficult at first, but you'll get better at it over time.

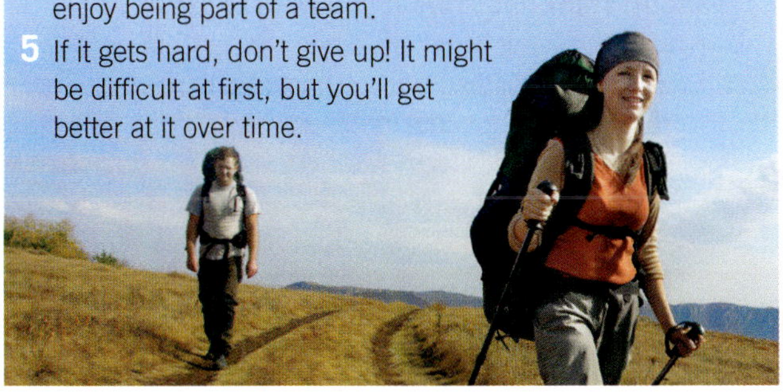

b **Find the phrases in the box in the text and underline them. Some of them are in different forms. Check the meaning of any words you don't know.**

be part of a team   do something for fun
find out about   give up   join a club
learn about something   spend time doing something
start doing something   try something new

c **Complete each sentence with one word. Use the phrases in Exercise 6b to help you.**

1 I'd like to ______ something new, like kite-surfing. But first I need to ______ out more about it.
2 I recently ______ a football club. Some people there are really serious about it, but I just do it ______ fun.
3 I love spending ______ repairing old cars. It's not easy but I'm learning more ______ it all the time.
4 Andy wants to ______ something new. I suggested he could ______ doing cookery classes.

7 **Work in pairs and discuss the question. Have you tried anything new or given anything up recently?**

Go to page 145 or your app for more vocabulary and practice.

Speaking

PREPARE

8 a 10.6 **You're going to talk about your hobbies/interests. First listen to Megan and Rob and tick (✓) the hobbies/interests they mention.**

chess   collecting dolls   football   gardening
making model planes   playing video games
running   tennis

b **Listen again and answer the questions.**

1 What did Megan buy every week?
2 How many planes did she make?
3 What was Rob interested in when he was a boy?
4 What does he like doing now?
5 Which hobby does Rob suggest for Megan?

9 **Make notes about your own hobbies/interests. Answer the questions below to help you.**

- What hobbies/interests did you have as a child?
- What did you use to do?
- What hobbies/interests do you have now?
- Why do you like them?
- Have you ever joined a club or team?
- What hobbies would you like to try? Why?

SPEAK

10 a **Work in pairs and discuss your hobbies/interests. Use the questions in Exercise 10 to help you.**

A: *So, Eva, do you have any hobbies?*
B: *No, not anymore, but I used to love photography.*

b **Share three interesting facts about your partner's hobbies/interests with the class.**

Develop your listening page 115

10D English in action

Goal: ask for clarification

Listening

1 Work in pairs and discuss the questions.

1. Do you ever find it difficult to understand English? In what situations?
2. Do you ever find it difficult to understand people in your own language? When?

2 a 10.10 Listen to two conversations. How well do Kim and Tania understand the people they are talking to?

b Listen again and decide if the statements are true (T) or false (F).

1. Kim knows what a potluck party is.
2. At a potluck party, the guests cook at home then bring their food to the party.
3. People can arrive late to the party if they want.
4. Tania doesn't know what a DX4518 form is.
5. She needs to complete the form and first give it to Sally in Human Resources.

3 Listen again. In which conversation (1 or 2) do you hear each of the Useful phrases?

Useful phrases

Asking for more information

What's a (potluck party)? *1*

What do you mean (exactly)?

Asking someone to repeat something

(Sorry) can you say that again/repeat that (please)?

What was the first part (again)?

Saying you don't understand

I'm not sure what you mean.

(Sorry) I don't understand.

Saying you understand

OK, got it.

I see.

4 a 10.11 Listen to the phrases in the Useful phrases and underline the stressed words in each one.

b Listen again and repeat.

5 a Complete the conversation with one word in each gap. Use the Useful phrases to help you.

A: I made chicken jalfrezi last night, it was delicious!

B: I'm not sure what you [1]_______ . What's that?

A: Oh, it's a type of curry.

B: [2]_______ a curry?

A: It's a type of Indian food, a hot and spicy dish.

B: Ah, OK, [3]_______ it. What's in it?

A: Well, chicken, obviously. Also tomatoes, spices and lots of coriander.

B: What was the [4]_______ part?

A: Coriander. It's a kind of herb.

B: Oh, I [5]_______ ! I think in the US it's called cilantro.

b 10.12 Listen and check.

PREPARE

6 You're going to practise asking for clarification. First, choose two topics below to tell another student about. Think about what you want to say.

- a dish or event or activity where you're from
- a hobby or interest that you know a lot about.
- something about your job
- a place you've visited
- an unusual food you've tried

SPEAK

7 Work in pairs. Take turns to tell each other about your topic. Listen to your partner and ask for clarification. Use the Useful phrases to help you.

A: *I'm going to talk about a piñata.*
B: *What's a piñata?*
A: *It's something which you break open to get sweets.*
B: *What do you mean exactly?*

Go online for the Roadmap video.

Check and reflect

1 a Match the sentences halves.

1 If the weather is nice this weekend,
2 I'll go to bed early tonight
3 If I earn a lot of money this year,
4 If I go to the supermarket when I'm hungry,
5 I shouldn't go out tonight

a I might buy myself a new car.
b We can have a picnic in the park.
c I'll spend too much money on food.
d if there's nothing to watch on TV.
e if my teacher gives me lots of homework.

b Work in pairs. Write different endings for sentences 1–5 so they are true for you. Take turns to read them to your partner and say which sentence they are finishing.

2 a Complete the sentences with the correct form of the verbs in the box.

borrow cost earn lend pay save

1 I don't ______ for things with cash these days.
2 I never ______ money to people.
3 I don't spend more than I ______ each week. I don't like ______ money from my friends.
4 I can never ______ money. I don't have enough left at the end of the month.
5 In general, things ______ more money in shops than they do online.

b Work in pairs. What was the last thing you borrowed from someone? What was the last thing you lent someone?

3 a Choose the correct alternatives.

1 The book 1984 *was/is* written by George Orwell.
2 Coffee is *grow/grown* in my country.
3 Coffee *aren't/isn't* grown in the UK.
4 Last night's show was *watched/watching* by millions.
5 How many mobile phones *does/are* sold each year?
6 The chocolate bar *was/were* invented by JS Fry & Sons.

b Complete the prompts so that they're true for you.

1 My favourite film was directed by ______________.
2 ______________ grown in my country.
3 ______________ recycled in my town.

4 a Correct the mistake in each sentence.

1 Cars were not common in my country about the 1950s.
2 I was born in the 20th years.
3 I couldn't drive a car during I was 16.
4 I don't write with a pen and paper much this days.
5 My country won the World Cup a few years before.

b Work in pairs. Are any of the sentences true for you?

5 Complete the text with the correct form of the verbs in brackets.

My best friend's name [1]______ (be) Sandy. She was born in New York, but when she was seven her family [2] ______(move) here to Sydney. I [3]______ (know) her for 13 years and we get on really well. Once, when I [4]______ (have) problems at school, she [5]______ (help) me, and I passed all my exams. At the moment she [6]______ (study) maths at university, so I don't see her much, but I [7]______ (stay) with her next weekend. I'm going to go to university one day. I think we [8]______ (be) great friends for the rest of our lives.

6 a Complete the prompts with sentences about you.

1 I've never …
2 I hope one day I'll …
3 Last week I …
4 I've known …
5 Next year I'm going to …

b Work in pairs. Compare your sentences with a partner.

7 a Complete the sentences with the correct form of the verbs in the box.

be do find join spend start try

1 Before you ______ doing a new sport it's a good idea to have a health check with your doctor.
2 I'd like to ______ a running club..
3 When I was a child I ______ a lot of time playing video games.
4 Some people hate studying history, but I ______ it just for fun!
5 The best way to ______ out about a hobby is to speak to people who already do it.
6 I've always ______ interested in cars.
7 Phil ______ something new every year.

Reflect

How confident do you feel about the statements below? Write 1–5 (1 = not very confident, 5 = very confident).

- I can present money-saving ideas.
- I can share information on a topic.
- I can ask and answer questions about hobbies and interests.
- I can ask for clarification.

Want more practice?
Go to your Workbook or app.

1A Develop your listening

Goal: understand a short talk

Focus: understanding the main idea

A

B

C

D

E

F

1 a Which greetings below can you see in photos A–D.

- bow your head
- hug someone
- kiss someone on the cheek
- put your hands together
- shake hands
- show your tongue
- press your noses together
- touch someone's hand or arm
- put your hand on your chest

b Do you know which countries the different greetings are from? If not, can you guess?

c 1.3 **Listen to the introduction of a radio programme. Which greetings in Exercise 1a does the radio presenter talk about?**

2 Read the Focus box. How can you identify key words?

Understanding the main idea

It isn't always necessary to understand every word when you listen – you can use key words (e.g. verbs, adverbs, nouns, adjectives) to understand the main idea.

It's easier to hear key words when listening because they are usually stressed.

***People** around the **world greet** each other **differently**.*

3 a Read what the radio presenter says about greetings and underline the key words.

How we greet someone for the first time is important because we want people to like us.

b 1.4 **Listen and check.**

4 1.5 **Listen to the next part of the radio programme and choose the correct alternatives.**

1 Men and women in the US usually *kiss/shake hands* when they meet new people.
2 Men and women in the US sometimes *bow/hug*.
3 Men in Brazil usually *kiss/shake hands*.
4 People in Brazil *sometimes/always* kiss three times.
5 Men and women in Qatar *put their right hand on their chest/shake hands* when they meet.
6 Men in Qatar sometimes *put their hands together/press their noses together*.

5 1.6 **Listen to the last part of the radio programme and complete notes 1–7 with one key word from the box.**

bow chest hands head high low tongue

South Korea

1 Friends: Bow their ______
2 Business people: ______ with top half of their body
3 Younger people: Bow ______

Thailand

4 Traditional greeting: People put their ______ together and bow their head
5 Friends: Hands are low in front of their ______
6 Older/important people: Hands are ______, fingers near top of their head

Tibet

7 Traditional greeting: People put their hands together and show their ______

6 Work in pairs and discuss the questions.

1 Which greeting in the radio show do you think is the most interesting? Why?
2 Can you think of any other greetings?
3 How do you usually greet the people below?

- family
- friends
- people you don't know
- people you work/study with

1B Develop your writing

Goal: complete a questionnaire

Focus: explaining reasons and results

1 a Work in pairs and discuss the questions.

1 What are the best ways to learn English?
2 What do you use English for?

b Read the questionnaire and match questions 1–6 with gaps A–F.

1 Do you prefer working alone or in pairs/groups?
2 What do you find difficult about learning English?
3 What do you like using to learn English (e.g. books, video, the internet, etc.)?
4 What do you do outside class to practise English?
5 What do you need English for?
6 What do you like doing in class (e.g. listening, speaking, pronunciation, etc.)?

Learning English Questionnaire

Name: *Miguel García*
Teacher: *Diana Norman*

A ________________________
I need to pass an exam at university. That's why I'm studying English. I think my reading and writing skills are OK, but I really need to improve my speaking for the exam.

B ________________________
I like having conversations in class because I can't practise speaking English at home. But I also like reading interesting articles, because I can learn new things.

C ________________________
I like watching videos and I use my phone all the time to look up new words.

D ________________________
I like working with other students so I can practise speaking, but I don't mind working on my own.

E ________________________
Pronunciation is the hardest thing for me because of all the different sounds in English.

F ________________________
When I'm at home I like watching TV programmes in English. I prefer watching them in the original language because I learn a lot of new vocabulary this way.

2 Read the questionnaire again. Decide if the sentences are true (T) or false (F).

1 Miguel has finished university.
2 He doesn't often speak English outside class.
3 He likes working in pairs or groups.
4 He finds it difficult to pronounce words correctly.
5 He learns English while doing something he enjoys at home.

3 Read the Focus box. Then underline the phrases Miguel uses to give examples in the questionnaire.

Explaining reasons and results

Use *because* (*of*) and *so that* to give reasons.
*I was late for class **because** I missed the bus.*
*I couldn't sleep **because of** the noisy traffic.*
*I'm saving money **so that** I can go to University.*
Use *that's why* to explain a result.
*I missed the bus. **That's why** I was late for class.*
*I want to learn new vocabulary – **that's why** I watch TV in English.*

4 Match the sentence halves.

1 I like using social media because
2 I would like to move to the UK. That's why
3 I try to learn ten new words every day, so that
4 I find reading the most difficult skill, because of

a I can quickly improve my vocabulary.
b I can chat with people in English from all over the world.
c all the new words.
d I'm interested in British English.

5 Choose the correct alternatives.

1 I like listening to songs in English *so that/that's why* I can learn fun words.
2 I need to practise writing emails *because/so that* it's important for my work.
3 I like working in groups *because/because of* the people I meet.
4 I find listening difficult. *Because/That's why* I need to practise it more in class.
5 I would like to have more homework *because of/so that* I can practise at home.

Prepare

6 You're going to answer the questions in Exercise 1b. First, make notes about each one.

Write

7 Write your answers to the questions. Use the Focus box and the Useful phrases to help you.

Useful phrases

I need English for (my job/an exam/my studies).
I really enjoy (speaking in class).
I don't mind (doing exercises for homework), but I prefer (doing online research).
It's difficult to (pronounce some words).

1c Develop your reading

- **Goal:** understand a short article
- **Focus:** reading for specific information

1 **Read the title and introduction to the news article. How has Morris recorded his life?**

A LIFE IN PHOTOS

Over the past few years, Morris Villarroel from Madrid has recorded everything in his life using a special camera and making lots of notes.

It started in 2010, when he decided to record what happened to him by writing things down in a notebook. He enjoyed it so much that, in 2014, he started taking photos every 30 seconds. He uses a small camera that he carries on his body and it takes about 1,200 photos every day. Most of them aren't very interesting – for example, a picture of his breakfast or his hands when he's driving, but he doesn't delete any of them.

As well as the photos, he has 245 notebooks with his thoughts and ideas inside. He reads his notes regularly to check them.

This sounds strange to a lot of people. Even Morris says that he hasn't seen all of his photos, but he feels it's important to keep a record of his life so that he can look at it when he's older and see what it was like – just like a personal diary. He also wants to create a collection of thoughts and activities to give to his son, who was born at 4.36 p.m. on 4th November, 2014. While most fathers have a few photos of mother and child, Morris recorded the whole day and then every day of his life so far. He hopes that when his son is older he can look back and see what his mother looked like on the day he was born, as well as every day after that.

2 **Read the Focus box. What are some examples of specific information?**

Reading for specific information

When reading, you often only need to understand specific pieces of information.

Before reading, think about the type of information you need. If you want to know a date, look for a number. If you're looking for a name, then capital letters will help you find it.

Elvis Presley was born in Tupelo, Mississippi, on 8th January 1935.

It also helps to think about where in the text the information will be - at the beginning, in the middle or at the end.

3 a **Read the text and answer the questions.**

1. How many photos does Morris take every day?
2. When did he start recording things?
3. What time was his son born?
4. What's Morris's surname?
5. How often does he take photos?

b **What do you think of Morris's project? Would you like to do something like this?**

4 a **Read the title and introduction to the text below. Are you interested in this kind of film?**

LIFE IN A DAY

In 2010, film-maker Kevin Macdonald asked people from all over the world to spend a day filming their lives. He then edited their videos into a film called *Life in a Day*.

In total, he asked 80,000 people from 192 countries. To make sure he had videos from lots of different countries, Kevin sent out 400 cameras to people in poorer places. They all made their films on 24th July 2010.

He asked people to answer three questions during their films: *What do you love? What do you fear?* and *What's in your pocket?* Kevin directed the film, and he worked closely with Ridley Scott as producer. In the end, they made a film that's 94 minutes and 53 seconds long – from *4,500 hours* of original videos! It was a lot of work.

The film starts with people waking up in the morning, and continues through the day, until night. It shows people with very different lifestyles from all over the world. It was first shown at the Sundance Film Festival in 2011 and, later that year, YouTube made it free to watch on their website.

b **Find the following information in the text.**

1. The name of the producer.
2. The day people made their films.
3. The number of people that were asked to make films.
4. Where you can watch the film for free.
5. The length of the film.

5 **Work in pairs. Talk about a typical day in your life.**

2A Develop your reading

Goal: understand a short story

Focus: narrative structure

1 **Work in pairs. What kind of stories do you like reading (e.g. adventure, romantic, traditional)? What do you like about them?**

2 **Read the Focus box. How many parts does a traditional story usually have?**

Narrative structure

Many traditional stories follow a similar structure:

A **Background:** stories usually begin by talking about where and when things are happening, as well as who the important people in the story are.
A long time ago, there was a mother duck with lots of baby ducks.

B **Problem(s):** then the story changes, often because something bad or unlucky happens.
One of the baby ducks was very ugly, and the other baby ducks laughed at him.

C **Solution(s):** to make sure the story is interesting, there is a solution to the problem.
When they all grew up, the ugly baby duck became a beautiful swan.

D **Conclusion:** this is the message of the story.
Don't treat people differently because of how they look.

Use expressions such as *a long time ago, one night, the next day, a week later* to help structure a story.

3 **Read the whole story and match paragraphs 1–6 with parts A–D in the Focus box. There is more than one problem and solution in the story.**

4 a **Read paragraphs 1–3 of the story again and answer the questions.**

1 Where is the story set?
2 Who are the important people in the story?
3 Which animals were important to them?
4 What's the problem in paragraph 2?
5 Was the old man sad about it?
6 What happened when the horse returned?
7 Did the old man think it was good luck?

b **Read paragraphs 4–6 of the story again and answer the questions.**

1 What's the problem in paragraph 4?
2 Did the old man think it was bad luck?
3 Why did the army come into the village?
4 Why didn't they take the old man's son?

5 **Work in groups. Do you agree with what the old man says in the last paragraph of the story? Why/Why not?**

The old MAN and his HORSE

1 A long time ago in ancient China, there was an old farmer who lived with his son in a small village in the countryside. He loved his son more than anything in the world. They worked together every day on the farm and rode their horses. They loved their horses very much.

2 One night, one of the horses ran away. When the people in their village heard that the horse was missing, they came to the old man and said 'We're so sorry about your bad luck!' However, the old man wasn't sad about it. 'There was nothing we could do', said the old man, 'so don't be sad. It wasn't bad luck. It just happened.' The people in the village were surprised and went away.

3 The next day, the horse came back, bringing with it another white horse. This was a beautiful horse, worth a lot of money. When the people in the village saw this, they were happy for the old man and talked about his good luck. But the old man said, 'It wasn't good luck. It just happened.'

4 The old man's son loved the new horse and rode it every day. But one day, he fell off the horse and broke his leg. Once again, the people in the village said to the old man 'We're sorry about your bad luck!' The old man replied in the same way as before, 'It wasn't bad luck or the horse's fault. You shouldn't feel sad about what happened.'

5 A week later, a war started and the army came into the village. They said that every young man should join the army and fight in the war. However, because the old man's son had a broken leg, they decided he could not join the army.

6 The old man explained to his son, 'When people think you have bad luck, the end result can sometimes be positive, so you shouldn't be too sad. In the same way, when people think you have good luck, you should be careful not to become too happy.'

2B Develop your writing

Goal: write a story

Focus: using adverbs to describe actions

1 **Work in pairs. Have any of the things below ever happened to you? What happened? How did you feel?**

- you called someone by the wrong name
- you took something that isn't yours by mistake
- you missed a bus, train or plane
- you sent a message to the wrong person

2 **Read the story *Taking the biscuit* and answer the questions.**

1 Which situation in Exercise 1 does it describe?
2 Whose were the biscuits on the table?
3 How did the woman and the man feel during the train journey?

TAKING THE BISCUIT

It all started when a businessperson bought a coffee, a packet of biscuits and a newspaper, and got on a busy train. She quickly found an empty seat and put her things on the table. She took off her coat, put her handbag carefully on the floor, and sat down. Then she opened her newspaper and started to read.

The young man sitting opposite her was looking at his phone. After half an hour, he calmly and quietly opened the packet of biscuits on the table and took one. The woman couldn't believe it — they were her biscuits! She looked at him angrily, but he just looked back at his phone. So she picked up her coffee, and took a biscuit herself. The man looked up at her and then looked away. After a minute or two, he took another biscuit, and she did the same. This continued until there was only one biscuit left.

Just before the next station, the woman got up slowly, and put her coat on. She took the final biscuit, put it into her mouth, and smiled at the man. He watched her, but he didn't say anything. Then she picked up her handbag, turned around, and got off the train. On the platform, she opened her bag to get out her train ticket. Inside was her unopened packet of biscuits.

3 **Read the Focus box. Then find two more adverbs which describe actions in the story.**

Using adverbs to describe actions

Use adverbs like *angrily*, *calmly*, *quickly* and *slowly* to describe how an action happens. They help the reader imagine the events in a story.

Adverbs are usually formed by adding *-ly* to the end of adjectives.

*She got up **slowly**.*

They can come before or after the verb.

*She quickly **found** an empty seat.*

*She looked at him **angrily**.*

Some adjectives have irregular adverbs.

fast - *fast*

good - *well*

4 a **Complete the man's story with the adverbs in the box. Sometimes more than one answer is possible.**

angrily calmly carefully quickly quietly slowly

I [1]______ put my coffee and biscuits on the table in the train. After a while, I opened the packet and took one. The woman who sat down opposite me looked at me [2]______ . I didn't know why, so I looked back down at my mobile phone and [3]______ ate my biscuit. Then the woman [4]______ took one of my biscuits and ate it. I was really surprised! We each continued to take one biscuit at a time, and eat them [5]______ . We didn't say a word to each other. Just before the next stop, she stood up and [6]______ took the last one. So strange!

b **Work in pairs and compare your answers. Do you agree with each other's choice of adverbs?**

Prepare

5 a **You're going to write a story about something that happened to you. It can be real or imagined. First, answer the questions below and make notes.**

- Where did the story happen?
- When did it happen?
- Who is in the story?
- Did something good/bad/funny happen?
- What happened in the end?
- How did you feel?

b **Write down any verbs and adverbs you can use in your story.**

Write

6 a **Write your story. Use your notes in Exercise 5 and the story in Exercise 2 to help you.**

b **Work in pairs and read each other's stories. Which adverbs did your partner use in their story?**

4A Develop your writing

Goal: write and respond to an invitation

Focus: inviting and responding

1 a Read Chris and Lily's invitation. What's it for?

Come and celebrate with us!

Lily and I are going to celebrate our birthdays together this year – we're having a dinner for all our friends at our house on 26th June. There'll be food, music and a few games, too.

We'd love you to come and have fun with us!

Our address is 26A Station Road and dinner is at 7 p.m. (but feel free to come any time after 6). Children are welcome, so please bring them!

Please let us know if you can come by 10th June.

We hope you can make it.

Chris and Lily

b Read the invitation again. What time can people come to their house?

2 Read the Focus box. What phrases can you use to respond to an invitation?

Inviting and responding

You can use some specific phrases when you write an invitation in English.

We'd love you to come.

We hope you can make it.

You can also use similar phrases when responding to an invitation.

We'd love to come.

Of course we'll be there!

If you can't accept an invitation, it's always a good idea to say why and use expressions like *but, unfortunately*, *I'm afraid* and *have fun/a great time* to be polite.

Sorry, but unfortunately we can't make it. We're on holiday then.

I'm afraid I can't come – it's my sister's birthday. Have a great time!

3 a Read the replies to Chris and Lily's invitation. Who can come?

Sue Watts

Thanks for inviting us, we'd love to come. Could you tell us the best way to get to your house? Do you want us to bring anything?

Sue and Phil

Henrick Souza

Hi Chris and Lily,

I'm afraid I can't come on the 26th. I'm going to be away on a business trip that week. I'll think of you all though. Have fun while I work hard!

b Read the replies again and answer the questions.

1 What phrase do Sue and Phil use to accept?
2 What two things do they ask?
3 What phrase does Henrick use to say *no*?
4 What reason does he give?

4 Read another invitation and the replies. Choose the correct alternatives.

Dear friends,

It's my 30th birthday next month, and I've decided to have a party. I'd [1]*love/want* to see you there.

It's going to be at my house on 7th September. It will start at around 7 p.m., and there's going be lots of music and dancing!

Let me know if you need any more details. I hope you can all [2]*do/make it*!

Best wishes,

Jonathan

Hi Jonathan,

Wow, 30 already? I can't believe it! [3]*I'd/I'll* love to come, but [4]*badly/unfortunately* it's the same day as my friend's wedding. Have a [5]*great/big* time and let's do something when you get back.

Suzanne

Hi Jonathan,

Fantastic news! Of course [6]*we/we'll* be there. It's going to be the party of the century!

Do you want us to bring anything?

Marsha and James

Prepare

5 You're going to invite people to an event. First, make notes about the things below:

- what the event is
- what will happen at it
- the location
- the time
- if people need to bring anything
- any other important information

Write

6 a Write your invitation.

b Work in pairs. Read each other's invitations and write a reply to accept.

c Work in different pairs. Read each other's invitations and write a reply to say you can't come.

4B Develop your listening

› **Goal:** understand instructions

› **Focus:** sequencing words

A

B

C

1 Work in pairs. Look at the photos and discuss the questions.

1 Do you use any apps to help you in these places?

2 What other apps do you use regularly?

2 a 4.4 Listen to Alicia and Jake talking about two apps, Buzz Tree and Eventroots. What does each app do?

b Listen again. Decide if the statements below refer to Buzz Tree (B) or Eventroots (E).

1 You add where the event will be.

2 You enter information about what you like.

3 It gives you ideas about places to go.

4 You can invite people from your contacts.

5 It shows you who's coming.

3 Read the Focus box. Do you know any other sequencing words?

Sequencing words

When people give instructions, they often use sequencing words (*first*, *next*, etc.) to introduce each stage (start, middle or end) of the instructions. These words help the listener follow the conversation.

***First**, type in your name.*

***Next/After that**, it asks you to create a password.*

***Finally**, press 'invite', and you're finished!*

Try to listen for sequencing words so that you can follow instructions better.

4 a 4.5 Listen and underline the sequencing words you hear.

1 *First/Next*, you answer some questions about you.

2 *Next/After that* you press 'Go'.

3 And *then/finally* it gives you ideas for things to do.

4 Well, *finally/to start with*, you add the details in this box here.

5 *Next/Then*, you invite people by adding their email addresses.

6 *First/After that*, people can reply and say if they can come or not.

7 *Finally/Then* you can update the event.

b Complete the table with the sequencing words in Exercise 4a.

start	middle	end
First		

5 a 4.6 Listen to someone explaining how to use another app and number stages a–f in the correct order.

a The person can see your location.

b Download the Famsafe app. *1*

c Share your location with that person.

d Turn on GPS.

e If something happens, you can send an emergency message.

f Find someone in your contacts.

b Listen again and complete the extracts.

1 ______, make sure you have GPS turned on, like this.

2 ______ find me in your contacts.

3 ______, select 'share my location with this user'.

4 ______, when I open the app I can see where you are in real time.

5 ______, if you need to call me in an emergency, just say 'call mum' and your phone will call me.

6 Work in pairs and discuss the questions.

1 What's your favourite app? What's it for? How often do you use it?

2 Do you use any apps you think other people might not know about?

4C Develop your reading

Goal: understand a review
Focus: understanding pronouns

1 **Read the advert. What's a *bootcamp*?**

2 **Read reviews A–C and match them with headings 1–3.**

1 Not very relaxing
2 A weekend to repeat
3 Everyone was helpful

3 **Read the Focus box. Can you think of any other examples of pronouns?**

Understanding pronouns

We use pronouns (e.g. *she, it, they, this, that, etc.*) in a text when we don't want to repeat a word, phrase or sentence. This makes the text sound better.

Last year I went to a bootcamp. The staff there were strict but kind. ***They*** *gave me a lot of help.* ***It*** *was actually a lot of fun and* ***this*** *surprised me.*

It's important to understand which word or phrase a pronoun refers to so that we can read texts more quickly.

They *= The staff*
It *= bootcamp*
this *= a lot of fun*

4 a **Look at the words in bold in review A. What does each one refer to? Choose the correct option, a or b.**

1 it: **a** the farmhouse **b** the countryside
2 this: **a** guests have their own room **b** guests share a bathroom
3 it: **a** other guests are tidy **b** sharing a bathroom
4 it: **a** have a great time **b** go to the boot camp

b **Find pronouns in reviews B and C that refer to:**

1 noise
2 building a bigger gym
3 a wedding ring
4 a mobile phone and TV

5 **Read the reviews again and answer the questions.**

Which reviewer(s) A–C ...

1 liked the evening activities?
2 didn't expect to share a bathroom?
3 had good things to say about the trainers?
4 plans to go to the bootcamp again in the future?
5 felt good after doing the bootcamp?
6 wants to continue doing one of the activities in future?
7 had to do an activity in an unusual place?
8 almost lost something important?

6 **Work in groups and discuss the questions.**

1 Would you like to go to a bootcamp? Why/Why not?
2 Why do you think people like going to bootcamps?

BURTOWN BOOTCAMP

› DO YOU WANT TO GET FIT?
› DO YOU WANT TO CHALLENGE YOURSELF?

Then come and spend a weekend with our excellent trainers. Spend two days running, walking and exercising in the gym, as well as lots of other fun activities! It doesn't matter if you can run only 20 metres or if you often run 20 km – we can help you get fitter. Stay in our beautiful farmhouse and enjoy the countryside around you. You'll leave feeling healthier and more relaxed.

A

I really enjoyed myself at the bootcamp. The farmhouse is big and very pretty and the countryside around [1]**it** is beautiful. Guests have their own room but they have to share a bathroom. I didn't know [2]**this** when I booked the weekend so I was surprised and a bit angry when I arrived. However, [3]**it** was actually OK because the other guests were tidy. The activities were enjoyable and I felt much better when I left. I really enjoyed the clean, fresh air. It wasn't a cheap weekend away but I had a great time so I'm going to do [4]**it** again.

B

I was unhappy with the weekend. I have a very stressful job in the city so I really needed some peace and quiet. They were building a bigger gym when I was there, so there was a lot of noise all of the time. It was really loud. Also, this meant that we had to do a lot of the classes in the car park instead of the gym, which wasn't very relaxing. It was a bit of a shame because the trainers were great and I especially liked the team games after dinner. So, I enjoyed being out of the city and away from my computer, but I needed a stress-free weekend and it wasn't stress-free at all.

C

I enjoyed the weekend. The trainers gave me lots of ideas and the chef cooked vegetarian meals especially for me. They weren't always the nicest meals but they were healthy. On the second day, my wedding ring fell off in the forest. I was so worried! But all the staff and guests were lovely and helped me find it. The bedrooms are fine but I didn't know that we had to share bathrooms. You can't use your mobile phone or watch TV, either. I talked to other people more without them, so maybe it was a good thing. I felt heathier at the end of the two days, and that's what I wanted. I'm going to do yoga every day now!

5A Develop your reading

Goal: understand an article

Focus: identifying positive and negative points

1 a Work in pairs. Do you think technology is making our working lives easier or more difficult? Why?

b Read the article and compare your ideas with those in the text.

2 Match the headings A–E with paragraphs 1–4 in the article. There is one extra heading that you don't need.

A Communication problems
B Faster but busier
C In control of our time
D Technology and health
E Too much time at home?

3 Read the Focus box. Then underline the phrases that introduce positive and negative points in the first paragraph of the article.

Identifying positive and negative points

Articles often include both positive and negative sides to an argument.

Look for key words and phrases to help you decide if an idea is positive or negative.

Positive

It's good that …
This has one main advantage …
The main benefit is that …

Negative

It's difficult to …
One problem is …
It's not good that …

You can also use the linking words *however* and *but* to introduce opposite ideas.

However, is this really true?

4 a Read the article again and answer the questions.

What are the positive and negative points about …

1 working anywhere and at any time?
2 working from home?
3 working in international teams?
4 sharing information?

b Work in pairs. Which language in the article helped you decide if a point is positive or negative?

Technology in the workplace: *a help or not?*

Technology is changing fast and work is changing with it. For some people these changes are positive but for others they are not. We had a look at four ways in which our working lives have changed because of new technology

1 ______________

Technology helps us to work anywhere at any time and this has one main advantage – we can choose the hours we want to work. We don't have to start and finish work at a specific time like our parents did. We can start late when we want to do some exercise first. We can start early and finish early when we have to pick up the children from school. We can pay more attention to our social lives. However is this really true? With a smartphone in our hands, we're always available. It's difficult to find time for ourselves because we take our work with us. Think about that next time you're reading a work email on a beach in Spain.

2 ______________

More and more people work from home these days. This means that workers don't see their colleagues as much. This is good when you prefer to work in a quiet place, but it's bad if you don't like spending time too much on your own. Of course, there are other advantages. People spend less time travelling to and from work and companies save money by having smaller offices. Is work only about money though?

3 ______________

In the past, meetings with people in other countries were only possible after long journeys. Today, people regularly work in international teams and meet online. The main benefit of this is that people in the company can work together easily and cheaply. But online meetings can sometimes have problems. It can be difficult to hear when people speak quietly or at the same time. The internet connection can often be bad, too. Sometimes it's better to get on a plane and meet face-to-face!

4 ______________

Technology helps us to find and share information really fast these days. We can work more quickly because we don't have to wait for hours or even days for information to arrive. The problem is that it's so easy to share information, our email inboxes are often completely full. We spend most of our working life reading and responding to these messages. When do we have time to actually do some work?

5B Develop your listening

Goal: understand a short talk

Focus: understanding linkers

B

E

1 **Work in pairs. How does each colour in the photos make you feel? Which photo do you like the most/least? Why?**

2 a 5.6 **Listen to three people describing what colours mean in their culture. Which two colours does each person talk about?**

b **Listen again. Complete the statements with a colour, according to what the speakers say.**

1 ______ can have a negative meaning in the US.
2 ______ can be both peaceful and sad in the US.
3 ______ can mean you are strong in India.
4 You shouldn't wear ______ if you go surfing in Indonesia.

3 **Read the Focus box. Do you know any other linkers for each category?**

Understanding linkers

When listening, recognising linkers (linking words) can help you follow what the speaker is going to say next.

Words like *and* mean that you'll hear some additional information.

Blue shows strength ***and*** *being brave.*

Words and expressions like *but* and *on the other hand* mean you'll hear a different idea.

I like dark colours, ***but*** *I don't like black.*

Anyway means that you'll hear a change of topic.

Yes, it was great. ***Anyway****, tell me about your holiday.*

4 **Look at the linkers in bold in sentences 1–5 below. Decide if each one gives additional information (A), a different idea (D) or a change in topic (C).**

1 I think green is very relaxing. Light blue is relaxing, **too**.
2 I love my city. **Anyway**, where do you live?
3 Red can show danger. **On the other hand**, it can be lucky.
4 We love the blue curtains. We **also** love the blue sofa.

5 5.7 **Listen to the extracts and complete them with the correct linkers.**

1 ______, we can use it to describe someone who's sad.
2 India is mostly Hindu, ______ some colours have special meanings in Hinduism.
3 It ______ shows how everything is connected.
4 ______, don't wear green if you go surfing here.

6 **Complete the sentences with linkers.**

1 My favourite colour is green. It's my sister's favourite, ______.
2 I don't usually like black ______ I love this black dress.
3 I love all these colourful paintings. ______, where shall we go for dinner?

7 a 5.8 **Listen to two more people talking. Which colours do they talk about?**

b **Listen again and answer the questions.**

1 What does red mean in China?
2 What do people give to married couples in China?
3 What does orange mean in the Netherlands?
4 Does orange have a positive or negative meaning in the Middle-East?

8 **Work in pairs. Which colours have special meanings in your culture? What do they mean?**

5c Develop your writing

Goal: write a guide

Focus: linking ideas

1 **Read the guide to shopping in Tokyo. Which area would you most like to visit? Why?**

Shopping in Tokyo

From fashionable clothes to electronics, Tokyo has a shopping area for everything.

Fashion

For designer brands you should visit Ginza. All the international fashion companies have stores there, but they're not cheap. If you want cheaper, younger clothes, go to Harajuku and visit the shops that Japanese teenagers go to.

Electronics

The most famous area for electronics is Akihabara, so you should go there if you want the latest technology. You can also go to Shinjuku, where you can find the largest electronics shops in the city.

Gifts and souvenirs

You can find traditional products like rice bowls in the area of Nihonbashi or in department stores across the city. You can also find cheap chopsticks to eat Japanese food with in Tokyo's 100 Yen shops. They make great gifts and you can find the shops all over the city.

Shopping and entertainment

In Odaiba, a man-made island in Tokyo Bay, there's both shopping and entertainment. That's why it's the best place to go if you want to go to a mall and then visit the beach or a museum. There's a theme park there too, which the whole family can enjoy.

Food

Fish lovers should visit the Tsukiji Market. You can buy fish, fruit and vegetables there. However get there really early in the morning because that's when the big fish arrive and go on sale.

2 **Read the Focus box. Then underline the linkers in the guide.**

Linking ideas

When we write, we join two ideas or sentences together with linkers.

To add information use *and*, *also* and *too*.

You can visit the market. There are ***also*** *some shops.*

To give opposite or surprising information use *but* and *however*. To give a choice use *or*.

The west side is better for clothes. ***However***, *the east side is cheaper.*

You can pay by cash ***or*** *credit card.*

To give reasons or results use *because* (*of*), *so* and *that's why*.

People come here ***because of*** *the choice.*

Everything was too expensive ***so*** *I didn't buy anything.*

Shops often have sales. ***That's why*** *you can always find a bargain.*

3 **Choose the correct alternatives.**

1. There isn't a department store *but/ too* there's a shopping mall.
2. You can buy fish at the market *so/ or* at the supermarket.
3. I need to buy some gifts, *however/ so* I'm going to Nihonbashi.
4. You can shop in Harajuku and you can relax in a café there *too/ however*.
5. The shops in Ginza are amazing. *That's why/ Or* lots of people go there.
6. Lots of shoppers go to Harajuku, *too/ however* they're usually young people.

Prepare

4 a **You're going to write a guide to shopping in your area. First, make notes about each of the categories in the box.**

clothes electronics food gifts/souvenirs shopping and entertainment traditional products

b **Plan your guide. Use the guide in Exercise 1 and the questions below to help you.**

- Which headings do you want to include in your guide and in what order?
- What information do you want to include under each heading?

Write

5 **Write your guide. Include some linkers and use the Useful phrases to help you.**

Useful phrases

You should go to (Harajuku) because (you're young).
You can find (designer products) in (Ginza), too.
You could try (Nihonbashi) or (Ginza) for (local products).
You can get the best (electronics) in (Akihabara). However, (they can be expensive).

6A Develop your listening

Goal: understand a short talk

Focus: silent /t/ and /d/

A

B

C

D

1 **Look at the photos. Do you think the people are 'living well'? Can you think of any other ways of living well?**

2 6.3 **Listen to a talk on how to live well. Number the tips in the order that you hear them.**

- be active
- be kind to other people
- connect with other people
- learn something new
- live for the moment

3 6.4 **Read the Focus box and listen to the examples. When are the sounds /t/ and /d/ often not pronounced?**

Silent /t/ and /d/

There are some letters that we don't always pronounce in English, because it makes words and sentences easier to say. For example the sounds /t/ and /d/ are usually not pronounced when they come before another consonant sound.

*I don'**t** know.*
*She jus**t** came back.*
*They stoppe**d** talking.*
*You an**d** me.*

Knowing this helps you understand fast, natural speech.

4 6.5 **Listen and notice the underlined /t/ and /d/ sounds. Then listen again and repeat.**

1 I want to feel better.
2 I can't describe it.
3 They played games all day.
4 I stopped the bus.
5 Walk around town.
6 It's next week.

5 a **Work in pairs. Read the extracts and underline the silent letters.**

1 ... and you'll feel much better because of it.
2 Don't be afraid of your feelings and emotions.
3 Just small things like a smile ...
4 Don't worry if you're not a sociable person ...

b 6.6 **Listen and check.**

6 **Listen to the talk in Exercise 2 again and answer the questions.**

1 What three examples of doing regular exercise does the speaker give?
2 What do many colleges and universities offer?
3 What advice does the presenter give if you're feeling sad?
4 Which two examples of being kind does she give?
5 What good thing can happen if you are kind?
6 What's the most important point to remember?

7 **Work in pairs and discuss the questions.**

1 Do you agree with the advice in the talk?
2 What other things do you do to live a good life?

6B Develop your reading

› **Goal:** understand an article

› **Focus:** identifying main ideas in paragraphs

Is ***team work*** *always the best?*

We all have busy working lives these days so we need to make the best possible use of our time. We spoke to top chef Tim Richards about why it's better to work in a team, and designer Lauren Smith about why it's better to work alone.

Tim: Working in a team

1 When people are in a team, they work better because they share the work and help each other. Everyone brings different knowledge and skills to the team. This means that there's always someone who can give you the information you need to help you with problems.

2 Also, people in teams often have more ideas than those working alone. This is for two reasons. Firstly, everyone wants the team to be successful. No one wants to make a mistake and make the others angry. Secondly, people want the others in the team to like them, so they try to think of the best ideas possible.

3 Finally, when people work in a team, they learn to communicate well with others. When they communicate well, they make friends more easily. They also have more fun. This helps them to have a happier life because it's important to feel good at work.

Lauren: Working alone

4 I think that when you work on your own, you work much faster. You don't have to discuss things with other people before you do something. You can quickly decide what to do and then just do it. You don't waste time. You can ask someone for help if you need it, but you don't have to.

5 People who work alone have control over everything they do. No one is there to tell them what to do. This can be scary but it pushes you to do the best you can. If you don't, things can go wrong and it's all because of you. Of course, when things go right, everyone knows you did it and no one else can take that away from you.

6 Your relationships can also be better when you work alone because you don't argue as much. When there are a lots of people in an office with different ideas it's more likely that you'll disagree with each other, but when it's just you there's no one else to have an argument with. This can make life easier and less stressful for you.

1 **Do you think it's better to work in a team or work alone? Why?**

2 **Read the Focus box. How can you quickly understand the main ideas in an article?**

Identifying main ideas in paragraphs

Each paragraph in an article usually has one main idea. The main idea is often in the first sentence of each paragraph. The other sentences give more details.

To quickly understand the main ideas of an article, read the first sentence of each paragraph. Then, to get more details, read the rest of each paragraph.

For me, working in a team is the best way to work. *I enjoy being around other people and find I am more creative when I can discuss my ideas. I like to hear other people's ideas and learn from them.*

3 a **Read the article and match paragraphs 1–3 with main ideas a–c below.**

- a People use their imaginations more.
- b People talk to each other more successfully.
- c There are more people to do the work.

b **Match paragraphs 4–6 with main ideas a–e. There are two extra ideas you don't need.**

- a You don't feel bad when things go wrong.
- b You don't have problems with other people.
- c You are the boss.
- d You can do things more quickly.
- e You can finish your work whenever you want.

4 **Read the text again. Then match the reasons a–f that Tim and Lauren give for their ideas with paragraphs 1–6.**

- a There isn't anybody there to make you do things.
- b You learn skills which help you to have better relationships.
- c When things go wrong, there's another person who knows what to do.
- d More people means more arguments.
- e Everyone wants to do well.
- f You don't need to spend time talking about things.

5 **Work in pairs and discuss the questions.**

1. Do you prefer working in a team or working alone? Why?
2. Which of the activities below do you prefer to do alone? Which do you prefer to do with others?

- cooking
- shopping
- going to the supermarket
- doing housework
- organising an event
- studying
- watching a film
- working

6c Develop your writing

› **Goal:** write a description of everyday experiences

› **Focus:** organising ideas in paragraphs

1 **When you have time off, do you usually go away or stay at home? Why?**

2 **Read Max's blog post. What's a *staycation*?**

1 Ashley and I are enjoying our 'staycation'. We both find travelling stressful so we decided not to go away for our holiday this year. Instead, we're spending it at home, relaxing.

2 We're already having a great time. On Saturday, the first day of our holiday, we slept for half the day. We really needed it! On Sunday, we had a barbecue on the beach with some friends. The weather was fantastic and we had a lot of fun.

3 We have some great plans for the rest of the week, too. We're going to a local art gallery tomorrow and we might eat out afterwards. On Thursday we're meeting our parents for lunch at a lovely restaurant near the river. We might go cycling afterwards if the weather's nice.

4 Things are great but there's only one small problem – I get work emails every day that I have to reply to. So, if you're having a holiday at home, tell your manager you're in the Himalayas with no internet. That's my advice!

3 **Read the Focus box. Why is organising your ideas in paragraphs a good idea?**

Organising ideas in paragraphs

Organising information in paragraphs helps the reader follow it more easily. Each paragraph usually has one topic or main idea. The first sentence often introduces the topic or main idea. The other sentences give more details.

Tomorrow evening, we're going to a festival*. One of my favourite bands is playing there and I can't wait to see them. I last saw them ten years ago but I think they'll still be great.*

4 **Read the blog post in Exercise 2 again and match each paragraph 1–4 in with its purpose a–d below.**

a talk about past activities

b say what's happening now

c say what you think about the holiday

d talk about future plans

5 a **Read the text and organise the information into four paragraphs.**

Quiet weekends are something everyone should have in their lives. They help you to relax and get your energy back after a busy week. They also help you get ready for the week ahead. Last weekend, I had a lovely time with an old friend from university. We spent the whole weekend chatting and eating. It was great to see him again. Next weekend will be completely different. I'm helping my brother to move house on Saturday and on Sunday I'm helping my sister to paint her new flat. I think I'll be really tired at work on Monday! Relaxing is really important to me. I work hard during the week so at the weekend, I just want to stay in bed and do nothing all day. That's my idea of a perfect weekend!

b **Work in pairs and compare your paragraphs. Do you agree?**

Prepare

6 **You're going to write about a holiday at home that you're having at the moment. Imagine the details and write some notes. Use the ideas below to help you.**

- why you're staying at home and what you're doing now
- activities you've done on your holiday
- plans for the rest of the holiday
- what you think about having a holiday at home

Write

7 **Write your blog post. Organise the information into paragraphs. Use your notes and the Useful phrases to help you.**

Useful phrases

At the moment I'm (relaxing in the garden).
Last month/Last week/Yesterday I (visited a castle).
The day after tomorrow/Later in the week/At the weekend, I'm (going to a concert).
I may/might (stay for a few more days).

7A Develop your listening

Goal: understand a discussion

Focus: agreeing and disagreeing

1 **Work in pairs. Read the definition of *landmark*. Are there any landmarks where you live?**

Landmark noun (countable) /lændmɑːk/ *something that is easy to see, such as a tall tree or building, that helps you know where you are*

2 7.3 **Listen to four conversations. Match each one to photos A–D.**

3 **Read the Focus box. Can you think of any other ways to disagree politely?**

Agreeing and disagreeing

Agreeing

To understand if people agree with each other, listen for phrases like:

I agree.
You're right.
That's true.
Me too. / Me neither.

Disagreeing

To understand if people disagree with each other, listen for phrases like:

I disagree.
I can't/don't agree.
I don't think (that's true).
I'm not sure (I feel the same).
I'm afraid (I don't feel the same).

To disagree politely, people often start by agreeing and then give a different opinion. For example:

Yes, but ...
You're right, but ...

4 a **Listen to the conversations in Exercise 2 again and complete each extract with one word.**

1

A: It's a nice design. Simple but attractive.
B: I [1]________ .
A: Every city needs an area like that so that people can get together.
B: You're [2]________ .

2

A: It looks perfect, doesn't it? Like a painting.
B: That's [3]________ . It must be popular with tourists.
A: That's [4]________ . It's our country's biggest and most famous landmark.

3

A: Well, it means we're nearly home. It makes me happy whenever I see it.
B: Really? I'm not [5]________ I feel the same.

4

A: When I first moved here, I didn't like it at all.
B: Me [6]________ . It's too big for the area.
A: I know I'm in Warsaw when I see it.
B: That's true, but I'm [7]________ I don't feel the same.

b **Do the speakers in each conversation agree or disagree with each other?**

5 a 7.4 **Listen to Matt and Katy and answer the questions.**

1 Where in cities do the cows usually stand?
2 How many are there?
3 Why do the artists put the cows there?

b **Listen again and choose the correct alternatives.**

1 Katy believes that the model cows are in ...
   a the right place.
   b the wrong place.
2 Matt thinks that it's important to ...
   a spend time outside.
   b move the cows from city to city.
3 Katy believes that the cows are ...
   a easy for the artists to paint.
   b good examples of art.
4 Matt says that the cows ...
   a help people to learn to paint.
   b help people to become interested in art.

c **Listen again. Do Matt and Katy agree or disagree with each other about each opinion In Exercise 4b?**

6 **Work in pairs and discuss the questions.**

1 Is there much public art in your area? What is it?
2 Do you think it's important to have public art in a city or town? Why/Why not?

7B Develop your reading

Goal: understand an article

Focus: reading for general understanding

1 **Work in pairs. Do you think it's better to grow up in a city or in the countryside? Why?**

2 **Read the Focus box. What kind of words should you look for when reading for general understanding?**

Reading for general understanding

When you need to read a text for general understanding, you can read it quickly and only look for key words. You don't need to understand every word.

For example, in the sentence below, the key words are *child, lived, Madrid,* and *miss.*

When I was a ***child*** *I lived in* ***Madrid*** *for a few years. I really* ***miss*** *it now.*

3 **Read the article about growing up in the countryside and complete gaps 1–4 with sentences a–d. Use the key words to help you**

- **a** Traffic keeps you awake.
- **b** You know how to read a bus timetable.
- **c** You have friends you've known all your life.
- **d** You're a very good driver.

Four signs you grew up in the countryside

1 ____________. Having a car was the only way to travel anywhere in the countryside. You passed your test as soon as possible. You used to drive everywhere, usually on small roads, so now you're the best.

2 ____________. When you first spent a night in a big city, you found it difficult to sleep, because of the cars and buses in the street. You used to live in a really quiet area when you were a child and the only sounds you could hear came from nature.

3 ____________. You met them when you started nursery and you went to the same schools together. It wasn't easy to meet other people so you stayed together all the time. Your parents are probably friends with your friends' parents, too!

4 ____________. In the city you can catch a train or bus every few minutes so you don't have to worry about public transport. It's not like that in the countryside – you have to know what time the next bus is and then plan your day.

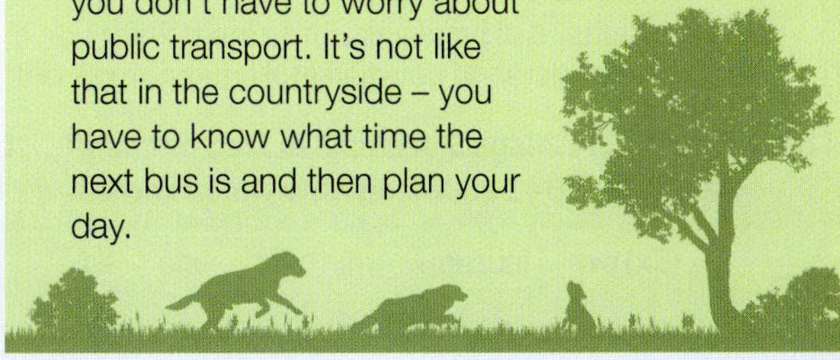

4 **Read the article again and answer the questions.**

Why do people who grew up in the countryside ...

1. know how to drive a car well?
2. sometimes find it hard to sleep in cities?
3. have the same friends for a long time?
4. find out the times of public transport before they plan their day?

5 **Quickly read the article about living in a large family and match the headings a–e to paragraphs 1–5.**

- **a** You answer to different names.
- **b** You talk fast.
- **c** Cold showers aren't a problem for you.
- **d** You're very good at sharing.
- **e** You didn't wear new clothes until you were an adult.

Five signs you grew up in a large family

1 ____________

You used to speak quickly because it was the only way people heard you at meal times. Everyone else was speaking so you needed to say what you wanted to say fast. Nowadays you sound like you're always in a hurry.

2 ____________

Nothing was just for you because it was for your brothers and sisters as well. For example, if you had something nice to eat, you had to cut it into small pieces to make sure everyone got some. You can cut a small chocolate bar into six pieces easily!

3 ____________

When your parents wanted to speak to you they called you by your brothers and sisters' names before they remembered yours, especially if they were in a hurry. Sometimes they'd even call out the name of the dog before they remembered yours!

4 ____________

Everything came from your older brothers or sisters. You wore your brother's shirts when he was too big for them or your sister's jeans. It was only when you left home and started working that you were able to experience wearing something new.

5 ____________

If you didn't wake up really early you had to wait to use the bathroom in the morning until your brothers and sisters were finished. By the time you got in the shower, there was no hot water left.

6 **Work in pairs and discuss the questions.**

1. Where did you grow up? What was it like?
2. Did you grow up in a small or large family? Did you like it?

8B Develop your listening

Goal: understand a short story

Focus: understanding the order of events

A

B

C

D

1 **Work in groups. Where do you think the places in the photos are? What problems might you have in each one?**

2 8.5 **Listen to the first part of Paul's story and answer the questions.**

1 Where was he going?
2 Who was he going with?
3 How did he travel?
4 What did the announcement on the radio say?
5 Did Paul and his friends hear the announcement?

3 **Read the Focus box. What can help you understand the order of events?**

Understanding the order of events

When listening to a story it's important to understand the order of events. You can do this by paying attention to the tenses and time expressions.

Past simple and past continuous

*I **was driving** through the mountains one day, when I suddenly **got lost**.*

Time expressions

Time expressions such as *one weekend, suddenly, at the time* and *as soon as* tell us when something happened and how long it happened for.

***As soon as** I got home, I called my friends.*

*I was living on my own **at the time**.*

4 **Match the sentence halves. Then listen to the first part of the story again and check.**

1 So this happened when
2 One weekend my friends and I decided
3 We had a great time
4 While we were travelling, we
5 When we were driving up into

a when we got there.
b saw a road through the mountains.
c I was living in Surabaya, in Indonesia.
d to visit Malang.
e the mountains the weather was fine.

5 a 8.6 **Listen to the next part of the story and answer the questions.**

1 What happened on the other side of the mountain?
2 How did they feel when they saw people running towards them?

b **Listen again. Decide if the sentences are true (T) or false (F).**

1 The people helped them.
2 They showed Paul and his girlfriend how to get home.
3 They never saw each other again.

6 **Work in pairs. Have you ever had any problems when travelling? What happened?**

8C Develop your writing

Goal: write a blog post

Focus: time expressions

1 **Work in groups and discuss the questions.**

1 Do you read blogs? If so, which ones do you read?

2 Have you ever written a blog? What was it about?

2 **Read the introduction to Kara's blog. What's she doing?**

Hi! My name's Kara and I'm spending a year teaching children in Cape Town, South Africa. I love working here and I'm going to share everything on this blog. If you have any questions then I'd love to hear from you. Thanks!

3 **Read Kara's latest post below. Number the topics in the order she writes about them.**

- what she's doing next week
- the weather
- what she did today
- other future plans
- what she did last week

Hello from Table Top mountain! I've got a day off today so I decided to come here. I've wanted to visit the mountain for ages. As you can see, the view is beautiful!

This morning I got up at early so I could get the first cable car before it got too busy.

It's still quite cold here, which I didn't expect. I know it's winter but I'd like to see some African sun at some point!

Anyway, last week we were teaching the kids about animals and the day before yesterday we took them to visit the Cape Peninsula. It was great – they loved it.

Afternoons are always fun because we play sport. The children really like playing football and next week we've organised a big game between them and the adults. I used to hate playing football but now I really like it, even though I'm not very good!

The week after next I have another day off, so I'd like to visit the lighthouse at Cape Point. It has interesting history and I've heard the views there are amazing, too. I'll definitely write and tell you all about it.

4 **Read the Focus box. Then read Kara's blog again and find six time expressions.**

Time expressions

Use time expressions to say when things happened or are going to happen. They can usually go at the beginning or end of a phrase or sentence.

*I started a new job **last week**.*

***Next Friday** I'm going to have dinner with Rob.*

*Shall we go out **tonight**?*

*I'm going on holiday **the week after next**.*

Some other common time expressions are: *yesterday, the day before yesterday, last Tuesday/month, today, this morning/afternoon/evening/Friday, tomorrow, next week/month/year, the day after tomorrow and in two weeks' time.*

5 a **Imagine it's 1pm on Wednesday 3rd April. Write the days and times using time expressions in the Focus box.**

1 2–5pm on 3rd April
this afternoon

2 Monday, 1st April

3 Monday, 15th April - Friday, 19th April

4 May this year

5 8am–11am on 3rd April

6 March this year

7 Friday, 5th April

8 Thursday, 4th April

b **Work in pairs and compare your answers.**

Prepare

6 a **Imagine you're having a year off work and you're going to write a blog post. First, decide what you're doing on your year off. Choose an idea below or think of your own.**

- teaching a skill you know well, e.g. painting
- studying a language in another country
- doing a completely different job
- going on a special trip

b **Make notes about:**

- where you are
- what you're doing
- the things you do every day
- your free time

Write

7 **Write your latest blog post. Say what you're doing today, then describe what you've done recently and talk about any future plans. Use the Focus box and Kara's blog post to help you.**

9A Develop your listening

Goal: understand a radio interview

Focus: identifying examples

A

B

C

1 **Work in pairs. Which animals can you see in the photos? What do you notice about them?**

2 9.3 **Listen to the first part of a radio interview about animal friendships and answer the questions.**

1 Where does Emily work?

2 Can all animals make friends with each other?

3 How do monkeys sometimes choose their friends?

3 **Read the Focus box. Why is it helpful to identify examples when you listen?**

Identifying examples

Identifying examples can help you listen for more information about something and understand the meaning of words or phrases you don't know. The most common words and phrases for giving examples are *for example*, *like* and *such as*.

Some pets are easy to look after, ***for example*** *goldfish.*

Some wild animals are dangerous, ***like*** *lions and tigers.*

I'd like to work in a place with lots of animals, ***such as*** *a zoo.*

4 a **Listen to the interview again. Match sentences 1–3 with examples a–c below.**

1 A lot of animals live in groups.

2 Some animals make friends.

3 Animal friendships can be like human friendships.

a Monkeys, elephants and horses

b Lions and penguins

c Monkeys

b **Listen again. Which word or phrase from the Focus box is used to give examples a–c?**

5 a 9.4 **Listen to the second part of the interview. Number the topics in the order that you hear them.**

a Animal friendship stories make us feel good.

b Animals become friends when one of them has no mother.

c Dangerous animals make friends when they're on their own.

d People like watching and reading about animal friendships.

e Animals sometimes become friends because they live in places made by people.

b **Listen again. Match each example below to a topic in Exercise 5a.**

a in a zoo or on a farm

b a gorilla caring for a cat, and a cat playing with a rabbit

c a baby tiger and a dog

d a tiger and a goat

e a video of a dog and a cat

6 a 9.5 **Listen to the first half of five sentences. Write the example you think each person will give in the second half.**

b **Work in pairs and compare your ideas.**

c 9.6 **Listen and check your ideas. What example does each speaker give?**

7 **Work in pairs. Which do you think are the friendliest animals? What about the least friendly? Why?**

9B Develop your reading

Goal: understand a report

Focus: understanding numbers in a text

What's HOT? The results of last month's survey are in!

Last month, we asked you to complete a survey on your TV watching habits. How much TV do you watch? When do you watch it? And what's your favourite way to watch it? We finally have all the results in and explain them in more detail below.

We all know that TV watching habits have changed a lot in recent years, and they're still changing really quickly. In the first four months of the year, we watched an average of forty-two hours per week of live TV. From May to August, we watched forty hours, and from September to December we watched just thirty-seven hours of live TV per week.

So what are the most popular types of TV these days? Unsurprisingly, online TV is at the top – everyone wants to watch their favourite programmes at any time they want. After that, websites like YouTube are really popular, where users can upload their own videos. People love to follow their favourite people and share the films that they upload. But there are some that still enjoy live TV, and usually they're over fifty-five. However, only nineteen percent of young people aged 13–18 watch live TV, and an amazing fifty percent of them prefer watching short videos online.

So what about how we watch things? Do most people still prefer a good old-fashioned TV? Is bigger better? Well, no, is the short answer. Half of the people in the survey said that they watch programmes on their tablets because it's easier. A quarter of the people replied that they use a normal TV or a computer, and the same is true for smartphones.

The most popular time of the day to watch TV isn't very surprising – seventy percent of people said that they only watch TV in the evening. After that, the morning was quite popular, while people have their breakfast before going to work. The least popular time is immediately after lunch – only seven percent of people said that they watch TV during this time.

1 Work in pairs and discuss the questions.

1 Do you prefer watching TV with other people or on your own? Why?
2 Do you think you watch more or less TV than you used to? Why?

2 Read the Focus box. Then match words and phrases 1–5 to numbers a–e below.

Understanding numbers in a text

Texts such as reports and surveys often contain numbers written as words. For example:

- *ninety-two* = 92
- *fourteen percent* = 14%
- *half* = ½
- *a quarter* = ¼

1 half	a ¼
2 a third	b 70%
3 three quarters	c ½
4 a quarter	d ¾
5 seventy percent	e ⅓

3 a Read the introduction to the article and answer the questions.

1 When did the survey happen?
2 What's the report about?

b Read the report. Do some young people still like to watch live TV?

4 Read the report again and match the numbers in the box to sentences 1–8.

40 50% 7% over 55 19% ¼ 37 ½

1 The number of hours of live TV we watched between May and August.
2 The number of hours of live TV we watched between September and December.
3 The age of people who like to watch live TV.
4 The number of young people who watch live TV.
5 The number of young people who watch videos online.
6 The number of people who watch TV on tablets.
7 The number of people who watch on a normal TV or computer.
8 The number of people who watch TV after lunch.

4 Read the text again and decide if the statements are true (T) or false (F).

1 People watch more live TV now than in the past.
2 Younger people watch less live TV than older people.
3 Teenagers watch more short videos online than live TV.
4 The most popular device to watch TV on is a tablet.
5 Most people watch TV in the morning.

5 How much TV do you watch? Do you usually watch live TV or watch programmes online? Why?

9c Develop your writing

Goal: write an email application

Focus: formal phrases

1 Work in pairs. Look at job advertisements A–C and discuss the questions.

1 Where do you usually look for jobs?
2 How do you usually apply for jobs?
3 Would you like to apply for any of the jobs below?

A Junior journalist

The Daily News has an exciting position available for a junior journalist. The right person will be a graduate with good writing and communication skills. You should also be able to speak good English. You must enjoy working in a team.

B Sales assistant

Namico supermarkets are looking for a part-time sales assistant. We are looking for someone who has good communication skills and has experience working in sales.
We offer a minimum of 35 hours a week.

C Personal assistant

Personal assistant to the CEO of TEF ltd. We need someone who:
- can work long hours
- has excellent IT skills
- has at least 5 years' experience

2 a Read Carla's email application. Which job in Exercise 1 is she applying for? Does she have the right qualifications for the job?

Dear Sir or Madam,
I am writing to apply for the position of junior journalist, as advertised on your website. Please find attached a copy of my CV.
I have a degree in English, and two years' experience as a part-time journalist for a local newspaper. During this time, I learnt how to write professional articles. I have excellent writing skills and I also enjoy working in a team.
I believe I that I have the right skills and experience to do the job and I am available for an interview at any time. If you would like any more information, please contact me at this email address or by phone.
I look forward to hearing from you.
Yours faithfully,
Carla Watts

b Read Carla's email again and put the topics in the correct order.

a her experience and qualifications
b her contact details
c why she's writing

3 Read the Focus box. Why are formal phrases useful?

Formal phrases

It's important to use formal phrases when writing an application for a job because they make it sound polite and professional. They can also help you with the structure of the letter or email. Some formal phrases which are useful in a letter or email application are:

1 *Dear Sir or Madam,*
2 *I am writing to apply for the position of …*
3 *Please find attached …*
4 *During this time …*
5 *I am available for an interview at any time.*
6 *I look forward to hearing from you.*
7 *Yours faithfully,*

4 Match phrases 1–7 in the Focus box with informal phrases a–g below.

a I hope you reply soon
b I want the job of
c Hi
d Goodbye
f While I was there
g I'm sending with this email
h I'm free to talk to you whenever you like

Prepare

5 You're going to write an email application. First, choose one of the jobs in Exercise 1 to apply for or use your own idea. Answer the questions below and make notes.

1 Why do you want this job?
2 What qualifications and experience do you have?
3 What skills do you have?
4 Why would you be good for the job?

Write

6 Write your email application. Use the Focus box and your notes in Exercise 4 to help you.

10A Develop your reading

Goal: understand a blog post
Focus: identifying opinions

1 **Work in pairs. How much time do you spend doing the activities below? How do you feel when you do them?**

- cooking
- travelling to work
- cleaning

2 **Read the first paragraph of the blog post and answer the questions.**

1 What do most people spend 547 hours a year doing?
2 What does the writer do for an hour every day?

3 **Read the Focus box. What's the difference between an opinion and a fact?**

Identifying opinions

An opinion is our own idea or something we believe. To identify an opinion, look for expressions such as *I think*, *I feel*, *in my opinion* and *for me*.

I think *people spend too much time at work.*
I feel *that I don't have enough time.*
In my opinion*, a great way to save time is to work from home.*
For me*, phones are the biggest waste of time.*

Texts also often contain facts. A fact is a piece of true information.

She lives in Moscow.
I do six hours of exercise a week.
There are 24 people in the class.

4 a **Read the whole post. Then decide if each sentence 1–10 is a fact (F) or an opinion (O).**

b **Work in pairs and compare your answers. Which words/phrases helped you decide if the sentences are opinions or facts?**

5 **Read the post again and answer the questions.**

1 How does the writer decide what she is going to do each day?
2 Which two activities does she do together?
3 What does she do instead of going to the gym?
4 How does she save time preparing meals?
5 Why does she turn off her phone for one hour a day?
6 What does she do instead?

6 **Work in pairs and discuss the questions.**

1 Do you think you have enough time to do the things you want?
2 How do you try and save time?
3 How do you think you waste time?

HOW TO MAKE MORE TIME FOR **YOURSELF**

By Annie Craft

[1]We're all so busy these days, most of us don't have time to enjoy the things we love doing. I read a report recently that says [2]we spend 547 hours a year cleaning, travelling to work and queueing, but [3]I don't think many people spend 547 hours a year doing things they enjoy! Until recently, I was always in a hurry and had no time to just sit down and relax. Then one day I decided to change all that, and now I spend an hour each day doing what I want to do. You could do the same if you save some time every day.

[4]In my opinion, one of the most useful things to do is plan every day. Every morning, I make a list of all the things I need to do. I do the important things that day. The things that aren't so important can wait for another day.

Another thing I find really useful is to do two activities at the same time. [5]The report says, we spend 27 days of our lives queuing for public transport. Sometimes I feel like I do that in one week! Now, in the morning, I answer work emails while I'm waiting for the bus. [6]I think this helps me get a lot more work done when I'm in the office. Then, on the way home, I walk instead of getting the bus. That means I don't waste time waiting and I get some exercise, too. I save three and a half hours a week by not going to the gym (and quite a lot of money, too!).

[7]For me, another great way to save time is to cook lots of meals at once. I usually spend an hour cooking a big meal at the weekend, eat some and then freeze the rest. During the week, I just put something I've already prepared in the oven and cook some fresh vegetables. [8]The average time people spend cooking is 45 minutes a day and I think that was also true for me. Now cooking only takes me 15 minutes a day so [9]I save three and a half hours each week.

So, in total, I save seven hours a week. And how do I spend that time? I give one hour to myself each day. [10]I feel we all use our phones too much, so I turn mine off and don't waste time on social media. Instead, I read a book, listen to music or practise the guitar. I started learning five years ago, and now with all this extra time I might improve at last!

10B Develop your writing

Goal: write a description of an object

Focus: order of adjectives

1 **Have you ever been to a lost property office? Why?**

2 **Read the lost item report and answer the questions.**

1. What has Andy lost?
2. When did he lose it?
3. Where does he think he lost it?
4. What was inside it?

Lost item report

Name:	Andy Davis
Email:	andrewKdavis@email.uk
Date item was lost:	19th June
Time item was lost:	5.30 p.m.

Where the item was lost:
I travelled between Manchester and Bolton with my wallet in my coat pocket. When I left Bolton station at around 5.30, I realised the wallet wasn't there. I think it fell out somewhere between platform 5 and the exit.

Detailed description of lost item:
It's an old, brown, leather wallet. It's made by Warlis and the name is on the front. Inside the wallet, there's a £20 note and about £3 in coins. There's a credit card and debit card as well as my driving licence. There's also a small, thin, silver key. It's on a round, metal key ring from Moscow.

3 a **Read the report again. What adjectives does Andy use to describe each item?**

1. The wallet
   old, ...
2. The key
3. The key ring

b **Look at the order of adjectives in the lost item report. Which comes first in each pair?**

1. age/material
2. colour/size
3. material/shape

4 **Read the Focus box and check your answers to Exercise 3b.**

Order of adjectives

To describe something using more than one adjective, use this order: size, age, shape, colour, material + object. However, try not to use more than two or three adjectives at a time. To do this you should choose the adjectives that best describe the object.

I've lost my ***big, red*** *scarf.*
It's an ***old, leather*** *bag.*
They're new ***blue, cotton*** *trousers.*

5 **Write the adjectives in the correct order.**

1. I've lost a ________________ (grey, cotton) sweater.
2. I'm trying to find my ________________ (brown, thin) glasses.
3. I left a really ________________ (black, leather, old) purse on the bus.
4. I've lost a ________________ (silver, big, long) key.
5. I've lost a pair of ________________ (round, gold, thick) earrings.

Prepare

6 a **Imagine you've lost your bag in a shopping centre and you need to complete a lost item report. Think about the questions below.**

- Where were you?
- Where do you think you lost it?
- When did you lose it?
- What items were in the bag?

b **Write some adjectives to describe the bag and the items in it. Use the Focus box to help you.**

Write

7 **Write a lost item report for your bag. Include the information below.**

- where and when you lost it
- a description of the bag
- a description of some of the items in the bag

10c Develop your listening

Goal: understand a TV interview

Focus: recognising discourse markers

1 Work in pairs and discuss the questions.

1 Do you like watching reality TV programmes? Why/Why not?

2 Would you like to take part in a reality TV programme? Why/ Why not?

2 Read the programme information and answer the questions.

1 What do the people on the TV programme have to do?

2 How can they win the prize?

3 How much money can they win?

In this new reality TV show, fifteen ordinary people have to live together in an old-fashioned house for three months. They must eat, sleep and have fun in the same way that people from 150 years ago did. Each week, people are voted out of the house by the public and the last person in the house wins £100,000!

In tonight's episode, three people are voted off – who will it be? Presenter Linda Cox interviews them as they leave the house.

3 a 10.7 Listen to an interview with Stacey and Kenny. Who is happy to be leaving the house? Who is sad?

b Listen again and answer the questions for each speaker.

1 What will they miss in the house? Why?

2 What didn't they like in the house?

4 Read the Focus box. What sounds do people make to give themselves time to think?

Recognising discourse markers

When we speak we often use words, phrases or sounds to give us time to think.

Some common sounds we use are *um*, *er* and *oh*.

***Oh**, I've seen that programme before.*

*I thought it was a bit, **um**, boring.*

*I, **er**, really liked that new, er, reality TV programme.*

Some common words and phrases we use are *let me see*, *well*, *you know*.

***Let me see**, I think it's about an hour long.*

***Well**, we can stay in if you like.*

*It was, **you know**, an interesting experience.*

These words, phrases and sounds don't help with the meaning of a sentence, but recognising them can help you focus on the more important words.

5 a 10.8 Listen and complete the extracts from the interview with the word, phrase or sound you hear.

1 I liked it at first but I miss, __________ , I miss my family.

2 He's always there for me and , __________ , I just miss him lots!

3 __________ , the food in the house was terrible.

4 __________ , I think the thing I'll miss the most is the clothes.

5 So yeah , __________ , I'm really sad to be leaving!

b Work in pairs and compare your answers.

6 a 10.9 Listen to Jackie leaving the house. Number the questions the presenter asks her in the order you hear them.

1 Do you have anything to say to the people still in the house?

2 How are you feeling right now, Jackie?

3 What are you going to do when you get home?

b Listen again and decide if the sentences are true (T) or false (F).

1 Jackie didn't like her time in the house.

2 She wants to go home.

3 She doesn't want to see her family.

4 She knows what she's going to do when she gets home.

5 She wants to have a nice meal.

6 She likes the people in the house.

7 Work in pairs. Do you use any sounds, words or phrases in your language to give you time to think? Which do you use most often?

Grammar bank

GRAMMAR

1A Word order in questions

Some questions only require a yes or no answer (*yes/no* questions).
For questions in the present and past simple, use *do/does/did* before the subject.
Does she *study English here? Yes, she does.*
For questions with *be*, use *be* before the subject.
Is he *from London? No, he isn't.*
For questions which require more information, use a question word (*who, what, where* etc.) Use the same word order for *yes/no* questions.

question word	auxiliary verb (*do/does/did*)	subject	infinitive	adjective/ noun/verb +*ing* etc.
Where	*do*	*you*	*live?*	
What	*does*	*she*	*do?*	
	Do	*they*	*want*	*a coffee?*
	Does	*he*	*like*	*his new bike?*

question word	*be*	subject	adjective/ noun/verb +*ing* etc.
What	*'s*	*your name?*	
When	*are*	*you*	*coming?*
	Is	*she*	*a teacher?*
	Are	*those shoes*	*new?*

1B Adverbs of frequency

Use adverbs of frequency to say how often something happens.
With *be* and modal verbs, adverbs of frequency come after the verb.
Thomas ***is always*** *on time.*
Is *he* ***always*** *on time?*
You ***should always*** *practice what you learn.*
With other verbs, they come before the verb.
We ***sometimes go*** *away at the weekend.*
Do you ***sometimes go*** *away at the weekend?*
Sometimes, often and *usually* can also go at the beginning of a sentence.
Sometimes*, I walk to work.*

However, *always, hardly ever, rarely* and *never* can't go at the beginning of a sentence.
I ***never*** *walk to work.*
It's possible to use *always, often* and *usually* in negative statements. They come after *not*.
Martina ***isn't usually*** *in the office on Monday.*
We ***don't often*** *eat out.*
Sometimes, hardly ever, rarely, and *never* can't be used in negative sentences.
~~I don't sometimes~~ play sport.
It's possible to use other expressions of frequency. These usually go at the end of the sentence.
She calls me ***every day****.*
We order pizza ***once a week****.*
I listen to music ***all the time.***

1C Present simple and present continuous

Use the present simple to talk about facts, habits and things which are always or generally true.
The Earth ***moves*** *around the Sun.*
He ***doesn't cycle*** *to work every day.*
Is *she a teacher?*
We often use adverbs of frequency with the present simple, e.g. *usually, often, sometimes* etc.
Use the present continuous to talk about actions happening now.
*He****'s doing*** *his homework in his room.*
They ***aren't working*** *at the moment.*
Are *you* ***waiting*** *for someone?*
Use the present continuous to talk about a temporary situation, or something happening around now.
*I****'m living*** *in Amsterdam for a few months.*
*She****'s studying*** *for her Master's degree this year.*

Form the present continuous with be + the *-ing* form of the verb.
Some verbs describe actions (active verbs), e.g. *go, buy, speak* etc., and some verbs describe states (state verbs), e.g. *be, now, like, love, prefer, understand, want.*
You can use active verbs with both the present simple and continuous.
I ***take*** *a bus to work every day.*
*I****'m taking*** *the bus early today.*
Only use state verbs with the present simple.
I ***understand*** *what you're saying.*
Not: ~~I'm understanding~~ what you're saying.
We often use these words and phrases with the present continuous: *now, at the moment, currently, today, this month* etc.
I'm staying with my brother ***at the moment****.*
She's cooking dinner ***now****.*

PRACTICE

1A

1 Correct the mistake in each question.

1 How long ~~are~~ *is* this lesson?
2 Whose bag this is?
3 Does she lives near here?
4 Why it is hot in here?
5 How much costs this shirt?
6 What kind of car drives he?
7 You want some cake?
8 How many do you have children?
9 Is he speak French?
10 Do she like Italian food?

2 Write questions for answers 1–8. Use the question words in brackets.

1 He's got one sister and two brothers. (How many)
2 I go to work by bus. (How)
3 I buy clothes from the department store. (Where)
4 The lesson starts at 7 o'clock. (What time)
5 I usually visit my friends at the weekend. (What)
6 I check my messages every 20 or 30 minutes. (How often)
7 My sister is happy because she passed all her exams. (Why)
8 They speak English and a little French. (Which)

1B

1 Choose the correct alternatives.

1 Work is *never/always/rarely* stressful – I'm not enjoying it at all.
2 *Sometimes/Never/Always* I get up at 6.30.
3 I *usually/often/hardly ever* go to the cinema – probably just once a year.
4 Diana has a Spanish class *every/never/always* Wednesday.
5 They don't *always/sometimes/never* arrive on time.
6 I see my brother *once/twice/three times* a year, on his birthday.
7 Jay *sometimes/always/hardly ever* has a big breakfast because he wakes up hungry every morning.
8 The children don't *sometimes/never/usually* come home this early.

2 Put the words in the correct order.

1 go / once a year / on holiday to France / they
2 rarely / she / late / is
3 play tennis / I / on Friday / usually
4 hardly ever / TV / we / watch
5 go / they / to the beach / often / don't
6 usually / free / at the weekend / aren't / we
7 he / drive / normally / to work / doesn't
8 every day / have breakfast / don't / I
9 sometimes / you / weekend / do / the / at / work / ?
10 late / he / always / is / ?

1C

1 Complete the sentences with the correct form of the verbs in the box.

check	clean	get	go	read	study	play	watch

1 I always _______ dressed before breakfast.
2 My friends and I never _______ video games.
3 I _______ a fantastic TV drama at the moment.
4 I never _______ to sleep late.
5 My brother _______ his messages every five minutes!
6 My dad _______ his car now.
7 I always _______ a book before I go to bed.
8 My sister _______ in Paris at the moment.

2 Complete the text with the correct form of the verbs in brackets.

I usually [1]_______ (eat) a lot but this month I [2]_______ (try) to be healthier. Every morning, I [3]_______ (have) some yoghurt and fruit. For lunch, I usually [4]_______ (go) to a cafe and [5]_______ (buy) a salad. I [6]_______ (eat) one right now, actually. I [7]_______(learn) to cook at the moment too. I often [8]_______ (cook) pasta because it's quick and easy. Sometimes I [9]_______(make) dinner for my housemate - he [10]_______ (loves) it! I [11]_______(not like) the diet much but I [12]_______ (know) it's good for me.

Want more practice? Go to your Workbook or app.

GRAMMAR

2A Past simple

Use the past simple to talk about finished actions and states in the past.

*I **arrived** in Lisbon at 2.45 p.m.*

*I **lived** in Rome for a few years.*

Form the past simple of *be* with *was* or *were*.

*I **was** late for work.*

*They **were** at work yesterday.*

Form the past simple of regular verbs by adding *-ed* to the verb.

*play - play**ed***

*listen - listen**ed***

If the verb ends in *-e*, add *-d*.

*love - love**d***

*hope - hope**d***

If the verb ends in consonant + *-y*, delete the *-y* and add *-ied*.

*hurry - hurr**ied*** *try - tr**ied***

If the verb ends in consonant + vowel + consonant, double the consonant and add *-ed*.

*stop - sto**pped*** *plan - pla**nned***

Many verbs have irregular past simple forms. See the irregular verbs list on page 160.

go - went *do - did*

give - gave *have - had*

2B Past simple negative and questions

Form the past simple negative with *didn't* + infinitive.

*I **didn't give** him any money.*

*They **didn't go** anywhere yesterday.*

Form the past simple negative of *be* with *wasn't* or *weren't*. Don't use *didn't*.

*He **wasn't** very well on Saturday.*

*They **weren't** in class last Monday.*

Not: They ~~didn't be~~ in class last Monday.

Form questions with *did*. Questions in the past simple have the same word order as questions in the present simple.

When did you go to Russia?

What band did she see?

Did they meet yesterday?

Did he call you?

Do not use *did* for questions with *be*.

***Was Amira** at the party?*

Not: e.g. ~~Did Amira be~~ at the party?

2C Quantifiers

Some nouns are countable and can be singular or plural.

egg/eggs, onion/onions, book/books

Some nouns are uncountable.

bread, milk, water, air

Some can be both.

I'd like a salad/ice cream, please. (countable)

Can you buy some salad/ice cream from the shop? (uncountable)

Use *a*, *an* or a number to talk about singular countable nouns.

*There's **a train** at 6.30.*

*I'd like **an apple**, please.*

*There are **15 people** in this company.*

Use *some* and *any* with uncountable nouns to talk about a general amount.

Use *some* in positive statements, use *any* in negative sentences and questions.

*There's **some fish** in this salad.*

*There **isn't any** money in my bank account.*

*Is there **any milk** at home?*

It's also possible to use *no* instead of *any*.

*There's **no juice** on this menu.*

Use *a lot of/lots of* to talk about a large quantity with both countable and uncountable nouns.

*There are **a lot of students** in this school.*

*There's **lots of sugar** in this cake.*

Use *a few* to talk about a small quantity with countable nouns.

*There are **a few lemons** in the bowl.*

Use *a bit of* and *a little* to talk about a small quantity with uncountable nouns.

*There's **a bit of milk** left.*

*There's **a little chocolate** in the cupboard.*

PRACTICE

2A

1 Choose the correct alternatives.

Yesterday I [1]*have/had* a really bad day. Firstly, I [2]*woke/waked* up late. I [3]*leaved/left* the house quickly and got into my car. I [4]*tried/try* to start it but it was broken! So I [5]*run/ran* to the bus stop. I [6]*waiting/waited* for a long time but there [7]*weren't/were* any buses. Then I [8]*read/readed* a sign on the bus stop which said, 'Sorry, no buses today.' So I [9]*go/went* home again and got my bicycle. Finally I [10]*arrived/arrive* at work, hot and tired, and walked into the office. 'That's strange' I thought, 'It's empty'. And then I remembered - it was Saturday!

2 Complete the sentences with the correct form of the verbs in the box.

arrive   begin   buy   eat   move   plan   teach   watch

1 Jake ______ his job three years ago.
2 I ______ a great film at the cinema last night.
3 Micky ______ into her new flat last weekend.
4 Arianna ______ the fish, but she said it wasn't nice.
5 He ______ late to the party.
6 Angelo ______ maths at the university.
7 They ______ a new car at the weekend.
8 Hanna ______ a trip to Ibiza for her birthday.

2B

1 Complete the story with *didn't* and a verb in the box or *wasn't/weren't*.

have   know   meet   say   start

I got a new job as a designer for an online magazine. Unfortunately, the day [1]__________ well because I woke up with a cold. I [2]__________ my manager until the end of the day. He [3]__________ in the office for most of the day because he was in a meeting. Anyway, he asked me what I thought about the company website. He said that he and his team [4]__________ afraid of hearing the truth, so I told him it [5]__________ very good. It [6]__________ the right information and it looked old. He then told me that his team designed the new website only last month. I [7]__________ what to do so I [8]__________ anything more. The day started badly and ended badly!

2 Make questions in the past simple using the prompts.

1 What / you / do / yesterday /?
2 How long / be / your journey to school today /?
3 Who / you / see / last weekend /?
4 Where / you / go / last night /?
5 How / you / feel / yesterday /?
6 Where / you / at six o'clock yesterday /?
7 What time / you / get up / this morning /?
8 What / be / your favourite game / when you were a child /?
9 When / you / start / this English course /?
10 What / your favourite TV programmes / when you were a child /?

2C

1 Choose the correct alternatives.

This week we're in Greece, looking at some delicious local dishes. Let's begin with a starter known as taramasalata. [1]*There's/There are* some fish in it and some lemon juice and olive oil. Some people also like to add an [2]*onion/onions* or some garlic. When it's ready, enjoy it with some fresh [3]*bread/breads*.

For the main course, we're having moussaka. It's made with meat, garlic and [4]*wine/wines* and [5]*there's/there are* a few tomatoes, onions, herbs and spices, too. On the top, there are some [6]*potato/potatoes*.

And for dessert, there's baklava! It's a really sweet dish, and there [7]*is/are* nuts and spices inside. There's also some butter, [8]*sugar/sugars*, honey and lemon juice.

2 Correct the mistake in each sentence.

1 I'm hungry and there isn't ~~no~~ *any* food in the fridge!
2 You shouldn't eat a lot sugar. It isn't good for you.
3 I'm going to add bit of chilli to this soup. Is that OK with you?
4 There are a few of blueberries in this recipe, which really adds to the flavour.
5 I love cheese. I always eat any at the weekend.
6 There's no good cooks in my family – we're all really bad at cooking!

Want more practice? Go to your Workbook or app.

GRAMMAR

3A Comparatives

Use a comparative adjective + *than* to compare two things.

This part of town ***is quieter than*** *the centre.*

The modern art museum ***is more interesting than*** *the national gallery.*

You can use (*not*) *as* + adjective + *as* to say two things are or aren't the same.

My town is as ***as big as*** *yours.*

It ***isn't as expensive as*** *London.*

We can use *a lot, much* and *a (little) bit* to make large and small comparisons.

Cafés in the square are ***much more expensive*** *than in the streets nearby.*

The park is ***a bit cleaner*** *than last week.*

type of adjective	example	comparative	example
short adjectives (one-syllable and some two-syllable adjectives)	*old* *quiet*	add *-er*	old**er** quiet**er**
short adjectives ending in *-e*	*nice*	add *-r*	nice**r**
short adjectives ending in *-y*	*noisy*	delete *-y* and add *-ier*	nois**ier**
short adjectives ending in one consonant, one vowel and one consonant	*big*	double the final consonant and add *-er*	big**ger**
long adjectives (most two syllable adjectives and all with three or more syllables)	*modern* *beautiful*	use *more*/*less* + adjective	**more** modern **less** beautiful
irregular adjectives	*good* *bad* *far*	no rules	*better* *worse* *further*

3B Superlatives

Use *the* + superlative adjective to compare more than two things. Superlatives describe something that is unique – there is only one of them.

This is ***the smallest*** *car we have.*

The Vacation Inn is ***the most comfortable*** *hotel in the area.*

type of adjective	example	superlative	example
short adjectives (one-syllable and some two-syllable adjectives)	*small* *quiet*	add *-est*	*small**est*** *quiet**est***
short adjectives ending in *-e*	*nice*	add *-st*	*nice**st***
short adjectives ending in *-y*	*busy*	delete *-y* and add *-iest*	*bus**iest***
short adjectives ending in one consonant, one vowel and one consonant	*big*	double the final consonant and add *-est*	*big**gest***
long adjectives (most two syllable adjectives and all with three or more syllables)	*interesting* *popular*	use *most*/*least* + adjective	*the **most** interesting* *the **least** popular*
irregular adjectives	*good* *bad* *far*	no rules	*best* *worst* *furthest*

3C Present perfect with *ever* and *never*

+	I	've	been	to India.
-	She	hasn't	finished	the report.
?	Have	you	seen	that film?

Use the present perfect to talk about experiences that happen in the past but it's not clear exactly when. Form the present perfect with *has/have* + past participle.

Use the past simple to talk about specific past experiences or a specific time in the past. It is common to start talking generally about a past experience in the present perfect, and then use the past simple to talk about the details.

A: Have *you* ***been*** *to the campsite near the river?*

B: *Yes, I* ***went*** *there last year.*

A: Did *you* ***like*** *it?*

B: *I* ***loved*** *it!*

The past participle of regular verbs is the same as their past simple form.

visit - visited, dance - danced, study - studied

Many verbs have irregular past participle forms. See the irregular verbs list on page 160.

be - been, buy - bought, eat - eaten, drink - drunk, fall - fallen, have - had, go - gone

Notice the difference between *been* and *gone*.

Gina's ***been*** *to the supermarket.* (She went and came back.)

Gina's ***gone*** *to the supermarket.* (She went and is still there.)

Use *ever* and *never* with the present perfect to mean 'in all your life'. Use *ever* in questions and *never* in negative statements.

Has Amanda ***ever*** *stayed at your house?*

I've ***never*** *eaten sushi.*

PRACTICE

3A

1 Correct the mistake in five of the sentences.

1. This area is ~~beautifuler~~ *more beautiful* than the city centre.
2. Moss park is less popular than Green park.
3. The west side of the city is more richer than the east.
4. My street is dirter than it was last year.
5. This house is a lot bigger than our house.
6. My house is farer than your house from the train station.
7. New York is the more expensive than Philadelphia.
8. The view from Primrose Hill is better then the view in Hyde Park.

2 Rewrite the sentences using the words in brackets so that they mean the same.

1. The main square is noisy and the park is quiet. (quiet)
   The park is quieter than the main square.
2. Shopping centres are boring. Museums are really interesting. (much/interesting)
3. The countryside is clean. The beach is dirty. (dirty)
4. The centre is old, but the rest of the city is modern. (modern)
5. Cafés in the High Street are expensive. Cafés in Green Street are cheap. (less expensive)
6. Oak End is a poor area. Greenfields is a rich area. (poor)

3B

1 Complete the description with the superlative form of the adjectives in brackets.

The [1]____________ (good) place to stay in my area is the Founder's Hotel. It's the [2]____________ (big) and the [3]____________ (beautiful) hotel in the area, although it's also the [4]____________ (expensive). It's a very old building from the 17th Century, when it was built as a house for the [5]____________ (rich) family in the area. It's in [6]____________ (quiet) part of town, so you can sleep really well. My friend stayed there last year and she loved it. She recommended staying in the Arbor room because it's the [7]____________ (nice).

2 Make true sentences using the prompts.

1. expensive / hotel in my city
   The most expensive hotel in my city is the Capitale.
2. interesting / place to stay in my city
3. small / room in my house
4. noisy / person in my family
5. beautiful / place I know
6. busy / time of the week for me
7. old / person in my family
8. cheap / place to eat in my area
9. popular / place to visit in my country
10. nice / person I know

3C

1 Choose the correct alternatives.

I [1]*'ve done/did* some interesting things in my life. I [2]*'ve travelled/travelled* a lot. When I was 20, I [3]*'ve cycled/cycled* across the US with a group of friends. We [4]*'ve been/were* there for six months and we met lots of great people. I [5]*'ve seen/saw* the Northern Lights. I [6]*'ve seen/saw* them in Finland in 2014. They [7]*'ve been/were* beautiful. I love diving. I [8]*'ve dived/dived* in the Pacific Ocean but I [9]*'ve never/never have* dived in the Atlantic Ocean. For my honeymoon, my wife and I [10]*'ve visited/visited* The Maldives. We [11]*'ve stayed/stayed* in a fantastic hotel and [12]*'ve swum/swam* in the Indian Ocean. Last year we [13]*'ve driven/drove* from the north to the south of New Zealand. We [14]*'ve taken/took* some photos of some amazing beaches, mountains and lakes. Next year, we'd like to go to China and walk along the Great Wall.

2 Make questions using the prompts. Use the present perfect with *ever*.

1. you / ride a motorbike
   Have you ever ridden a motorbike?
2. you / be to a music festival
3. you / fall over in the street
4. you / bake bread
5. you / sleep outside
6. you / sing in public
7. you / climb a mountain
8. you / write a story
9. you / run a marathon
10. you / break a bone

Want more practice? Go to your Workbook or app.

GRAMMAR

7A *too* and *enough*

Use *too*, *too many* and *too much* to say something is more than necessary.

too + adjective	*It's **too hot** in here.* *This room is **too small** for all of us.*
too many + countable noun	*There are **too many people** in here.* *I had **too many things** to do yesterday.*
too much + uncountable noun	*I've got **too much homework** to do.* *There's **too much pollution** in this city.*

Use *very* + adjective to say something is positive.

*I like George. He's **very funny**.*

Use *enough* to say that there is the right amount of something.

enough + noun	*There are **enough chairs** for everyone.* *We have **enough time** to walk slowly.*
adjective + *enough*	*This car is **big enough** for me.* *Please don't turn up the music. It's **loud enough**.*

Use *not enough* to say something is less than necessary.

not + adjective + noun	*This suitcase **isn't big enough** for all my clothes.* *I can't have a bath. The water **isn't hot enough**.*
not enough + (adjective) + noun	*There **aren't enough English books** for every student.* *I **don't have enough energy**.*

Use *enough* with both countable and uncountable nouns.

*There **are enough computers** for everyone in the class.*

*There **wasn't enough time** to finish the film.*

It is common to use *for* + noun/pronoun after *too* and *enough* phrases.

*There aren't enough seats **for** everyone on the train.*

*This soup is too spicy **for** me.*

*There are too many messages **for** us to read.*

7B *used to*

Use *used to* + infinitive to talk about repeated activities or situations in the past which are not true now.

*We **used to go** on holiday to Croatia every year* (but we don't now).

*My brother **used to play** football* (but he doesn't now).

Form the negative with *didn't use to* + infinitive.

*I **didn't use to like** broccoli* (but I do now).

*They **didn't use to live** in this town* (but they do now).

Form questions with *Did* (*you*) *use to* + infinitive.

***Did you use to play** video games when you were young?*

*Where **did they use to live**?*

It is sometimes possible to use the past simple and *used to* to say the same thing.

***I used to have** a nice car.*

***I had** a nice car.*

With a single action, we only use the past simple.

I left school when I was 16.

Not: ~~I used to leave school when I was 16.~~

Use *usually* to talk about habits in the present, not *used to*.

I usually have dinner around 7 p.m.

Not: I ~~used to~~ have dinner around 7 p.m.

7C Articles

Use *a* or *an* when talking about singular countable nouns for the first time.

*There's **a** bookcase in my room.*

*There's **an** armchair in my study.*

Use *the* to talk about the same thing again or when both the speaker and the listener know which thing we're talking about.

*I've got a dog and a cat. **The** dog's name is Cookie and **the** cat's name is Swingle.*

*Can you switch **the** TV on?*

Also use *the* when there is only one of something, with superlatives, in some prepositional phrases and with times of the day/seasons.

*Wow, look at **the** moon tonight!*

*That's **the** best meal I've had for a long time.*

*There's a plant in **the** corner of the room.*

*It gets a lot of light in **the** morning / summer.*

Don't use an article before plural and uncountable nouns, most countries/cities or with sports.

I bought flowers for Michelle.

There's milk on the floor.

She's from Spain.

I love New York.

I play basketball twice a week.

We also don't use an article when talking about things in general.

I prefer dogs to cats.

PRACTICE

7A

1 Put the words in italics in the correct order.

1 I'm really thirsty but I *money / don't / enough / have* for a drink.
2 I can't work in here. There's *much / noise / too.*
3 There *chairs / enough / aren't* for everyone so I'll sit on the floor.
4 It's *me / hot / for / too* in here. Can I open a window?
5 There *many / too / cars / are* on the road these days. The traffic is terrible.
6 This bag *big / isn't / enough* for all my books. I need a bigger one.
7 We *food / have / for / enough / everyone.* No one will be hungry after!
8 My flat *small/'s / me / too / for* these days. I need a larger place.

2 Complete the article with the words in brackets and *too, too many, too much* or *(not) enough*.

I recently moved into a new flat but I don't like it. Firstly, it's [1]__________ (small). There are [2]__________ (cupboards) for all of my things in the bedroom so a lot of them are on the floor. The living room is [3]__________ (big) for my huge TV. The only room that's OK is the kitchen. There's [4]__________ (space) for me to cook so I'm happy with that. The flat is on a busy city road. There's [5]__________ (traffic) at night. It's [6]__________ (noisy) and I can't sleep. There are [7]__________ (noisy neighbours), as well. Unfortunately, I have to stay here for a few more months because I don't [8]__________ (have/money) to move to somewhere bigger.

7B

1 Complete the conversation with *use(d) to* and the verbs in the box.

have	not like	live	look	play	watch

A: Where did you [1]__________ when you were a child?
B: I grew up in a big city. My parents [2]__________ a flat on the tenth floor.
A: Really? What was that like?
B: It was great, I [3]__________ out of my bedroom window and see the whole city. I [4]__________ it when the lift broke and we had to use the stairs. That was annoying!
A: Where [5]__________ with your friends?
B: Mostly at home. We [6]__________ TV or play video games.

2 Make sentences and questions with *use (d) to* using the prompts.

1 Where / go / school?
Where did you use to go to school?
2 I / not / like / carrots.
3 We / go everywhere / by bike.
4 I / play / the piano.
5 you / drive?
6 We / not / go / holiday / much.
7 They / live / in a flat.
8 she / study / medicine?

7C

1 Choose the correct alternatives.

1
A: Do you like *the/-* animals?
B: Yes, I love them, I've got two pets: *a/-* cat and *a/the* dog.

2
A: Has she got any children?
B: Yes, *a/the* boy and *a/the* girl. *A/The* boy's name is Ben and *a/the* girl's name is Claire.

3
A: Can you switch *-/the* lamp on?
B: Which one?
A: The one in the corner of *-/the* room, next to *the/a* TV.

2 Complete the sentences with *a* or *an, the* or -.

1 There's ______ sofa in front of ______ bookcase on the right.
2 ______ milk is expensive these days.
3 I bought some T-shirts. I like ______ blue one best.
4 This is ______ most comfortable chair.
5 We've got ______ new oven. Do you like it?
6 I love ______ cats, but I also like ______ dogs.
7 Don't look directly at ______ sun, you'll hurt your eyes.
8 Where did we park ______ car?

Want more practice? Go to your Workbook or app.

GRAMMAR

8A Past continuous

+	I	was	working	from home yesterday.
-	We	weren't	living	in Germany in 2014.
?	Were	you	having	lunch at one o'clock?

Use the past continuous to talk about actions that were in progress over a period of time in the past. Form the past continuous with the past of be and the *-ing* form of the verb.

*I **was working** from home yesterday.*

*We **weren't living** in Germany in 2012.*

***Were** you **studying** in the library yesterday?*

Past continuous events are often interrupted by a past simple action.

*She **was running** up the stairs when **she fell** and broke her arm.*

***Andreas arrived** while she **was cooking**.*

It is common to use the past continuous and the past simple to tell stories.

Use *when* and *while* before the past continuous to describe the period that you're talking about..

***While I was watching** the film, I fell asleep.*

***When I was working** at my old company, I met lots of people from Japan.*

8B *because, so* and *to*

Use *because, so* and *to* to explain the cause (what made something happen), purpose (why something happened) and result (how something finished) of an action.

Use *because* to talk about the cause of something.

*I don't cycle **because** I don't have a bike.*

*They went to bed late last night **because** they were out with friends.*

Use *to* + infinitive to talk about the purpose of an action.

*I got up early **to finish** my homework.*

*She sometimes goes to the gym **to take** a yoga class.*

Use *so* to talk about the result of something.

*I wasn't feeling well **so** I decided to stay in.*

*The shops were open late **so** we went into town at 7 p.m.*

It is also possible to use *so that* to talk about the purpose of an action.

*I got up early **so that** I could finish a report for work.*

*We bought a huge cake **so that** everyone could have some.*

8C Verb patterns

When we use two verbs together, the second verb is usually either the *-ing* form or the infinitive with *to*.

*I love **working** here.*

*She hates **swimming**.*

*I don't want **to travel** by bus.*

*I'd like **to get** there early, if possible.*

It's possible to use both forms after some verbs.

*My son **started talking** when he was one year old.*

*My son started **to talk** when he was one year old.*

*After dinner, we **continued watching** the film.*

*After dinner, we **continued to watch** the film*

Use verb + *-ing* after verbs which describe how we feel about something: *love, like, enjoy, don't mind, hate*.

*I **love relaxing** in my garden.*

*They **like playing** football after work.*

*She **enjoys reading** in bed.*

*We **don't mind working** late.*

*He **hates getting up** early.*

With *love, like* and *hate*, it's also possible to use the infinitive with *to*.

*I **like to get** up early at the weekend.*

*I **hate to walk** in the rain.*

Use infinitive with *to* after verbs such as *want, would like*, and *need*.

*I **want to go** on holiday.*

*She**'d like to buy** a new phone.*

*They **need to leave** early.*

common verb patterns	
verb + *ing*	**verb + infinitive with *to***
avoid	choose
don't mind	decide
enjoy	expect
finish	hope
imagine	need
stop	want
	would like

PRACTICE

8A

1 Complete the sentences with the past simple or past continuous form of the verbs in brackets.

1 While we __________ (swim) in the pool, someone __________ (take) my towel!
2 My sister __________ (argue) with my parents when I __________ (get) home last night.
3 Dan __________ (lose) his keys while he __________ (cycle) to work.
4 I __________ (fall) down the stairs when I __________ (leave) the building.
5 It __________ (snow) when we __________ (leave) work.
6 I __________ (take) a photo of a friend when a bird suddenly __________ (fly) into her face!
7 Angela __________ (live) in Miami when she __________ (meet) Rico.
8 Brad __________ (break) his leg while he __________ (snowboard).

2 Make sentences using the prompts. Use the past simple and past continuous.

1 I / make / lunch / when / I / cut my finger.
I was making lunch when I cut my finger.
2 Greg / fall off / bike / while / he / cycle / to college.
3 I / find / a letter / while / I / read / an old book.
4 While / we / sit / on the beach / we / see / an unusual bird.
5 Fran / practise / the piano / I / get home.
6 She / tell them / the news / while / they / have dinner.
7 Dan / wear / a really strange coat / I / see / him.
8 Annie / fall over / while / she / run / after the ball.

8B

1 Choose the correct alternatives.

1 I want to become a nurse *because/so/to* I need to study hard.
2 We're going fishing *because/so/to* I find it relaxing.
3 Mick left school at 16 *because/so/to* become a builder.
4 I love chocolate *because/so/to* I eat quite a lot of it.
5 Paula bought a new dress *because/so/to* wear to the party.
6 It was a lovely day *because/so/to* we all cycled to the beach.
7 *Because/So/To* I like travelling so much, I had four holidays last year!
8 I couldn't do my homework *because/so/to* I asked my teacher for help.

2 Complete the sentences with *because, so* or *to*.

1 I enjoy travelling by train ______ I do it quite a lot.
2 My parents are taking an Italian course ______ have some fun.
3 We decided not to have a barbecue ______ it was raining.
4 Ian wanted to surprise Anne ______ he planned a weekend away.
5 Ella took a photo of her new hairstyle ______ share with her friends.
6 We went to the cinema ______ there was a really good film on.
7 I love the sea ______ I try and go sailing every few months.
8 Tony rented a car ______ pick up Helen from the airport .

8C

1 Choose the correct alternatives. Sometimes both answers may be possible.

Next year I'd like [1]*to take/taking* a year out from my job. I don't know what I want [2]*to do/doing* yet, but I have a few ideas. I enjoy [3]*to travel/travelling* and I like [4]*to meet/meeting* new people, so I might go backpacking somewhere far away. I wouldn't like [5]*to go/going* anywhere dangerous, but I don't mind [6]*to go/going* somewhere that's difficult to get to. A friend suggested going to South-East Asia, which sounds exciting, but I've always wanted [7]*to see/seeing* South America, so I might go there instead. The problem is I hate [8]*to fly/flying*, it makes me really nervous. Anyway, I have lots of time to decide!

2 Make questions using the prompts.

1 would / you / visit / Antarctica /?
2 you / like / flying /?
3 Why / you / hate / play / sport /?
4 you / want / go out / this weekend /?
5 would / you / hike / 100 km /?
6 you / enjoy / travel / by bus /?
7 you / need / get / a new passport /?
8 Where / you / decide / go / on your last holiday /?
9 you / avoid / work / at the weekend /?
10 What / you / hope / do / next weekend /?

Want more practice? Go to your Workbook or app.

GRAMMAR

9A Present perfect with *for* and *since*

Use the present perfect (*has/have* + past participle) to talk about things that started in the past and are still true now.

*He**'s lived** in Shanghai since 2010.*

*He**'s lived** in Shanghai for about 10 years.*

Use *for* to describe a period of time, e.g. *a few minutes, ten years, months, a long time, a while, ever.*

*I**'ve known** Jack **for** at least 30 years.*

*We **haven't seen** each other **for** years.*

Use *since* to describe when something started, e.g. *last summer, my birthday, last month, yesterday.*

***I've worked** here **since** last year.*

It's also possible to use *since* before a clause, e.g. *I was born, I was at university, he left his job.*

*They**'ve lived** here **since** they got married.*

*She**'s had** those glasses **since** she was at school.*

Use *How long ... ?* to ask questions about *for* and *since*.

***How long have** you **known** Sam?*

*I**'ve known** Sam for seven years.*

Use the past simple, not the present perfect for things which happened at a specific time in the past.

He bought a new car yesterday.

Jimmy moved house last year.

9B Present perfect with *already, just* and *yet*

It is common to use *already, just* and *yet* when talking about completed present perfect actions.

Use *already* to talk about something that happened in the past, possibly earlier than you expected. It comes between *have* and the main verb.

***I've already seen** that film.*

*The concert **has already finished**.*

Not: *The concert ~~already has~~ finished.*

Sometimes *already* comes at the end of a sentence, but this is less common.

*We**'ve spoken** to Cara **already**.*

Use *just* to talk about something which happened a short time ago. It comes between *have* and the main verb.

*We**'ve just watched** an interesting documentary. It finished a few minutes ago.*

*I**'ve just got** home.*

Not: *We ~~got just~~ home.*

Use *yet* to ask questions and talk about something that hasn't happened but you expect it to. It comes at the end of a question and negative sentence.

*We **haven't got** home **yet.***

***Have** you **finished** that report **yet**?*

Not: *We haven't got ~~yet home~~. / Have you finished ~~yet that report~~?*

Don't use *yet* in positive sentences. Use *already* instead.

***I've already** read that book.*

Not: *I've read that book ~~yet~~.*

9C *could/couldn't*

Use *could* + infinitive to talk about general ability in the past.

*Mika **could ride** a bike when he was three.*

*I **could speak** Russian better when I lived in Moscow.*

*They **could swim** long distances even when they they were little.*

Use *couldn't* + infinitive to talk about a lack of general ability in the past.

*I **couldn't understand** Russian when I first moved to Moscow, but I can now.*

*We **couldn't play** football that well when we were kids.*

*My mum **couldn't cook** until she was about forty.*

Use *Could* + subject + infinitive to ask questions.

***A: Could** you **ride** a bike when you were ten?*

***B:** Yes, I **could**.*

***A: Could** she **paint** well as a child?*

B:** No, she **couldn't.

PRACTICE

9A

1 Complete the sentences with *for* or *since*.

1 I've had this same hairstyle ______ I was in secondary school!
2 My parents have known each other ______ 1981.
3 We've had our car ______ 18 years but it still works well.
4 I've loved skateboarding ______ I was a child.
5 Mara's been a nurse ______ she left university.
6 They've been students here ______ about six months.
7 We've lived in this area ______ we were children.
8 Tom's wanted to be a singer ______ a really long time.
9 Dieter has been in our band ______ a couple of years.
10 Angie has had her job ______ 2017.

2 Complete the text with the present perfect or past simple form of the verbs in brackets.

I want to thank someone really important to me – my friend Lara. I [1]______ (know) her since we were children. She [2]______ (live) next door to me between 1995 and 2010 and had so much fun. We did everything together. Sadly she [3]______ (move) to Canada in 2010 for work. She [4]______ (meet) Ari there and they got married. They [5]______ (be) married for six years and I'm so glad that she's met someone lovely. We [6]______ (not/see) each other since she moved but we video chat all the time. This year has been a difficult year for me but Lara [7]______ (help) me whenever I needed it. So, thanks Lara – you're the best!

9B

1 Make sentences with the present perfect and the words in brackets.

1 I / not / have / dinner. (yet)
I haven't had dinner yet.
2 I / not / book / my flights. (yet)
3 Our teacher / give / us / homework / for / tonight. (already)
4 I / buy / a new phone. (just)
5 My parents / not / arrive. (yet)
6 Yolanda / do / homework / ? (yet)
7 Nina / woke up. (just)
8 I / finish / this exercise! (already)

2 Complete the sentences with *already, yet* or *just*.

1 I've ______ seen that film. Four times!
2 Have you cleaned the car ______?
3 Saskia hasn't got home ______.
4 My sister's ______ lost her keys. She had them in her hand a minute ago!
5 I don't want to eat at Renzo's tonight. I've ______ been there this week.
6 Has the match finished ______?
7 I don't want to go into the bedroom because the kids have ______ gone to bed.
8 Rudy hasn't finished eating ______.

9C

1 Choose the correct alternatives.

A: [1]*You could/ Could you* ride a bike when you were 5?
B: No, I learnt quite late. I [2]*could/ couldn't* ride a bike until I was 12!
A: Really?
B: Yes, though I learnt to when I was really young. I could actually [3]*drive/ to drive* a car when I was 14.
A: How did you do that?
B: Oh, we lived on a farm, so we could [4]*do/ doing* lots of things like that. Of course I [5]*could/ couldn't* only drive when my dad was in the car and I [6]______ (couldn't) drive on the roads, just around the farm.
A: Right, I [7]*could/ couldn't* drive at that age. In fact, I failed my driving test three times!

2 Correct the mistake in six of the sentences.

1 I could to write my name when I was three years old.
2 Maria could enjoy history because the teacher was boring.
3 Could you swimming when you were 5?
4 We couldn't afford to go on holiday every year when I was young.
5 Sorry, I couldn't not hear you. Can you repeat that?
6 Jamie and I not could sit together on the plane here.
7 I could drive a car when I was 16.
8 How old were you when you could first to ride a bike?

Want more practice? Go to your Workbook or app.

GRAMMAR

10A First conditional

Use the first conditional to talk about the possible result of an action in the future.

__If you wait__ for a minute, __I'll come__ with you.

__If I'm tired, I won't go out__ tonight.

A first conditional sentence has two clauses: *if* + present tense and *will/won't* + infinitive.

__If it's warm__ tomorrow, __I'll go__ to the beach.

__If I lose__ my keys again, __I won't be__ happy.

__If he doesn't feel__ well, __he won't come__ for dinner.

Swap the position of the subject and *will* to make questions.

If I give you some money, __will you drive__ me to the airport?

Use *when* instead of *if* for something that is more certain.

I'll pick you up __when you finish__ work.

It's also possible to use modal verbs such as *can, might* and *should* instead of *will*.

If you go to the cinema tonight, you __should see__ that new action film.

__We can meet__ up tomorrow __if you're free__.

__I might go__ to bed early tonight if I'm tired.

10B Present and past passive

Use the passive when we don't know who or what is responsible for an action or if it's not important.

Form the passive with *be* and the past participle.

Present passive: subject + *am/is/are* + past participle.

__Stamps are sold__ in the post office.

__This meat isn't cooked__ properly.

Past passive: subject + *was/were* + past participle

__The post office was built__ in 1934.

__Smartphones weren't used__ in the 1990s.

Swap the subject and *be* to form a question.

__Was the post office built__ a long time ago?

__Were smartphones used__ in the 1990s?

If necessary, use *by* to say who or what is responsible for an action.

My room wasn't cleaned __by the hotel staff__ this morning.

English is spoken __by millions of people__ around the world.

10C Review of tenses

The present

Use the present simple for habits or something which is always true.

I __walk__ to work every day. I __don't get__ the bus.

Cara __is__ a chef.

Use the present continuous for an activity in progress at the time of speaking, or a temporary situation.

We__'re having dinner__ at the moment.

__I'm staying__ with friends while I look for a new flat.

Use the present perfect for activities or states which started in the past and are still true.

__I've lived__ on Old Street for five years.

__How long has__ Fiona __worked__ here?

The past

Use the past simple for finished activities and states.

I __went__ to bed late last night.

I __didn't live__ in the city when I was a child.

Use the past continuous for activities in progress over a period in the past.

I __was having__ dinner at 7 p.m. last night.

When __I left__ work, it __was raining__.

Use the past simple and past continuous together to show when one activity interrupts another.

My phone __rang while__ I __was watching__ the news.

We __were talking__ about Janice __when__ she __walked__ in the room.

Use the present perfect for a past action or event, but we don't know (or it's not important) when it happened.

Sam can tell you about Borneo, he__'s been__ there several times.

__I've never been__ in a helicopter.

The future

Use (*I think*) *will/won't* + infinitive for future predictions.

We__'ll be__ much healthier this time next near.

Manchester United __won't win__ the Premier League this year.

__Do you think__ mobile phones __will get__ smaller again in the future?

Use *be going to* + infinitive for future plans and intentions.

__I'm going to get__ a new job next year.

__Are__ you __going to tell__ her when you see her?

Use the present continuous for future arrangements.

__I'm having__ lunch with my mother __on Saturday__.

We__'re staying__ at a really nice hotel __next weekend__.

PRACTICE

10A

1 Choose the correct alternatives.

1 If people *like/will like* the idea, we *organise/'ll organise* a food festival in our area.
2 The local restaurants *cook/will cook* food for people if we *ask/'ll ask* them.
3 Visitors from other areas *come/will come* if we *tell/'ll tell* them about it.
4 If people *visit/will visit* our area, they *see/should see* what a great place this is.
5 If people *try/will try* the food, they *want/'ll want* to come back again.
6 No one *come/will come* if we *don't/won't* advertise the event.
7 The event *don't/won't* be successful if we *don't/won't* get help from local people.
8 If it *rains/will rain*, we *don't have/can't have* a barbecue.

2 Make first conditional sentences using the prompts.

1 I / send / you a message / if /I / be / free tomorrow.
I'll send you a message if I'm free tomorrow.
2 If / we / get / home early / we / make / dinner.
3 If / they / not get / here soon / we / should / give them a call.
4 We / go out / tomorrow / if / the weather / be / nice.
5 I / drive to the shop / if / we / not have / any bread.
6 I / not see / you tomorrow / if / you / not be / at work.

10B

1 Choose the correct alternatives.

Jeans [1]*was/were* first made by Jacob Davis.
The first jeans were [2]*make/made* of heavy cotton.
The first Levis 501 jeans were [3]*design/designed* in 1890.Jeans [4]*wasn't/weren't* worn by everyone, only some men. Today, hundreds of millions of pairs of jeans [5]*are/were* bought each year in the US.
Jeans [6]*are enjoy/are enjoyed* by people everywhere. Around the world, over one billion pairs of jeans [7]*are sold/were sell* each year.
These days, jeans [8]*are worn/were worn* by all kinds of people.

2 Complete the sentences with the correct passive form of the verbs in brackets.

1 Paper ___________ first ___________ (make) in China around 2,000 years ago.
2 In the beginning, ___________ (not/use) for writing.
3 When ___________ it first ___________ (use) for writing?
4 Today, about 8,000 pieces of paper ___________ (make) from one tree.
5 Ten litres of water ___________ (need) to make one piece of A4 paper.
6 The first bank notes ___________ (make) with paper.

10C

1 Choose the correct alternatives.

I [1]*'ve always liked/always liked* cats, ever since I was a child. My first cat [2]*is/was* all black, and his name was Charlie. He [3]*has loved/loved* exploring different places around the house. One time when I [4]*came/come* home from school, he [5]*is sitting/was sitting* on the top of my bedroom door. When I walked in the room he [6]*was falling/fell* on my head! I [7]*'ve had/'m having* lots of cats over the years, and at the moment I [8]*'ve looked after/'m looking after* my friend's cats while she's on holiday. Next year. I [9]*open/'m going to open* up a cat sanctuary – a safe place for homeless cats to live. I think [10]*it's/it'll be* really popular, because there are a lot of homeless cats in my area. I[11]*'m meeting/'ll meet* someone next month to talk about it.

2 Complete the sentences with the correct form of the verbs in brackets.

1 I ___________ (live) in New York since I was 20.
2 When I got home last night, my brothers ___________ (play) a board game in the living room.
3 I think we ___________ (use) bicycles a lot more in the future.
4 Last week I ___________ (send) over a thousand emails!
5 I ___________ (learn) Chinese at the moment.
6 I ___________ (not like) pizza.
7 Janine ___________ (write) three reports this morning.
8 We ___________ (stay) by the lake this weekend.

Want more practice? Go to your Workbook or app.

Vocabulary bank

1C Everyday activities

A

B

C

D

E

F

G

H

I

J

K

L

M

N

1 Match the everyday activities 1–14 with photos A–N.

1 get the bus to work/school
2 chat to your friends
3 bake a cake/bread/biscuits
4 make a meal/breakfast/lunch/dinner
5 go to the gym
6 have a rest
7 do the housework
8 iron your clothes
9 order pizza/a takeaway
10 go online
11 get ready for work/to go out
12 brush your hair
13 go for a walk/run/drive
14 stay in

2 Complete the sentences with one missing word.

1 I usually get the bus ______ work.
2 I go ______ the gym early every morning before work.
3 Sally's tired so she's having ______ rest.
4 You need to do your homework, don't just chat ______ your friends online.
5 It's your turn to wash ______ dishes!
6 This weekend I'm making ______ meal for my friends.
7 I really tired. I just want to stay ______ in tonight.
8 It's 7 a.m. – I need to get ready ______ for work.

3 Describe a typical day for you. Use as many of the phrases in Exercise 1 as possible.

I get up at around 7 a.m. I have a shower and then I make breakfast. I don't get the bus to college. I usually go by bike.

2A Feelings

1 **Choose the correct alternatives.**

1 exhausted/cheerful

2 annoyed/calm

3 upset/annoyed

4 frightened/calm

5 annoyed/miserable

6 cheerful/worried

7 upset/confident

8 annoyed/worried

2 a **Choose five of the adjectives in Exercise 1. Think about the last time you felt this way and why.**

b **Work in pairs. Share your ideas with your partner.**

I felt exhausted yesterday because I had too much work.

2C Food

1 **Match the food and drink 1–15 with photos A–O.**

1 burger
2 butter
3 cereal
4 chilli
5 crisps
6 fish
7 fizzy drinks
8 grapes
9 juice
10 lamb
11 mango
12 mushrooms
13 salad
14 steak
15 yoghurt

2 **Work in pairs and discuss the questions.**

1 Which of the food and drink in the photos do you like/dislike? Why?
2 Which do you think are healthy/unhealthy?

3A Places in a town

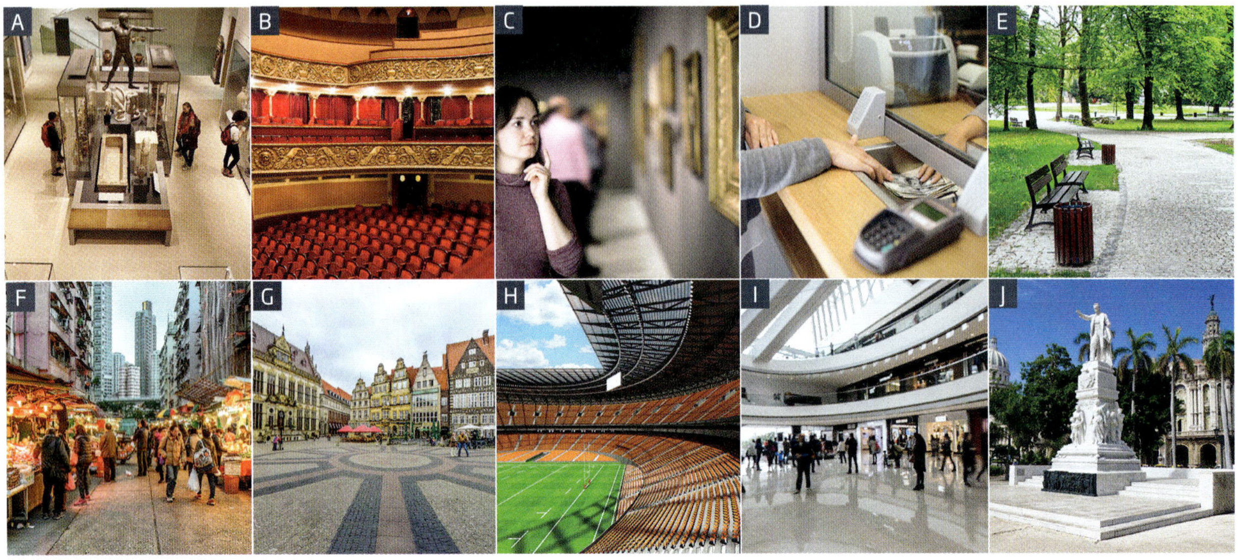

1 **Match the places 1–10 with photos A–J.**

1 a street market
2 an art gallery
3 a museum
4 a park
5 a monument
6 a stadium
7 a theatre
8 a shopping centre
9 a square
10 a bank

2 **Work in pairs. Compare the places using different adjectives.**

A: *I think art galleries are more interesting than museums.*

B: *I'm not sure. I think pictures are more beautiful than old things!*

3B Places to stay

1 **Match the places to stay 1–8 with photos A–G.**

1 an apartment
2 a Bed and Breakfast (B&B)
3 a campsite
4 a holiday cottage
5 a resort
6 a caravan
7 a hostel
8 a hotel

2 **Choose the correct alternatives.**

1 Last holiday we stayed in a big tent on a lovely *campsite/caravan*.
2 We want to cook our own meals, that's why we usually rent *a B&B/an apartment*.
3 I can recommend a lovely little *resort/holiday cottage* that you can rent there.
4 The *resort/B&B* has everything: a swimming pool, three restaurants and lots of things for the children to do.
5 We love our *holiday cottage/caravan* because it means we can stay anywhere we want to.

3 **Which of the places in Exercise 1 do you prefer staying in? Why?**

4C Sport

1 Match the sports vocabulary 1–14 with photos A–N.

1 coach
2 fan
3 team
4 winner
5 match
6 race
7 bat
8 racket
9 hit the ball
10 kick the ball
11 score a goal
12 throw the ball
13 pitch
14 court

2 Match the sentence halves.

1 This hotel is great – it's got a swimming pool
2 The players listened to
3 The winner of the
4 Dale Parker scored
5 Alice hit the ball
6 The fans ran on the pitch
7 I'm not good at basketball because
8 Kate kicked the

a race was only 16.
b really hard.
c and a tennis court.
d ball a really long way.
e two goals in his first match.
f when their team won.
g their coach.
h I don't know how to throw the ball.

3 Work in pairs. Cover the vocabulary in Exercise 1 and take turns to say what each photo shows.

5A Jobs

1 **Match the jobs 1–15 with photos A–O.**

1 plumber
2 pilot
3 accountant
4 computer programmer
5 hairdresser
6 builder
7 vet
8 actor
9 telesales agent
10 waiter/waitress
11 translator
12 estate agent
13 PA (Personal Assistant)
14 receptionist
15 lawyer

2 **Which jobs do these sentences describe?**

1 They help people organize their money.
2 They cut and style people's hair.
3 They appear in films and TV.
4 They sell houses.
5 They defend people in a court of law.
6 They create apps.
7 They repair water pipes.
8 They serve people in a restaurant or café.

3 **Work in pairs and discuss the questions.**

1 Which of these jobs would/wouldn't you like to try? Why?/Why not?
2 Which job do you think is the most ...
- interesting?
- boring?
- stressful?
- well-paid?
- fun?
- difficult?

6C Weekend activities

1 **Complete the activities with *do, go* and *play*.**

2 **Choose the correct alternatives.**

1. Paul often *goes/does* hiking at the weekend.
2. I *did/went* for a meal with my friends last night.
3. Dad's *doing/going* fishing on Sunday.
4. Have you ever *gone/played* climbing?
5. Eliza will *do/go* the cleaning when she gets home.
6. Marco *does/plays* board games with his children every Saturday morning.
7. Do you know how to *play/do* table tennis?
8. I try to *do/play* exercise three times a week.

3 **Complete the sentences with the correct form of *do, go* and *play*.**

1. The children ______ board games all day yesterday.
2. Tom sometimes ______ fishing with his dad in the holidays.
3. Can you ______ the cleaning today?
4. We're going to ______ table tennis. Do want to come?
5. Rachel and Josh are ______ for a meal in town tonight.
6. I'm ______ climbing this weekend.
7. Have you ever ______ hiking in Scotland.
8. Sam ______ with the children as soon as he came from work.
9. How often do you ______ exercise?
10. I can't ______ to the concert tomorrow because I have to work.

4 **Work in pairs. Choose one of the activities and discuss the questions below.**

1. Where did you do it?
2. Who did you do it with?
3. Did you enjoy it?

1 ______ to a concert

2 ______ for a meal

3 ______ table tennis

4 ______ board games

5 ______ hiking

6 ______ the cleaning

7 ______ exercise

8 ______ with the children

9 ______ fishing

10 ______ climbing

7C Rooms and furniture

1 Answer the questions. Use the words in the box to help you.

bathroom bedroom
garden garage kitchen
living room study

1 Which room do you cook in?
2 Which room do you have a shower in?
3 Which room do you sleep in?
4 Which room do you relax and watch TV in?
5 Which room do you work in?
6 Where do you park the car?
7 Where do you spend time outside?

2 Match the furniture 1–14 with photos A–N.

1 armchair
2 bed-side table
3 blind
4 coffee table
5 chest of drawers
6 cupboard
7 curtains
8 dishwasher
9 lamp
10 shelves
11 stool
12 rug
13 wardrobe
14 washing machine

3 Work in pairs and discuss the questions.

1 Which rooms do you usually find the furniture in Exercise 2 in?
2 What furniture do you have in your bedroom?
3 What's your favourite piece of furniture at home?

8B Travel and transport

1 **Match the travel and transport words 1–12 with photos A–L.**

1 bus stop
2 car park
3 motorway
4 garage
5 passenger
6 petrol station
7 platform
8 ticket machine
9 timetable
10 traffic
11 traffic light
12 zebra crossing

2 **Match the sentence halves.**

1 We need to stop at the petrol
2 There's a bus
3 Stop! The traffic
4 I can't drive at the moment
5 We can get our tickets from the ticket
6 Stop at the car

a light is on red.
b station. The car's almost empty.
c machine over there.
d park and I'll get out there.
e stop about five minutes from here.
f because my car is in the garage.

3 **Complete the sentences with a word or phrase from Exercise 1.**

1 You have to use the ________ to cross the roads in this city.
2 There's too much ________ on the roads these days.
3 If we take the ________ instead of the country roads, we'll get there much faster.
4 Which ________ does the train to London leave from?
5 Do you have a ________? I want to know when the next bus is.
6 I was the only ________ on the bus home today.

A

B

C

D

E
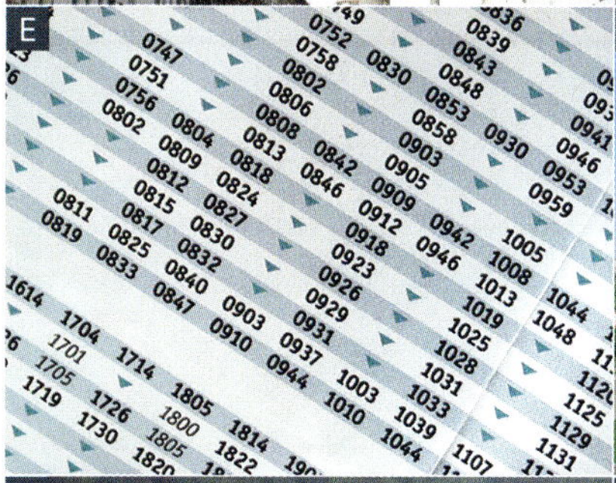

F

G

H

I

J

K

L

9B TV genres

1 **Match the types of TV programme 1–10 with pictures A–J.**

1 cartoon
2 chat show
3 comedy
4 drama
5 quiz show
6 sitcom
7 soap (opera)
8 the news
9 weather forecast
10 wildlife programme

2 **Which are your favourite types of TV programme?**

9C School subjects

1 **Match the school subjects 1–8 with photos A–H.**

1 P.E. (Physical Education)
2 maths
3 history
4 art
5 music
6 geography
7 computer science
8 science

2 **Work in pairs and discuss the questions.**

1 What subjects were you good/bad at when you were at school?
2 What was your favourite subject? Why?
3 What other subjects did you study?

10A Money and shopping

1 **Match the money and shopping words and phrases 1–12 with photos A–L.**

1 ATM
2 bank statement
3 cheque
4 coins
5 contactless payment
6 counter
7 credit/debit card
8 notes
9 receipt
10 till
11 voucher
12 wallet

2 **Read the sentences. What does each one describe?**

1 A ticket that we can use instead of money.
2 A round, flat piece of metal that we use for money.
3 A machine that you use to get money from your bank account.
4 A piece of paper that shows how much you have paid for something.
5 A piece of paper that shows you how much money you have in your bank account.
6 The place where you pay in a shop.

3 **Complete each sentence with a word or phrase from Exercise 1.**

1 Have you seen my __________ ? It's got all my cards and cash in it.
2 Have you got any __________ for the coffee machine?
3 If you want to return that shirt to the shop, you'll need to take the __________ with you.
4 My __________ says I took more money out than I put in.
5 This car park machine doesn't take __________ or cards, just coins.
6 I need to get some cash out of the bank. Is there an __________ near here?

4 **Which ways of paying do you prefer to use? Why?**

A
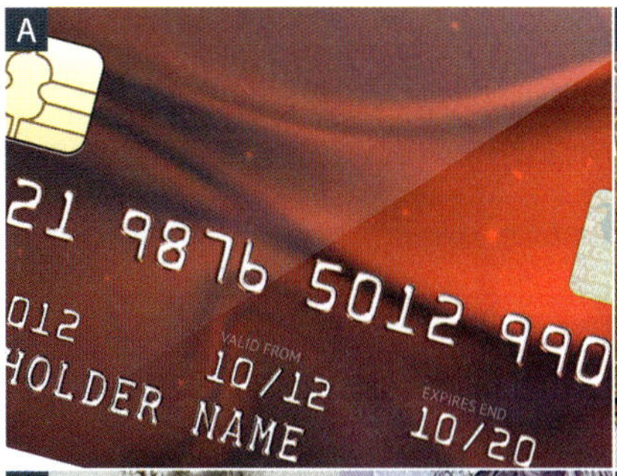

B

C

D

E

F
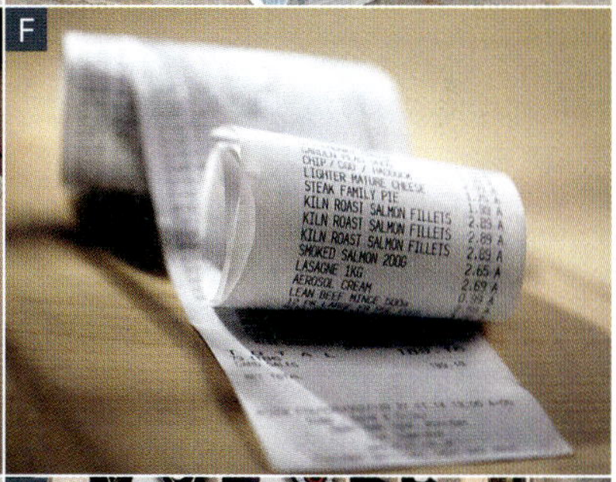

G

H

I
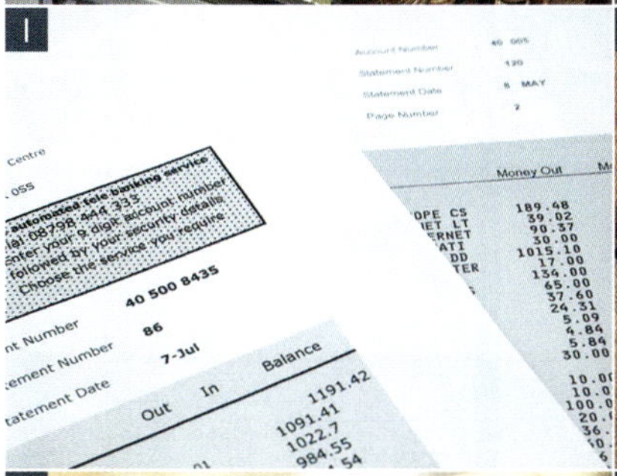

J

K

L

Communication games

Four in a row (Units 1-2 review)

Play in two teams. Take turns to choose a square and answer the question. If you answer correctly you win the square. The first team to win four squares in a row (down, across or diagonally) wins!

How does a person feel when there's nothing to do?	What's the past simple form of *feel, laugh, hear?*	Read the answer. What's the question? *I listen to classical music.*	Say three countable nouns.	Say three things you have a few of.
Correct the mistake in this sentence. *I go often to the park.*	Say three past simple sentences with time expressions.	Correct the mistake in this sentence. *I read a good book at the moment.*	Complete B's reply and sound excited: *A: I want to join a gym.* *B: That ...*	Say four adjectives that describe the taste of food.
What two questions could you ask after someone tells you this? *I found some money yesterday.*	What's the missing word? *The first thing people often do in the morning is c_______ their messages.*	Look at the answer. What's the question? *I go to the supermarket about twice a week.*	What's the missing word? *I'll pay for dinner. I've got _______ of money.*	Say three things that you have a lot of.
Make this sentence negative. *Marc said hello.*	What's the missing word? *I went to the cinema _______ night.*	Say three sentences about what your family or friends are doing now.	How do you pronounce the past simple tense of *need, stay* and *watch*?	Read the answer. What's the question? *I usually get here at about six.*
What's the missing word? *I started my English course four weeks _______.*	What's the missing adjective? *I always feel r_______d before interviews. They don't make me nervous.*	Complete the sentence. *To be successful, it's important to have clear g_______.*	Does a countable or uncountable noun come after *a few*?	Say two things you have a little of.
Say three things you did last week using the past simple.	Say one thing you often do, one thing you hardly ever do and one thing you never do.	How does a person usually feel when something unexpected happens?	Say two nouns that can go with the verb *spend*.	Say two nouns that go with the verb *take*.

Keep talking (Units 3-4 review)

- Play in two teams. Each team chooses a topic from the table. You have two minutes to plan what to say.
- Try to talk about your topic for 30 seconds to win one or two points.
- Repeat four more times, choosing different topics.
- The team with the most points wins!

• Describe a city you've visited. (1 point) • Use at least four different adjectives. (2 points)	• Describe some interesting activities you've done in your life. (1 point) • Use at least three present perfect simple verbs. (2 points)
• Describe the best food you've ever eaten. (1 point) • Use at least one present perfect simple verb and two superlative adjectives. (2 points)	• Compare your home to a friend's home. (1 point) • Use at least three comparative adjectives. (2 points)
• Compare the area where you live with another area in your town or city. (1 point) • Use at least two comparative adjectives. (2 points)	• Describe the most beautiful place in your country. (1 point) • Use at least three comparative or superlative adjectives. (2 points)
• Talk about three things you've never done but would like to do. (1 point) • Use two irregular past participles. (2 points)	• Describe a hotel, hostel, B&B or resort you have stayed in. (1 point) • Describe at least four things that were there. (2 points)
• Talk about your plans for the next week. (1 point) • Use *going* to at least twice. (2 points)	• Talk about things you would like to do next year. (1 point) • Use both *want* and *would like* correctly. (2 points)
• Imagine you're organising a party. Talk about your plans. (1 point) • Use *will* + infinitive at least twice. (2 points)	• Describe your favourite place to spend time. (1 point) • Use at least four adjectives. (2 points)
• Talk about the laws in your country. (1 point) • Use *can* or *can't* and *have to* or *don't have to.* (2 points)	• Talk about what you did last weekend. (1 point) • Use at least four *-ed/-ing* adjectives. (2 points)
• Talk about your plans for next weekend. (1 point) • Use *going to* at least twice. (2 points)	• Talk about some of the things you have to do in your life. (1 point) • Use *have to/don't have to* at least three times. (2 points)

Roadmap race (Units 5-6 review)

Work in groups. Write numbers 1-6 on pieces of paper and put them in a bag. Take turns to take a number and move along the squares. If you answer the question correctly, stay on the square. If your answer is incorrect move back to the square you were on before. The first person to reach FINISH wins.

START

1 What's the missing word? *I work ______-time 20 hours a week.*

2 What's the missing word? *______ an excuse/an appointment.*

3 Say three words to describe someone's appearance.

4 Correct the mistake. *I might not to go the show this evening.*

5 What's the missing word? *I want a job ______ is unusual.*

6 Tell the group three things you might do next week.

7 Your friend has lost their credit card. Give them two pieces of advice.

8 Correct the mistake. *My brother looks like very happy in this photo.*

9 Which verb comes before the words *homework*, *nothing* and *yoga*?

10 Say two words which describe hair on the face.

11 What's the missing word? *If you are funny you have a good sense of ______.*

12 Make three predictions about future transport.

13 You're calling your dentist to cancel an appointment. What do you say?

14 What kind of word follows *look like*? A noun, a verb or an adjective?

15 Tell the group three things you may do at the weekend.

16 Correct the mistake. *You shouldn't taking a taxi. It's expensive.*

17 When do we use the relative pronoun *which*? When do we use *who*?

18 Make two predictions about the future of schools.

19 Which verb goes before *shopping*, *cycling* and *running*?

20 Say two adjectives to describe hair shape.

21 Your friend wants to buy a present for someone who loves football. Make two suggestions.

22 Tell the group something you think will happen tomorrow.

23 Tell the group an arrangement you have next week.

24 What's the missing word? *I go to the gym because I like to keep ______.*

25 What's the missing word? *I have a very busy ______ life - I see my friends almost every day.*

26 What's the missing word? *Did you have a good holiday? What was the hotel ______?*

27 What's the missing word? *It's always a good idea to ______ something on before you buy it.*

28 Correct the mistake. *You never should be late to a job interview.*

29 Tell the group two plans you have for tomorrow.

30 What's the missing word? *I like people ______ are kind and friendly.*

FINISH

True or false? (Units 7-8 review)

1 **Choose eight topics and write one true and one false answer for each, in any order.**

- a place you want to travel to

____

____

- something you hate doing

____

____

- something you don't have enough of these days

____

____

- something you love doing

____

____

- an activity you used to do a lot when you were younger

____

____

- a job you wouldn't like to do

____

____

- what you were doing yesterday at 8 p.m.

____

____

- something you have too much of these days

____

____

- an item of furniture in your favourite room

____

____

- the best thing you did last year

____

____

- a place you got lost in

____

____

- a type of transport you often use

____

____

2 **Work in pairs. Ask your partner questions and try to guess which answers are true. If you guess correctly you win a point. The person with the most points wins!**

Talk about ... (Units 9-10 review)

Work in groups. Write numbers 1–6 on pieces of paper and put them in a bag. Take turns to take a number and move along the squares. Talk about what's in the square and answer any questions from your group. The first person to reach FINISH wins.

START

1. a TV programme that you like
2. your relationship with a friend
3. **GO BACK TO START**
4. a scary film you've seen
5. something you find difficult
6. something that's made in your country
7. a subject at school that you liked
8. something you're terrible at
9. **GO FORWARD TWO SQUARES**
10. something you disagree with your friends about
11. something you waste money on
12. a person you've known since you were a child
13. something you've just done
14. something you're going to do next weekend
15. something you've worked hard at
16. something you did on your last holiday
17. **GO BACK TWO SQUARES**
18. something you've had for a long time
19. something that happened in your life two years ago
20. **GO FORWARD THREE SQUARES**
21. something you like spending money on
22. someone you sometimes argue with
23. a boring film that you've watched
24. **MISS A GO!**
25. what you do when you meet up with your friends
26. what you'll do at the weekend if you have time
27. something you're getting better at
28. what you were doing at ten o'clock last night
29. something you could do when you were younger
30. **GO BACK THREE SQUARES**
31. how you made friends with your closest friend
32. something you need to do today but haven't done yet
33. something that you think will happen tomorrow.
34. something you'd like to have a go at

FINISH

Communication bank

Lesson 1D

6

Student A

1 Ask Student B for the information below. Check the details they give you.

1 what time the concert tonight starts
What time does the concert start?
2 what the homework for tonight is
3 when the shop is open

2 Answer Student B's questions with the information below and check they understand.

1 The film starts at 6:30 p.m., but everybody is meeting at Café Central at 5 p.m.
2 You'd like some pasta, tomatoes, bread, some salt and a newspaper.
3 You have to go onto the company website, search for the job and then complete the online form.

Lesson 2D

5a

Student A

1 You recently did something exciting (e.g. went to a sports event, went skydiving, passed an exam). Get ready to tell Student B:

- what it was
- where you were
- why you did it
- what happened
- how you felt

2 Student B is going tell you about something exciting that happened to him/her recently. Get ready to ask questions about what, where, why, etc.

Lesson 5D

6

Student A

You and Student B went to another country for a language course. You stayed with different families. You'd like to buy the family you stayed with some gifts. Read the information about your family below.

Gail: 50, doctor, likes running
Martin: 52, businessman, likes golf
Gail's mum: 82, likes reading
Gail's dad: 80, likes films

Now go back to page 44 and ask Student B to help you think of ideas. Give some suggestions for his/her family.

Lesson 10B

2c

Quiz results

1 20 billion
2 minute
3 Jacob Davis. Levi Strauss was his business partner.
4 2,500
5 3,500
6 a Danish king who helped people communicate better.
7 Humphry Davy.
8 more

Lesson 3B

11b

The Blue Arrow Hotel

Popular with business travellers, this hotel is in a quiet area just outside the city.

Average customer reviews:

Price (1 = the cheapest; 5 = the most expensive):	1	2	**3**	4	5
Noise (1 = the quietest; 5 = the noisiest):	1	**2**	3	4	5
Size of rooms (1 = the smallest; 5 = the biggest):	1	**2**	3	4	5
Close to the centre (1 = the closest; 5 = the furthest):	1	2	3	4	**5**
Age (1 = the oldest; 5 = the most modern):	1	2	3	4	**5**

Facilities: air conditioning, wifi, free parking, 24-hour reception

The Embassy Hotel

A five-star hotel in the centre of town, close to the business centre and great shopping areas.

Average customer reviews:

Price (1 = the cheapest; 5 = the most expensive):	1	2	3	4	**5**
Noise (1 = the quietest; 5 = the noisiest):	1	2	3	**4**	5
Size of rooms (1 = the smallest; 5 = the biggest):	1	2	3	**4**	5
Close to centre (1 = the closest; 5 = the furthest):	1	**2**	3	4	5
Age (1 = the oldest; 5 = the most modern):	1	2	**3**	4	5

Facilities: air conditioning, wifi, free parking, pool, gym, spa, room service, restaurant, 24-hour reception

Homestyle Bed & Breakfast

This is a cheap option if you want to stay in the centre of town. It's basic and inexpensive.

Average customer reviews:

Price (1 = the cheapest; 5 = the most expensive):	**1**	2	3	4	5
Noise (1 = the quietest; 5 = the noisiest):	1	2	3	4	**5**
Size of rooms (1 = the smallest; 5 = the biggest):	**1**	2	3	4	5
Close to centre (1 = the closest; 5 = the furthest):	**1**	2	3	4	5
Age (1 = the oldest; 5 = the most modern):	1	**2**	3	4	5

Facilities: breakfast included, wifi, free maps

Lesson 2D

5a

Student B

1. **Student A is going to tell you about something exciting he/she did. Get ready to ask questions about what, where, why, etc.**
2. **Something exciting happened to you recently (e.g. you got a new job, you won a competition, you found something interesting). Get ready to tell Student B:**
   - what it was
   - when and where it happened
   - why it happened
   - what happened
   - how you felt

Lesson 1D

6

Student B

1 Answer Student B's questions with the information below and check they understand.

1. The concert starts at 8 p.m., but you can go in anytime after 6 p.m.
2. You have to go to page 95 and do Exercises 2, 5 and 7.
3. The shop is open from 8 a.m. until 6 p.m. from Monday to Friday, and from 10 a.m. until 4 p.m. at the weekend.

2 Ask Student A for the information below. Check the details they give you.

1. what time the film at the cinema starts
   What time does the film at the cinema start?
2. what you need to buy from the shops
3. how you apply for the job

Lesson 4B

2b

Check your score:

1	a 5	b 2	c 0
2	a 0	b 5	c 2
3	a 0	b 2	c 5
4	a 5	b 0	c 2
5	a 0	b 2	c 5
6	a 5	b 2	c 0

0-4

You should let someone else organise things for you. Please don't ever invite me to one of your parties!

5-17

Organising events is difficult, but you try your best – sometimes it goes well, sometimes you need a bit of help.

18-30

You're a super organiser! You have the best parties in town and if there are any problems at the last minute, you don't get stressed. Can I come to your next party, please?

Lesson 7D

5 Work in pairs. Read the information below and think about an excuse you can make for each situation. Then go back to page 60.

Student B

1. You broke A's pen.
2. You're late for A's birthday party.
3. You're taking A somewhere but you went the wrong way.
4. You borrowed A's USB stick and lost it.
5. You can't meet A tomorrow for lunch.

Lesson 5B

7c

8c

A

Name: Amit
Age: 45
Job: has his own business
Hobbies: spending time with his kids and cooking
Character: describes himself as hard-working and funny.

B

Name: Lena
Age: 22
Job: Biology student
Hobbies: cycling, dancing salsa
Character: describes herself as friendly and hard-working

C

Name: Marcus
Age: 29
Job: Video game designer
Hobbies: watching films. playing the guitar
Character: describes himself as quiet

D

Name: Alice
Age: 79
Job: Artist
Hobbies: runs marathons for charity
Character: describes herself as sometimes serious, sometimes fun

E

Name: Chris
Age: 31
Job: Restaurant manager
Hobbies: going to the gym, and he likes to DJ in his free time
Character: describes himself as relaxed

F

Name: Tallah
Age: 33
Job: Personal assistant
Hobbies: sport, going out with friends
Character: describes herself as active and sociable

Lesson 6B

8 **Choose eight of the activities in the box and add them to the calendar at different times. Then go back to page 49 and make arrangements with other students.**

bake a cake   barbecue   buy new car   cook for friends   dentist appointment
dinner with family   do homework   finish report   lunch with a friend   meet a friend
party   tennis   work meeting

Monday	Tuesday	Wedneday
8 a.m. ________	8 a.m. ________	8 a.m. ________
10 a.m. ________	10 a.m. ________	10 a.m. ________
12 a.m. ________	12 a.m. ________	12 a.m. ________
2 p.m. ________	2 p.m. ________	2 p.m. ________
4 p.m. ________	4 p.m. ________	4 p.m. ________
6 p.m. ________	6 p.m. ________	6 p.m. ________
8 p.m. ________	8 p.m. ________	8 p.m. ________
10 p.m. ________	10 p.m. ________	10 p.m. ________

Lesson 6D

5

Student A

You're going to practise leaving a voice message for Student B. Read the situations and think about what you want to say. Use the Useful phrases box on page 52 to help you.

Situation 1

You are Student B's boss and you need them to come to a meeting tomorrow morning at 7.30 a.m. Ask them to text or call you back to say if they can come.

Situation 2

You are Student B's friend. Leave a message to say that you can't meet them for dinner tomorrow because you have to work late. Ask them to call you back to arrange another time for you to meet.

Situation 3

You are a receptionist at the doctor's. You have to change Student B's appointment next week. Ask them to call you back to arrange a new appointment.

Situation 4

You are Student B's friend. You've just got back from your holiday and want to tell them about it. Ask them to call you back.

Situation 5

You are Student B's colleague. You're calling to ask them to bring in an important document to work tomorrow.

Student B

You're going to practise leaving a voice message for Student A. Read the situations and think about what you want to say. Use the Useful phrases box on page 52 to help you.

Situation 1

You are responding to an advertisement Student A posted online because they're selling their car. You're interested in buying it. Ask them to call you back on 07912 946 2121.

Situation 2

You are Student B's colleague. You're driving to work tomorrow and can pick them up at 7.45 a.m., but you're not sure what their address is. Ask them to call you back before 10 p.m.

Situation 3

You are Student A's friend. You have plans to go cycling on the 23rd, but you want to change the date to the 30th. Ask them to text or call you back to say if this is OK.

Situation 4

You are Student A's boss. You have an important meeting tomorrow at 10 a.m., but you need to change it to 9 a.m. Ask them to text or call you to say if they can come earlier.

Situation 5

You are Student A's friend. You're just calling for a chat. Ask them to call you back when they can.

Lesson 5D

6

Student B

You and Student A went to another country for a language course. You stayed with different families. You'd like to buy the family you stayed with some gifts. Read the information about your family below.

Kate: 38, receptionist, likes cycling

Jason: 37, nurse, likes music

Will: 15, school student, likes skateboarding

Emily: 9, school student, likes art

Now go back to page 44 and ask Student A to help you think of ideas. Give some suggestions for his/her family.

Lesson 7D

5 **Work in pairs. Read the information below and think about an excuse you can make for each situation. Then go back to page 60.**

Student A

1. You borrowed B's coursebook and lost it.
2. You meet B for coffee but you're late.
3. You can't go out with B next week.
4. You stood on B's bag and broke something in it.
5. You took B's jacket by mistake.

Lesson 8D

6a **Choose a place to start and finish on the map. Tell your partner where to start and give them directions. Do they arrive at the correct place? Swap roles and repeat.**

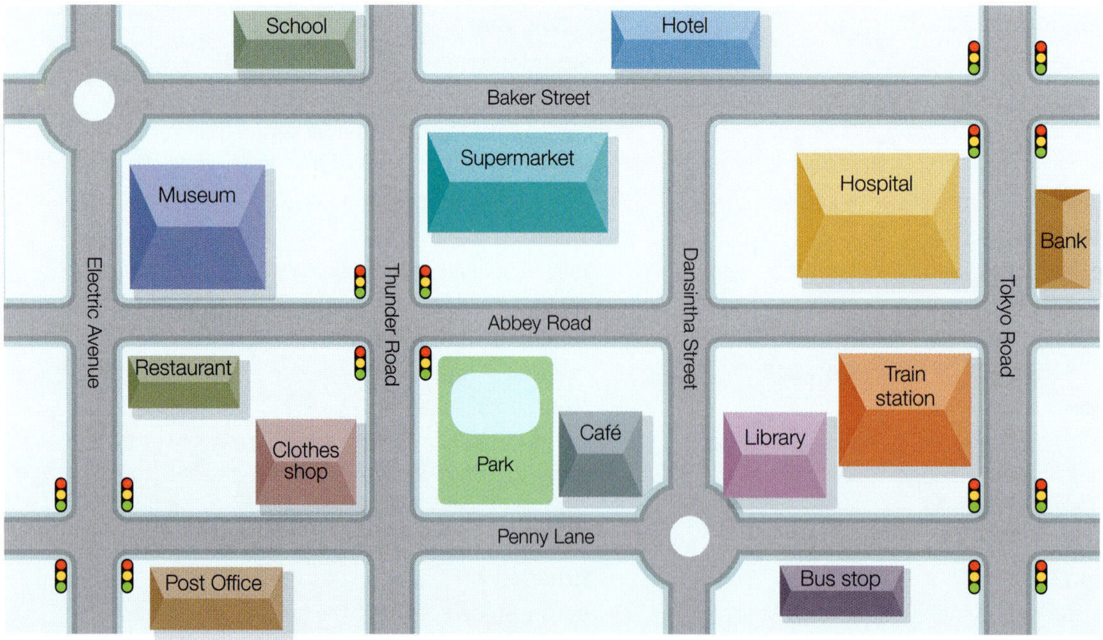

Lesson 9D

6 **You're going to have two conversations. Read the information below. First, Student A asks for some information and Student B answers. Then swap roles and repeat.**

Student A

Conversation 1

You're a guest at a hotel. Student B is the receptionist. Ask him/her for this information:

- what time breakfast is
  Do you know what time breakfast is, please?
- if there's a gym
- what time the gym opens and closes
- what the wifi password is
- if there's a supermarket nearby

Conversation 2

You're a receptionist at a college. Student B will phone you to find out about the art course.

This is the necessary information:

- The course starts in the first week of September and finishes at the end of June.
- There are two lessons a week – on Tuesday and Thursday afternoons.
- The course costs £950.
- You don't need any of your own equipment.
- There's a free car park for students at the college.

Lesson 10B

8b

Student A

Read the notes about the ballpoint pen and chewing gum. Prepare to tell your partner about them. Use complete sentences.

The first ballpoint pen was made by Laszlo Biro in 1938.

	Ballpoint pen	Tomato ketchup	Chewing gum	Paper
	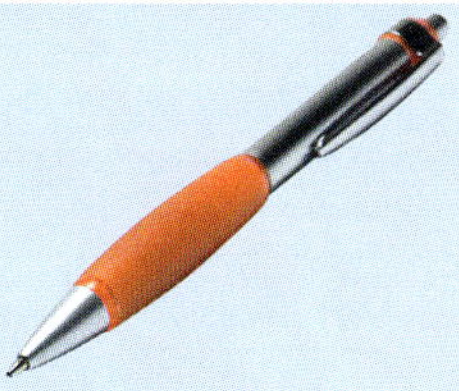		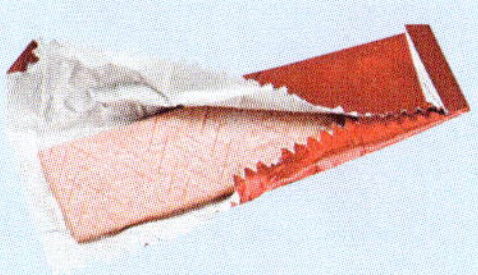	
Where and when was it first made? Who made it?	first made by Laszlo Biro, 1938		first made by early man, 6,000 years ago	
What was it first like?	first pens sold for £27 each in today's money		made with gum from a tree today's gum first made during the 1800s	
How much/ many … is/are sold each year?	15 million sold around the world each year		Trillions (000,000,000) of pieces sold each year	
Other interesting facts	the world's largest pen made in 2011 (5.5 m long)		first used to clean teeth	

Lesson 9D

6 **You're going to have two conversations. Read the information below. Student A asks for some information and Student B answers. Then swap roles and repeat.**

Student B

Conversation 1

You're a receptionist at a hotel. Student A is a guest and he/she will ask you some questions.
This is the necessary information:

- Breakfast is from 7 a.m. until 10 a.m.
- The gym is on the ground floor.
- The gym opens at 6 a.m. and closes at 9 p.m.
- The wifi password is hotel99.
- There's a supermarket about five minutes walk away. Go right out of the hotel, go straight down the road and it's on the right.

Conversation 2

You're interested in taking an art course at a local college. Student A is a receptionist there.
Call and ask for this information:

- when the course starts and finishes
  Could you tell me when the course starts and finishes, please?
- when each lesson is
- how much it costs
- if you need your own equipment
- if there's a car park nearby

Lesson 10B

8b

Student B

Read the notes about tomato ketchup and paper. Prepare to tell your partner about them. Use complete sentences.
The first tomato ketchup was made in the 17th century by the Chinese.

	Ballpoint pen	Tomato ketchup	Chewing gum	Paper
			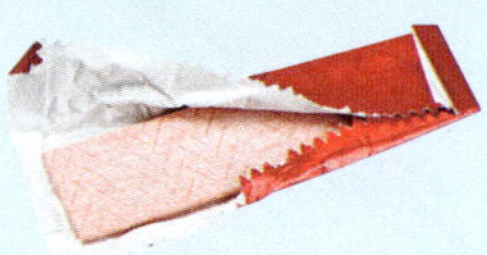	
Where and when was it first made? Who made it?		in the 17th century by the Chinese		2200 years ago by the Chinese
What was it first like?		made of fish and spices, not tomatoes first modern tomato ketchup made during the 1800s		made from old clothes, plants and tree wood
How much/ many … is/are sold each year?		650 million Heinz bottles bought each year		around 400 million tonnes sold each year
Other interesting facts		three bottles eaten by every American each year		around 10 litres of water used to make a piece of paper

Irregular verbs

Verb	Past simple	Past participle
be	was	been
become	became	become
begin	began	begun
bite	bit	bitten
blow	blew	blown
break	broke	broken
bring	brought	brought
build	built	built
buy	bought	bought
catch	caught	caught
choose	chose	chosen
come	came	come
cost	cost	cost
cut	cut	cut
do	did	done
draw	drew	drawn
drink	drank	drunk
drive	drove	driven
eat	ate	eaten
fall	fell	fallen
feel	felt	felt
find	found	found
fly	flew	flown
forget	forgot	forgotten
freeze	froze	frozen
get	got	got
give	gave	given
go	went	gone
grow	grew	grown
have	had	had
hear	heard	heard
hide	hid	hidden
hit	hit	hit
hold	held	held
hurt	hurt	hurt
keep	kept	kept
know	knew	known
learn	learned/learnt	learned/learnt
leave	left	left

Verb	Past simple	Past participle
lend	lent	lent
let	let	let
lie	lay	lain
lose	lost	lost
make	made	made
mean	meant	meant
meet	met	met
pay	paid	paid
put	put	put
read	read	read
ride	rode	ridden
ring	rang	rung
run	ran	run
say	said	said
see	saw	seen
sell	sold	sold
send	sent	sent
shine	shone	shone
show	showed	shown
shut	shut	shut
sing	sang	sung
sit	sat	sat
sleep	slept	slept
smell	smelled/smelt	smelled/smelt
speak	spoke	spoken
spend	spent	spent
spill	spilled/spilt	spilled/spilt
stand	stood	stood
swim	swam	swum
take	took	taken
teach	taught	taught
tell	told	told
think	thought	thought
throw	threw	thrown
understand	understood	understood
wake	woke	woken
wear	wore	worn
win	won	won
write	wrote	written

Pearson Education Limited
KAO TWO
KAO Park
Hockham Way
Harlow, Essex
CM17 9SR
England
and Associated Companies throughout the world.

english.com/roadmap

First published 2019

ISBN: 978-1-292-22795-5

Set in Soho Gothic Pro

Printed and bound by L.E.G.O. S.p.A., Italy

Acknowledgements

The Publishers would like to thank the following people for their feedback and comments during the development of the material:

Kate Browne, Louise Brydges, Sue Cable, Iñigo Casis, Claire Fitzgerald, Nikki Fořtová, Katy Kelly, Sylwia Kossakowska-Pisarek, Klara Malowiecka, Fran Perry, Susana Royo, Glenn Standish, Michael Turner, Nelita Vasconcellos, Milena Yablonsky

Illustration acknowledgements

Roy Hermelin (Beehive Illustration) p.144; Lauren Radley p.12, 60; Tony Richardson p.58, 68, 156

Photo acknowledgements

The publisher would like to thank the following for their kind permission to reproduce their photographs:

123RF.com: Alex Maxim 15, Alla Ordatii 44, Andriy Popov 136, 136, 140, Antonio Balaguer Soler 56, Antonio Diaz 136, Brian Jackson 145, Cathy Yeule 101, Cathy Yeulet 141, Cristina Ionete 142, Danilo Vuletic 138, Darryl Brooks 137, Dmitry Kalinovsky 40, 154, Galina Peshkova 142, Graham Oliver 144, Hans Geel 18, Hemant Mehta 40, 154, Ion Chiosea 75, Jacek Chabraszewski 91, Jan Novak 26, Jodie Johnson 142, Katarzyna Białasiewicz 137, 59, Maciej Błędowski 143, Michael Simons 50, 75, Mikhail Bulanov 141, Oleksandr Nebrat 145, Olena Danileiko 91, Olena Kachmar 145, Parinya Agsararattananont 137, Paweł Opaska 64, Petro Kuprynenko 142, Phongphan Supphakankamjon 78, Sergey Galushko 40, 154, Sergey Nivens 141, Sergii Koval 19, Viacheslav Iakobc 140, Viacheslav Iakobchuk 144, 144, atic12 75, belchonock 44, bialasiewicz 50, blasbike 101, chanwitohm 108, claudiodivizia 143, deksbakh 66, design56 15, dolgachov 136, 141, 141, dolphfyn 18, gbh007 141, hanschr 145, iloveotto 91, islander11 142, jakobradlgruber 138, jason cox 145, kavram 109, ladyann 145, lenanet 137, madbit 15, maxriesgo 50, mindof 143, moodboard 136, movingmomen 90, niserin 34, ocusfocus 137, olegdudko 145, 78, perutskyi 143, racorn 47, rez_art 137, rido 136, rilueda 138, saiko3p 64, scanrail 137, 157, 158, 81, scyther5 142, siraphol 44, smileus 139, stockbroker 144, 154, tashka2000 145, 91, tomertu 6, tonobalaguer 57, upperkase 145, velvetocean 59; **Alamy Stock Photo:** Buddy Mays 10, Chris Rout 14, ClassicStock 111, Douglas Peebles Photography 19, Efrain Padro 35, Everett Collection Historical 16, Grapheast 86, Hero Images Inc. 84, Jaroslaw Pawlak 57, Johann Hinrichs 22, Julia Gavin 152, Kevin Britland 152, Mint Images Limited 50, Nathaniel Noir 22, Nik Wheeler 115, P.D. Amedzro 114, Ryan Cardone / Stockimo / 6, Simon Maycock 18, Slick Shoots 138, Stephen Barnes / Lifestyle 82, Tony Eveling 65, ZUMA Press, Inc. 34; **Getty Images:** 10'000 Hours 28, Anton Petrus 62, Ascent / PKS Media Inc. 66, Bambu Productions 49, Boogich 86, Caiaimage / Sam Edwards 112, Cameron Davidson 22, Chris Minihane 73, Chris Williamson 8, Compassionate Eye Foundation / Hero Images 36, DigiPub 80, Dougal Waters 51, Frank Lukasseck 93, Franz-Marc Frei 22, Frederick Florin 38, Fredrik Telleus 10, Hero Images 113, 20, 50, Hugh Sitton 86, Igor Prahin 22, Image Source 94, James Whitaker 106, Janek Skarzynski 104, Jason Merritt 9, Jenny Dettrick 26, Jerod Harris / Stringer 16, Jo-Ann Richards 6, Joff Lee 30, Johnathan Ampersand Esper 94, Jose Cendon / Stringer 16, Jose Luis Pelaez Inc 86, 9, Knauer / Johnston 74, Lee Edwards 27, Liam Norris 48, Lisa-Blue 65, Mark Webster 103, Maskot 62, Mike Harrington 70, Mike Powell 63, MissKadri 7, MoMo Productions 17, Pekic 36, PeopleImages 10, 14, 84, Peter Cade 46, Peter Muller 70, PhotoAlto / Frederic Cirou 74, Photography by Simon Bond 11, Plume Creative 14, Robbie Jack 8, Soccrates Images 8, Spaces Images 24, Steve Debenport 74, Sven Hansche / EyeEm 66, Svetlana123 55, Taylor S. Kennedy 66, Thomas Barwick 14, 38, 40, 70, Thomas_EyeDesign 86, Tim Grist Photography 33, Tim Mosenfelder 8, Tim Robberts 50, Tom Merton 139, Viktor Drachev 34, 34, Vostok 42, Walter Bibikow 22, Westend61 14, 41, 46, 86, 154, Wibowo Rusli 24, Yellow Dog Productions 70, agustavop 24, chinaface 23, christian.plochacki 14, commerceandculturestock 46, danielvfung 42, franckreporter 41, 154, images by Tang Ming Tung 42, monkeybusinessimages 48, peeterv 100, picturegarden 43, piola666 38, sigenest 94, urbancow 49, william87 50, yanik88 80, zyxeos30 30; **Little Woodham:** 82; **Pearson Education Asia Ltd:** Joey Chan 142; **Pearson Education Ltd:** Debbie Rowe 143; **Shutterstock.com:** 81593 137, ARENA Creative 143, Aaron Kohr 143, AboutLife 145, Adisa 80, Africa Studio 137, Aleksey Stemmer 138, Alexander Raths 144, Andrey_Popov 139, Angelo Giampiccolo 140, Antonio Guillem 137, Boris Ryaposov 99, Bplanet 139, Brian A Jackson 78, Checubus 26, Coprid 44, Corepics VOF 32, Cre8tive Images 81, DGLimages 30, Dan Breckwoldt 6, Daniel Taeger 26, Diana Grytsku 102, Diego Cervo 137, Dmitry Kalinovsky 140, Dragan Grkic 50, Dusit Wongwattanakul 91, Elena Hramova 137, Elnur 140, Elzbieta Sekowska 138, Fashion iconography 78, Filipe Frazao 139, Flamingo Images 46, Gabriel Georgescu 140, GaudiLab 20, 38, George Dolgikh 137, Georgejmclittle 42, Glass and Nature 110, Golbay 78, Goodluz 140, 144, Graphical_Bank 152, Gregory Gerber 137, HBO / Kobal 72, Hartswood Films 73, HiltonT 109, ITV 72, Iakov Filimonov 138, Jaromir Chalabala 110, 62, Jaroslav Francisko 138, Jason Swalwell 81, Jo Ann Snover 57, Johann Helgason 137, Juriah Mosin 32, Kamira 138, Kataleewan Intarachote 138, Katran 157, 158, KoM-KoM 108, Krishna. Wu 104, Leonid Andronov 64, Lisa S 136, Lucky Business 136, 136, Maridav 141, 34, Marie C Fields 137, MaszaS 139, Matteo Ceruti 96, Mihai Simonia 138, Monkey Business Images 137, 138, 139, 139, 140, 141, 144, 144, Multiart 137, My Good Images 67, 83, Nadino 102, NadzeyaShanchuk 105, Nestor Rizhniak 140, Nickolay Khoroshkov 142, OPIS Zagreb 145, OPOLJA 38, OlegDoroshin 157, 158, PatrikV 78, Patryk Kosmider 108, Pavel L Photo and Video 143, PhIIIStudio 44, Photographee.eu 58, 74, 98, Pitchaya Pingpithayakul 140, Pitchayarat Chootai 143, Pix11 142, Pressmaster 137, 36, Preto Perola 78, Prod-akszyn 136, RCPPHOTO 139, REDPIXEL.PL 140, Radiokafka 108, Radu Bercan 96, Rawpixel 46, Rawpixel.com 141, 145, 76, 78, Richman21 58, Roman Babakin 54, Roman Sigaev 157, 158, Romanets 40, 154, RossHelen 101, S_L. 136, Sergey Novikov 71, Shaun Robinson 136, Song_about_summer 103, Stocker1970 104, Stuart Monk 139, Syda Productions 136, 138, 50, 52, Taina Sohlman 143, Thomas Barrat 138, Tim R 94, Tim UR 137, Tyler Olson 140, UltraOrto, S.A. 81, Uroš Medved 143, Ursa Studio 99, VP Photo Studio 110, Valentyn Volkov 137, Visions of America 56, Vitaly Korovin 137, Vytautas Kielaitis 138, WDG Photo 138, YIUCHEUNG 138, Yulia Grigoryeva 142, alice-photo 96, arek_malang 109, barytek86 99, cobalt88 88, cunaplus 15, dennizn 143, eWilding 138, godrick 23, goodluz 38, halitomer 142, horvathta 6, karamysh 56, kavione 142, keko64 47, kurhan 140, lorenza62 57, majivecka 105, maxpetrov 101, melastmohican 139, muratart 99, pavla 56, progressman 26, sagir 142, sharptoyou 104, sirtravelalot 136, 139, 139, 139, 140, siso_seasaw 142, spaxiax 137, themorningglory 54, wavebreakmedia 140, 141, 50, 97, wong yu liang 99; **The Chrismans:** 82.

Cover Image: *Front:* **Getty Images:** Posnov

Every effort has been made to trace the copyright holders and we apologise in advance for any unintentional omissions. We would be pleased to insert the appropriate acknowledgement in any subsequent edition of this publication.

MIX
Paper from responsible sources
FSC www.fsc.org FSC™ C128612